Contents

REISSUED WITH A NEW INTRODUCTION

Physical Knowledge in Preschool Education: Implications of Piaget's Theory

Constance Kamii
Rheta DeVries

FOREWORD BY JEAN PIAGET

Teachers College, Columbia University
New York and London

Published by Teachers College Press, 1234 Amsterdam Avenue, New York, NY 10027

Library of Congress Cataloging-in-Publication Data

Kamii, Constance.
    Physical knowledge in preschool education : implications of Piaget's theory / Constance
Kamii, Rheta DeVries ; foreword by Jean Piaget.
        p.   cm. — (Early childhood education series)
    Originally published: Englewood Cliffs, N.J. : Prentice Hall, c1978. Reissued with a new
introd.
    Includes bibliographical references (p.   ) and index.
    ISBN 0-8077-3254-0 (alk. paper)
    1. Education, Preschool.   2. Piaget, Jean, 1896–   .   I. DeVries, Rheta.   II.
Title.   III. Series.
LB1140.2.K32   1993
372.21—dc20   93-18388

Printed on acid-free paper

Manufactured in the United States of America

99 98 97 96   7 6 5 4 3 2

Foreword

Many educators have used our operatory tasks by transforming them into kinds of standardized "tests," as if their purposes were to diagnose the performances a child is capable of in a given situation. Our method of asking questions with free conversations, as well as the theory of the formation of structures which we have studied stage by stage, permit a much more nuanced use of these tasks—to know how a child reasons and what kinds of new constructions he is capable of when we encourage his spontaneity to a maximum. In this case the double advantage which can be obtained is: (1) from the standpoint of psychological diagnosis, to foresee in part the progress the child will be able to make later; and (2) from the pedagogical point of view, to reinforce his constructivity and thus find a method of teaching in accordance with "constructivism" which is the fundamental principle of our interpretation of intellectual development.

This is what the authors of this book have well understood. I had already visited with great pleasure in 1967 the Ypsilanti Public Schools (Michigan) and observed the efforts made there to develop the pupils' creativity. The new experiments done by the authors at the University of Illinois at Chicago Circle are inspired by the same principles: Focusing on physical knowledge more than on logico-mathematical knowledge, they centered their effort on inventing activities to permit children to act on objects and observe the reactions or transformations of these objects (which is the essence of physical knowledge, where the role of the subject's actions is indispensable for understanding the nature of the phenomena involved). The importance of errors is not neglected, as an error corrected is often more instructive than an immediate success.

In Part II (Chapter 4-10) the authors have illustrated these activities and principles in a concrete way with protocols taken from videotapes, showing in what precise context the teacher intervened in a constructive way and in what context he had done the opposite of what he was hoping to do.

In Part III (entitled "How to Go beyond This Book") they showed how to invent other activities and how to adapt pedagogical principles in various situations in the course of the day. The merit of this book is thus that it goes beyond generalities by giving practical ideas and concrete examples, but without giving recipes or a ready-made "method." The reader will find how a teacher can *and must* experiment in his own class by creating various situations and evaluating his interventions in view of his pupils' reactions.

It is thus a great service which C. Kamii and R. DeVries render to the pedagogy that emphasizes activity, by basing their principles on a psychology of which they have well understood (unlike so many others) the essentially "constructivist" character.

JEAN PIAGET

Acknowledgements

Many individuals have contributed to the development of our thinking and the progress of the research which led to the writing of this book. The one person to whom we owe the greatest debt is Professor Hermina Sinclair of the University of Geneva. Professor Sinclair has influenced us in many ways for over a decade through her critiques of our manuscripts, her observations of our classrooms, our numerous discussions, and the support of her friendship. Without her assistance, the publication of this book would not have been possible.

We also owe a large debt of gratitude to the teachers with whom we have worked. We ourselves are not classroom teachers, and without their perspective and insight, we could never have approached any level of practical application. To the administrators of the institutions in which these teachers worked, we also express thanks for enabling us to try our ideas in classrooms. We are especially grateful to the Director and teachers of Circle Children's Center, a day care facility at the University of Illinois at Chicago Circle. It was there that most of the activities of Part II were devised and carried out. The Director, Ms. Patricia Chronis, created an organizational and interpersonal milieu which made our research and teacher-training seminars possible. The teacher with whom we worked the longest and most intensively is Ms. Maureen Ellis, and we would like to express our particular appreciation for all we learned from her. The other teachers making significant contributions are Mr. Sargent Aborn, Ms. Colleen Blobaum, Ms. Robin Burgess, Ms. Nancy Fineberg, Mr. Thomas Gleeson, Ms. Laura Gross, and Ms. Jeanne Klauber. We are grateful for their openness, their willingness to have us in their classrooms, their reflective teaching, their comments and questions, and their reactions to drafts of this book.

Many other teachers contributed to earlier phases of research. In the Ypsilanti Early Education Program of the Ypsilanti (Michigan) Public Schools the following teachers and other personnel should be acknowledged: Ms. Emmalyn Anderson, Ms. Susan Morse Anderson, Ms. Arbedella Brown, Ms. Louise Derman, Ms. Marie Ezell, Ms. June Guthrie, Ms. Ann Hammerman, Mr. Raymond Kingston, Ms. Barbara Konieczny, Ms. Shirley Lai, Ms. Caroline Plummer, Ms. Kathy Miller, Ms. Honne Sonquist, Ms. Cheryl Wilbanks, Ms. Donna Williams, and Ms. Glorianne Wittes. Ms. Linda Kos and other teachers at the Christian Action Ministry St. Barnabas Day Care Center also contributed to this research.

Among our many colleagues, Dr. Norma Radin of the University of Michigan has provided constructive criticisms over the course of many years. Dr. Marianne Denis-Prinzhorn of the University of Geneva has also given valuable advice. Others we would like to mention for their reactions to earlier drafts of this book are Dr. Thomas Lickona of the College at Cortland, State University of New York, Mr. Robert Peper of the Ypsilanti Public Schools, and students at the University of Illinois at Chicago Circle, the University of Geneva, and the Erikson Institute for Early Education. To Dr. Frank Sinclair, now at Purdue University, we are grateful for his critique from the point of view of physics.

Indispensable was the financial support from a variety of sources. The bulk of the research reported in this book was funded since 1971 by the Urban Education Research Program of the College of Education, University of Illinois at Chicago Circle. The Spencer Foundation also provided a grant during 1971–72 which made our work possible at the Evanston (Illinois) Child Care Center and the St. Barnabas Day Care Center of Christian Action Ministry in Chicago. Earlier work was funded under Title III, ESEA, in the Ypsilanti Public Schools during 1967–70. Some of the material reported here was gathered in the course of our consultation during 1973–75 to a Title VII, Emergency School Aid Act, experimental kindergarten project in the District 65 Public Schools in Evanston, Illinois, under the direction of Ms. Corinne Kolen and Ms. Mona Golub. The postdoctoral study of the senior author at the University of Geneva was made possible by fellowships from the Social Science Research Council and the National Institute of Mental Health.

Finally, we would like to thank Rheta's mother, Ms. Lorraine Bradley Goolsby, for providing a retreat in Arkansas, where much of the final draft was written, and Ms. Margaret Halsey for her patience and reliability in helping us type the manuscript.

Introduction

In this book we attempt to show how Piaget's theory can be used in practical ways in early childhood education in one area—physical knowledge. As discussed in Chapters 1 and 2, physical-knowledge activities are similar to but different from "science education." The physical-knowledge approach centers around the child's action on objects and the construction of physical and logico-mathematical knowledge from within. By contrast, science education emphasizes content and specific bits of scientific knowledge, even when it attempts to be a "process," "discovery," or "concept" approach.

Although our emphasis is practical, we do not intend to provide a cookbook curriculum. Piaget's constructivism does not imply a cookbook curriculum that can be used to educate all children in the same way. Although children share basic similarities, constructivism implies that the teacher must respond to each child's unique ideas in a flexible fashion. What we have tried to do is to communicate a way of thinking about children and objects so that teachers will be able to invent their own activities. We also stress that the broad principles of teaching we outline must always be adapted by each teacher to a specific group of children at a given time.

In writing this book, we had three audiences in mind—teachers of young children, students of psychology, and people in various administrative capacities who are concerned with curriculum. To teachers and prospective teachers we attempt to present Piaget's theory as a practical framework for their teaching. We address ourselves particularly to those who are searching for alternatives to traditional methods that attempt to put knowledge into the child's head or to get them to "discover" it. Although the book focuses mainly on four-year-olds, teachers of three-year-olds, as well as of children in kindergarten and the primary grades, will also find the ideas applicable.

Students of psychology are often frustrated on the one hand by the difficulty of Piaget's books and, on the other hand, by the many conflicting interpretations of Piaget's theory. One of the reasons for frequent misinterpretations is that many people are unfamiliar with epistemological controversies and are thus unaware of Piaget's epistemological framework, which includes a basic distinction between physical and logico-mathematical knowledge. We hope that this book, particularly Chapters 2 and 3, will help the student understand Piaget's framework and make better sense of his books.

We also hope that curriculum specialists, principals, and other school personnel influential in making decisions about curriculum, especially in the early grades, will find in this book a new and different way of thinking about *what* to teach, *how,* and *why.*

We assume that the readers of this book bring some familiarity with Piaget's work, and our intention is not to repeat what can be found in books such as *Piaget's Theory of Intellectual Development: An Introduction* by Ginsburg and Opper (1969).

Although this book deals with subject matter related to science education, it cannot be compared directly with other programs such as *Science— A Process Approach, Elementary Science Study, Science Curriculum Improvement Study,* and *Science 5/13,*[1] because none of these programs deals with preschool education. The lowest grade considered by all of them is kindergarten. Moreover, even if one believed any of these programs to be ideal for elementary children, it is obvious that elementary-school science cannot simply be extrapolated to ages four, three, two, or one. The education of preschool children should be different in many ways from that of pupils in elementary schools. Two of the above programs *(Science Curriculum Improvement Study* and *Science 5/13)* claim explicitly to be inspired by Piaget's theory, and we leave to the reader the task of comparing the differences between these approaches and ours.

The book is organized in three parts. Part I is a theoretical introduction consisting of three chapters dealing with rationale, objectives, and principles of teaching. Part II (consisting of Chapters 4-10) provides seven concrete examples of activities that illustrate the principles of teaching presented in Chapter 3. Chapters 9 and 10 are written in the first person by the teachers who conducted the activities. In Part III, entitled "How to Go beyond This Book," we include ways of developing physical knowledge activities and integrating them in an ongoing program. The reader may want to begin by sampling one of the activity chapters in Part II.

[1]For more information on these programs, see "Programs and Materials for Science Education" in the Bibliography.

* * *

Although we still agree with the general goals, objectives, and principles of teaching discussed in Chapter 3, our conceptualizations of goals have changed somewhat in the 15 years since we first wrote this book. As can be seen in Kamii (1982, 1984, 1985), one of us came to agree with Piaget (1948/1973) that moral and intellectual autonomy should be the aim of education. Accordingly, Kamii would prefer to label the circle to the left in Figure 3.1 (p. 46) "Autonomy." She would also like to label the circle to the right "The goals of most educators and the public."

The term *autonomy* in Piaget's theory means something different from common usage. In Piaget's theory, autonomy means the *ability* to take relevant factors into account and make decisions for oneself about right and wrong in the moral realm, and about truth and untruth in the intellectual realm, independently of reward and punishment. Space does not permit an elaboration of this difficult concept, but suffice it to say that autonomy is the opposite of heteronomy, which means being governed by somebody else. By manipulating children with reward and punishment, traditional education often unwittingly promotes heteronomy (i.e., blind obedience, calculation, and revolt) rather than personal decisions based on relevant factors.

DeVries also values the concept of autonomy but views its role within the broader notion of development as the aim of education. She follows Piaget (1948) in advocating that "education shall be directed to the full development of the human personality" (p. 87). DeVries views Piaget's statement as referring to the highest stages of intellectual and moral development. To put the emphasis on development is to aim education toward promoting structural progress in the child's reasoning. Autonomy (from root words meaning self-regulation) may be taken to refer to an aspect of the transformative process by which development occurs. Taken as cognitive and moral ability, autonomy does not suddenly appear full-blown. It develops. Autonomy is therefore indissociably linked with structural transformation through Piaget's intellectual and moral stages. To say that development is the aim of education implies that teachers must focus on the specific qualitative ways in which children reason and the process by which reasoning evolves. Respect for developmental process leads to minimizing teacher heteronomy and encouraging the child's autonomous functioning.

While theorists like to debate the preceding points, the principles of teaching conceptualized and illustrated in this book remain the same whether we define our broad, long-range goal as autonomy or development. The reader interested in knowing more about constructivist early childhood education can find similar principles of teaching in the following books that were written after the present volume: *Group Games in Early Education*

(Kamii & DeVries, 1980), *Number in Preschool and Kindergarten* (Kamii, 1982), *Young Children Reinvent Arithmetic* (Kamii, 1985), *Young Children Continue to Reinvent Arithmetic—2nd Grade* (Kamii, 1989), and *Constructivist Early Education: Overview and Comparison with Other Programs* (DeVries & Kohlberg, 1990/1987).

Constance Kamii
Rheta DeVries

January, 1993

PART I

Rationale and Principles

Chapter 1

What Are
Physical-Knowledge
Activities?

What we mean by "physical-knowledge activities" can be best explained by contrasting these with activities typically found in "science education." For illustrative purposes we shall present two different ways of teaching an activity on crystals. The first, quoted from a text on preschool education, is an example of the "science education" approach:[1]

Theme: Crystals
Behavioral objective: At the end of the experience, the child will be able to

1. Pick out crystals when shown a variety of things.
2. Define what a crystal is.
3. Discuss the steps in making crystals at school.

Learning activities:
  The teacher will show the children different crystals and rocks. She will explain what a crystal is and what things are crystals (sand, sugar, salt, etc.). Then she will show some crystals she made previously. The children are given materials . . . so they can make crystals to take

[1]We are aware of the existence of such innovative programs as *Elementary Science Study* and *Science 5/13* (references in the Introduction), which warn against the verbalism of traditional science education. We are also aware of the fact that, in reality, most preschool teachers do not teach in such didactic ways. We nevertheless refer to the "science education" approach throughout this book as if it were one uniformly didactic approach for the following reasons: Innovators in science education have generally not considered preschool education, and their work begins at the kindergarten level. Authors of early-education texts, on the other hand, have not been influenced by these recent ideas, and their chapters on science education are invariably filled with verbalistic instruction and "scientific" content. When we refer to the "science education" approach in this book, we thus have in mind this characteristic of published texts in early education.

3

home. A magnifying glass is used so the children can examine the crystals.

Method 1: Mix ½ cup each of salt, bluing, water, and 1 T (tablespoon) ammonia. Pour over crumpled paper towels. In 1 hour crystals begin to form. They reach a peak in about 4 hours and last for a couple of days. (Taylor, 1964, pp. 80–81)

Maureen Ellis, one of our teacher colleagues, read the above lesson, modified it into a physical-knowledge activity, and wrote the following account of her teaching with crystals:

> While looking through an early-education text, I found the "recipe" for making crystals. I decided to try it, but not as a science project because I had no idea why crystals formed. It was as much magic to me as to the kids; so we used it like a cooking activity. I told them that we didn't know why it happened, but they got the idea that when some things mix together, sometimes something extraordinary happens. The activity was such a success that for days individual children were showing others how to make crystals, and some made their "own" to take home.
>
> This experiment inspired other experiments and a whole atmosphere of experimentation. One boy, during cleanup, decided to pour the grease from the popcorn pan into a cup with water and food coloring. He put it on the windowsill until the next day. He was sure "something" would happen and was surprised when nothing much did. Another child said she knew an experiment with salt, soap, and pepper (which she had seen on television). She demonstrated for those who were interested. A third child was inspired by the soap experiment to fill a cup with water and put a bar of soap in. She was astonished by the change in water level and then tested other things in the water—a pair of scissors, chalk, crayon, and her hand to see the change in water level.
>
> The next day, one child brought a cup filled with beans, blue water, styrofoam packing materials, and a Q-Tip. "This is my experiment. Cook it," he said. So I asked what he thought would happen to each of the things in the cup. He made a few predictions, and I told him we could cook it the next day. (I wanted to experiment first to see if there might be anything dangerous involved.) At group time, he told everyone about his experiment, and the group made predictions which I wrote on the blackboard. Among these were: "The whole thing will get hot," "The water will change color," "The beans will get cooked, and you can eat them," and "The beans will grow." When I asked, "Will anything melt?" the children predicted that the styrofoam would not melt, but that the Q-Tip would. The next day, the child did his cooking experiment, and wrote down the results with my help. Many of his predictions were found to be true, but there were some surprises: It smelled terrible, the Q-Tip did not melt, and the whole thing bubbled.

In the "science education" approach above, the teacher's objective is for the child to learn about crystals. More specifically, the objectives are to get children to become able to *recognize* and *define* crystals, and to *describe* how they can be made. In this content-centered approach, children listen to explanations, look at what the teacher shows, and do what he or she planned.

In the "physical-knowledge" approach, by contrast, the teacher's objective is for children to pursue the problems and questions *they* come up with. The purpose of making crystals is thus not to teach about crystals per se, but to stimulate various ideas within a total atmosphere of experimentation. In the situation reported above, the making of crystals inspired four children in four different ways—to make "something" with grease from the popcorn pan, to make specks of pepper "swim" in water, to watch what happens to the water level when various objects are dropped into a container, and to cook a variety of objects. It also stimulated other children to think about many possible outcomes, and encouraged decentering through exchange of ideas about what might happen. The physical-knowledge approach thus, emphasizes children's initiative, their actions on objects, and their observation of the feedback from objects.

All babies and young children are naturally interested in examining objects, acting on them, and observing the objects' reactions. Our aim in physical-knowledge activities is to use this spontaneous interest by encouraging children to structure their knowledge in ways that are natural extensions of the knowledge they already have. Thus, learning in the physical-knowledge approach is always rooted in the child's natural development.

As we saw in the lesson on crystals, "science education" basically unloads adult-organized content on children. At this point, we shall not discuss the relative merits of either approach but reserve considering the rationale for using physical-knowledge activities until Chapter 2. In the remainder of this chapter, we briefly describe types of physical-knowledge activities and give examples, in order further to clarify the difference between our approach and the "science" activities commonly found in early-education texts.

Types of Physical-Knowledge Activities

The child's *action* on objects and his *observation* of the object's reaction are both important in all activities involving physical knowledge. However, we see two kinds of activities based on the relative importance of action and observation. In the first type, activities involving *the movement of objects* (or mechanics), the role of the child's *action* is primary and that of *observation* is secondary. Aiming a ball down an incline toward a container is an example of this kind of activity. The role of action is primary here because there is a direct and immediately observable correspondence between where the child positions the ball and where it rolls down. If he varies his action by moving the ball six inches to the right, the ball rolls down about six inches to the right of the previous fall line, parallel to it.

The second kind of activity involves *the changes in objects*. Making crystals is an example of this kind of activity. In activities involving the movement of objects, the objects only move—they do not change. In making crystals, however, the object itself changes. The role of *observation* thus becomes primary and that of the child's action becomes secondary. The role of action is secondary because the reaction of the object is neither direct nor immediate; that is, the outcome is due not to the child's action as such, but to the properties of the objects. Action is secondary also because, for example, mixing grease, water, and food color involves basically the same action as mixing salt, bluing, water, and ammonia. Yet the reaction of the second set of substances is very different, which leads to the conclusion that only under certain circumstances do crystals begin to form. Of primary importance, therefore, is the role of observation—the structuring of what is observable. We shall now give specific examples of each of these two kinds of activities: the movement of objects and changes in objects.

The Movement of Objects (Mechanics)

Actions that can be performed on objects to make them move include pulling, pushing, rolling, kicking, jumping, blowing, sucking, throwing, swinging (a pendulum), twirling, balancing, and dropping. All activities in this category offer the advantage of being good for the structuring of space and logico-mathematical knowledge,[2] in addition to physical knowledge. In a blowing activity, for example, if the child tries to move a straw across the floor by blowing it with another straw (see Figure 1.1), he finds out that he has to blow in the middle at a right angle to make it go straight. As a function of where one blows relative to the center of the straw, it turns more or less to the right or to the left, sometimes turning a complete 360 degrees. As the child sees how the straw reacts to different actions, he structures spatial and logical relationships. How this happens can be seen more clearly in the following description of a blowing activity. After giving each child a straw, Ms. Ellis showed them a box containing several of each of the following items:

     Kleenex
     Round Tinker Toys
     Popsicle sticks
     Straws
     Empty cans (frozen orange juice and one-pound coffee cans)
     Marbles
     Small blocks

She said, "Can you find something that you can blow across the floor?" This question prompted the children to look at objects with their "blowability" in

[2]"Logico-mathematical knowledge" will be defined and discussed in Chapter 2 (pp. 16–23).

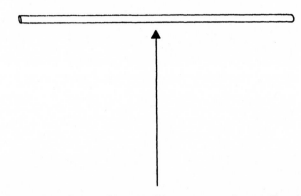

Figure 1.1 The place to blow on the straw to make it roll straight.

mind and to think, at some vague, intuitive level, about considerations such as the following: Is the object's weight relevant? Is its shape important? Are both important? How can we find out?

These questions illustrate the logico-mathematical structuring that takes place during a physical-knowledge activity. The child constructs logico-mathematical structures in the course of structuring specific contents. In this blowing activity, the child has an opportunity to create at least three categories—"things that *never* move" (a block), "things that *always* move" (a Kleenex, marble, straw, and popsicle stick), and "things that *sometimes* move" (an orange juice can and Tinker Toy which move only when they are in a certain position).[3] In addition, the child may observe that certain objects move by sliding, certain objects move by rolling, and still others (such as a straw) move in both ways. A classificatory scheme becomes also necessary to put into correspondence the result of blowing in the middle and the results of blowing on other parts of the straw. With this classificatory scheme the child can conclude that the only way to make the straw go straight is by blowing in the middle.

This blowing activity also involves serial correspondences. The child can put into correspondence the differences in weight of the objects and differences in their movability. He can also relate the variations in blowing hard or softly to the speed of the object's motion. As he varies the distance between his straw and the object, he may note that, although it is generally better to get close to the object, it is not possible to establish a simple correspondence between distance and movability. A particularly interesting problem is making the coffee can roll. Finding this task at first quite impossible, some children vary the position and direction of the airstream as shown

[3]This third category can be considered an intersection between the other two categories. That is, in one position, the can and Tinker Toy never move, and in another, they always move. At the preoperational level, however, we cannot expect children to have such a well-structured classificatory scheme with two categories which overlap partially.

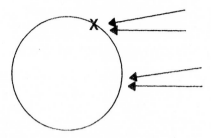

Figure 1.2. Various ways of blowing on a coffee can to make it roll.

in Figure 1.2. By watching the object's reaction, they discover that the best place to blow is the spot marked "X." When the can finally moves, it rolls away a little bit but then rolls back toward the child, and then away again! By coordinating his action with the can's movement and blowing only when it is rolling away from him, the child can succeed in blowing the object across the floor (in a way similar to our rocking a car back and forth to get it out of snow). There is a serial corresponcence between the can's rolling in one direction and its rolling in the opposite direction. Each successive movement is greater than the previous one, and the more it rolls forward, the more it rolls backward—until it builds up enough momentum to sail steadily forward.

In selecting phenomena involving the movement of objects, the following four criteria are important to keep in mind:

1. *The child must be able to produce the movement by his own action.* As stated earlier, the essence of physical-knowledge activities is the child's action on objects and his observation of the object's reaction. It is necessary, therefore, that the phenomenon selected be something that the child himself can produce. The movement of a piece of Kleenex in reaction to the child's sucking on it through a straw meets this criterion. The movement of objects caused by a magnet, on the other hand, is an example of a phenomenon that is produced only indirectly by the child's action and primarily by magnetic attraction.

2. *The child must be able to vary his action.* When the variations in the child's action result in corresponding variations of the object's reaction, the child has the opportunity to structure these regularities. In a pool game, for example, if the child misses the target by hitting a ball too far to the left, he can adjust the next attempt accordingly. In a pinball-type game, by contrast, the child's action is limited to pulling a lever, and there is very little variation possible in how he releases the lever. The child thus cannot significantly affect the outcome. Without a direct correspondence between the variations in actions and reactions, a phenomenon offers little opportunity for structuring.

3. *The reaction of the object must be observable.* Movement is a clearly observable reaction of an object to the child's action. That is why we stress this first category of activities, the movement of objects, as the best way to facilitate the child's structuring of correspondences. However, the materials the teacher selects can ensure or prevent observability. For example, an opaque tube for water play prevents observability.

4. *The reaction of the object must be immediate.* Correspondences are much easier to establish when the object's reaction is immediate. For example, the child can raise an object to the top of a jungle gym by pulling a rope as shown in Figure 1.3. He can also lower the object by letting go of the rope. As a function of his pulling the rope, the child can see that the object goes up. He can also see that as a function of his releasing the rope, the object goes down. The weights of a cuckoo clock work in exactly the same way, but the movement takes place so slowly that the correspondence between the lengthening of one end and the shortening of the other is difficult to see. The cuckoo clock is an example not only of an object which reacts slowly but also of a phenomenon that is not produced by the child's own action (criterion 1). The child can pull the free end of the chain down, but the action of pulling down on the other end is performed by a weight.

The Changes in Objects

Examples of physical-knowledge activities that rely heavily on the role of observation are the following:

Cooking
Mixing paints, or paint powder and water, and drying paint
Making pottery
Melting wax and making candles
Playing with ice and water

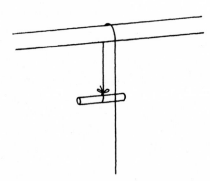

Figure 1.3. Raising and lowering an object by pulling and releasing a rope.

These activities are different from those involving the movement of objects in that the phenomena involve actual changes in the objects themselves. For example, dissolving Jello and mixing paints both produce changes in the objects. In this case, how such objects react to a certain treatment depends not on the child's action but on inherent properties of the objects. For example, the child mixing water and sugar performs exactly the same action when he mixes water and sand, yet the results of the two actions are very different. Furthermore, the action of mixing and stirring cannot be varied like the action of aiming a ball at a target. In addition, the object's reaction is neither direct nor unambiguous, since there is usually something other than the child's action that is at work (such as heat or chemical reactions). Finally, the object's reaction is not always immediate. For example, the child has to stir sugar for some time to make it dissolve in water. Likewise, he has to stir sand for some time before concluding that it does not dissolve. Thus activities involving changes in objects do not meet the criteria that pertain to the movement of objects. Only under *certain* circumstances, does the object change in *certain* ways. It is these circumstances and changes that the child has to observe and structure. For these reasons, we say that in activities belonging to this end of the continuum, observation is primary and action is secondary in relative importance.

Although there is a large element of "magic" in all the phenomena included in this second category, it is still important to distinguish between the kinds of action and observation that are possible in each activity. In cooking, for example, action and its variability still play a large part in contrast to this outline of the study of evaporation and condensation of water from an early-education text:

Experience	Related concepts
Notice early morning fog.	A cloud moves down onto the earth and is called *fog* by the people in it.
Make fog by boiling water under a pan of ice water.	When air is cooled, it cannot hold so much water vapor.
See the fog on a cold window pane.	
Put ice into a glass of water; set it aside until water condenses on the glass.	On the cold surface, see the water that came out of the air.
While having a hot bath, notice mirrors and windows. Feel their coldness and dampness. (Use flannelboard and pictures to show this at school.)	Water comes out of the air when the air touches a cold surface. (Todd and Heffernan, 1970, p. 319)

The only actions recommended in this activity consist of boiling water under a pan of ice water, and of putting ice into a glass of water. These actions are dictated by the teacher and do not offer the motivation that a cooking activity, for example, affords. From the standpoint of the observability of the phenomena, too, this activity must be questioned. Air and the water in it are both unobservable, and no amount of explanation with a flannelboard and pictures will help young children make sense out of the teacher's attempts to teach. For the same reasons of unobservability and incomprehensibility, we also reject contents such as the following which are recommended in the science chapters of other early-education texts:

> *Electricity* . . . Dry cell batteries can be used to ring bells and to light bulbs. Children can learn to complete the circuit to make it work. Show the children the electric element on the hot plate or electric frying pan used for cooking projects. They can learn such words as battery, circuit, outlets, plugs, bulbs, and switches. (Hildebrand, 1971, pp. 157–158)

> *Matter and energy* . . . Some machines burn fuel; some use electricity. (Leeper, Dales, Skipper and Witherspoon, 1974, p. 306)

In selecting activities involving changes in objects, a rule of thumb is to consider the objects that primitive people could act upon. Electricity and machines run by electricity were not invented until later in history. The history of science can thus serve as a guide as to what is probably appropriate for preschool children. In primitive times, people were interested in cooking, plants, animals, and art. Just as these people structured their observations, young children learn about the properties of objects and living organisms and their interactions by acting on them and observing the regularity of their reaction. For example, in kindergarten classes, we find each fall several children who think that a leaf found on the ground will grow if it is planted and watered. If we want to nurture an experimental attitude, we must encourage such children to act on the object to test their hypotheses.

Activities between the Two Categories

Between the two categories of movement and changes in objects are many other activities which cannot be categorized as neatly. Examples are:

Finding out whether an object sinks or floats
Sifting
Shadow play
Playing with mirrors
Producing echoes
Looking through a magnifying glass
Touching various objects with a magnet

The above activities share elements with the other two categories but cannot be placed in either of them. The child's actions clearly do not produce a change in the objects themselves; on the other hand, any movement that results from the action is caused more by the properties of the object than by the subject's action. For example, the fact that a nail sinks in water while a ping-pong ball does not is determined by the properties of the objects rather than by the child's action. This is why we say that these activities are situated between the two poles.

In each one of these activities, the structuring of observation plays a large role. A nail *always* sinks in water. A shadow is *always* on the side away from the source of light. A shadow is long under certain circumstances and short under others. When it is short, everybody's shadow is short. A certain glass *always* makes the object appear bigger. Certain objects *always* stick to a magnet, while others *never* do.

Most of the examples we have listed of activities which cannot be neatly categorized can be found in early-education texts under the heading of "science." However, these texts also include many other activities which we would not recommend. In selecting certain of these activities while rejecting most others, it is important to remember that the objective of physical-knowledge activities is not to teach scientific concepts, principles, or explanations. It is, rather, to provide opportunities for the child to act on objects and see how the objects react—to build the foundation for physics and chemistry. The four criteria of good activities given in connection with the movement of objects can therefore be used to evaluate all other physical-knowledge activities. Shadow play, sinking and floating, cooking, and making candles all encourage the child to produce a phenomenon, to vary his action, and to observe how the object reacts. In the next chapter, we present the rationale for physical-knowledge activities and show that the child constructs knowledge by acting on objects and people and not by having the teacher present or demonstrate ready-made concepts.

Before concluding this discussion of kinds of physical-knowledge activities, we would like to point out that there are countless incidental situations throughout the day when the child elaborates his physical knowledge. These, too, can be evaluated according to the same criteria discussed above with reference to the movement of objects. Examples which do not meet these criteria are why there are four seasons in the year, why flowers are beginning to bloom, how the room is heated, and how hot water comes to the bathroom. On the other hand, experiences which the teacher will do well to capitalize on include drying wet mittens, hanging up paintings to let them dry, pasting things together, noticing that ice cubes always float, watching ice and snow melt and make a mess, and spilling and mopping up milk. In the next chapter, we discuss why these kinds of activities are especially good for children's development.

Chapter 2

Why Use
Physical-Knowledge
Activities?

To answer this question in a nutshell, physical-knowledge activities are especially conducive not only to the development of children's knowledge of objects in the physical world, but also to the development of their intelligence, or knowledge, in a more general sense. In order to clarify this statement, we need to discuss the epistemological background of Piaget's theory, the distinctions he made among various aspects of knowledge, and their interdependence in the constructive process. The rationale for physical-knowledge activities versus "science education" will also become evident.

Upon first reading Piaget's work, most people appreciate its significance from the psychological perspective—that is, the insight it provides into the nature of children's thought and the stages of development. The developmental child psychologist finds the theory useful in answering questions such as "How does the child think?" and "How does the child think differently at different stages?" The thrust of Piaget's work, however, was not child psychology, but epistemology. As an epistemologist, the broader questions to which he addressed himself included: "What is knowledge?" "How did it develop?" and "How do we know what we know?" Piaget studied the development of thought in children because he was convinced that this was the best approach to epistemological questions about the nature of knowedge in adults and in the history of knowledge.

Philosophers have debated for a long time about how we attain truth, or knowledge. Two main currents—the empiricist and rationalist currents—developed in answer to this question, differing especially in the way they conceived the role of experience. We shall now discuss these briefly in order to highlight their differences as well as the relationship Piaget emphasizes between physical and logico-mathematical knowledge.

Empiricists (such as Locke, Berkeley, and Hume) argued in essence that knowledge has its source outside the individual, and that it is internalized through the senses. They further argued that the individual at birth is like a clean slate on which experiences are "written" as he grows up. As Locke expressed it in 1690,

> The senses at first let in particular ideas, and furnish the yet empty cabinet, and the mind by degrees growing familiar with some of them, they are lodged in the memory. . . . (1947, p. 22)

Although such rationalists as Descartes, Spinoza, and Kant did not deny the importance of sensory experience, they insisted that reason is more powerful than sensory experience because it enables us to know with certainty many truths which sensory observation can never ascertain. For example, we know that every event has a cause, in spite of the fact that we can obviously not examine every event in the entire past and future of the universe. Rationalists also pointed out that since our senses often "deceive" us in perceptual illusions, sensory experience cannot be trusted to give us reliable knowledge. The rigor, precision, and certainty of mathematics, a purely deductive system, remains the rationalist's prime tool in support of the power of reason. Yet this power of reason must itself be accounted for, and rationalists concluded by saying that it is an innate characteristic of human beings.

Piaget's position, called relativism, is in sharp disagreement with empiricism, and, although he does not agree completely with rationalism, when constrained to place himself in a broad sense in one tradition or the other, he aligns himself with rationalism. With reference to the empiricist belief that objects are known by the subject through the senses, Piaget argues that objects are never known as they are "out there" in external reality, but that they are known by assimilation into the schemes that the subject brings to each situation. The term *relativism* refers to the fact that the object-as-known is relative to the knowledge that the knower brings to a situation. For example, the same mobile is not the same object for the same child at the ages of six months, two years, five years, and ten years. Babies have no idea about the spatial connections among the parts of a mobile hanging over their cribs, and they have no appreciation of the fact that each one of a number of arms is delicately balanced in relation to all others.

Many of Piaget's research findings with his tasks can be cited to support his position on the rationalist side of the fence. For example, let us take the most famous task, that of the conservation of liquid.[1] Sensory experience alone will never enable the child to conserve because each time the liquid is put in a container of different dimensions, the child's senses can only tell him that the liquid *is* different (in a narrow, tall container compared to what it was in a wider beaker). It should be noted, furthermore, that the child's sensory experience includes watching the action of pouring and seeing that nothing has been added or taken away. It is thus not sensory information that enables the child to conserve, but rather reasoning, which gives him a feeling of *logical necessity* that the quantity of liquid remains the same when it is poured into a container of different dimensions.

The class-inclusion task is another example that illustrates the fact that sensory experience alone will never enable the child to reason logically. In this task, the child is given, for example, six blue blocks and two yellow ones. He is first asked, "What do we call these?" so the examiner can proceed with whatever word came from the *child's* vocabulary. If he says, "blocks," he is asked to show *all* the blocks. The examiner then asks the child to show "*all* the blue blocks" and "*all* the yellow blocks." Only after thus ascertaining that the child understands the phrases "all the blocks," "all the blue blocks," and "all the yellow blocks" does the examiner ask the following class-inclusion question: "Are there more blue blocks or more blocks?" Four-year-olds typically answer, "More blue ones."[2]

Note that the child has all the sensory information *and* all the language he needs to answer the question correctly. Yet, until he is about seven or eight years of age, the young child usually cannot give this answer. This task thus illustrates the inadequacy not only of sensory information but also of language in enabling young children to reason logically. It is but one of many

[1]In this task, two identical transparent glasses are filled with equal quantities of water. Then, one is emptied into a third glass (either wider or narrower), and the child is asked whether the two have the same amount to drink, or whether one has more. Until about the age of seven or eight years, children typically believe that the glass in which the water is higher has more to drink.

[2]The examiner thereupon asks, "Than what?" The four-year-old's typical answer is "Than yellow ones." In other words, the question the examiner asks is "Are there more blue blocks or more blocks?" but the question the child "hears" is "Are there more blue blocks or more yellow ones?" Young children "hear" a question that is different from the question the adult asks because once they mentally cut the whole into two parts, the only thing they can think about is the two parts. For them, at that moment, the whole no longer exists. They can think about the whole, but not when they are thinking about the parts. In order to compare the whole with a part, the child has to do two opposite mental actions at the same time—cut the whole into two parts and put the parts back together into a whole. This is precisely what young children cannot do. This inability to think simultaneously about the whole and a part explains why, when they are asked, "Are there more blue blocks or more blocks?" the only "blocks" they can see while thinking about the blue ones are the yellow ones.

that can be cited to disprove the common empiricist belief that what enables children to reason logically is language. In fact, Piaget has demonstrated the importance of reason in literally hundreds of experiments. For further examples, the reader is referred to Piaget (1946), Piaget and Inhelder (1941, 1948, and 1966a), Piaget, Inhelder, and Szeminska (1948), Piaget and Szeminska (1941), and Inhelder and Piaget (1955 and 1959).

While Piaget's position is thus squarely in the rationalist tradition, he disagrees with those who argue that the ability to reason is an innate characteristic of human beings. He insists that all knowledge, including the ability to reason logically, is constructed by the individual as he acts on objects and people and tries to make sense out of his experience. This view, called constructivism, is also in disagreement with the empiricist belief that knowledge has its source outside the child to begin with, and that each child acquires it by internalizing it through his senses and/or language.[3] Piaget believes that knowledge is acquired not by internalization of some outside "given" but by construction from within. This construction is a long process that begins at birth and continues throughout adulthood. To explain constructivism in relation to physical-knowledge activities, we would like to discuss a fundamental distinction Piaget adopted from epistemology between physical and logico-mathematical knowledge.

Physical and Logico-Mathematical Knowledge

Physical knowledge, as we saw in Chapter 1, is knowledge of objects which are "out there" and observable in external reality. The fact that a ball rolls down an incline, that a certain combination of stuff produces crystals, and that certain objects float on water are examples of physical knowledge. The fact that a ball bounces when it is dropped on the floor, while a glass usually breaks, are also examples of physical knowledge. The source of physical knowledge is thus mainly in the object, that is, in the way the object provides the subject with opportunities for observation.

Logico-mathematical knowledge, on the other hand, consists of relationships which the subject creates and introduces into or among objects.[4] An example of logico-mathematical knowledge is the fact that, in the class-

---

[3]The most common reason for the widespread misunderstanding of Piaget's theory is probably the fact that most psychologists and educators are raised in the empiricist tradition, completely unaware of the rationalists' point of view and of the fact that Piaget's theory flows out of the rationalist current. Many thus unconsciously deform Piaget's theory by assimilating it into their empiricist assumptions.

[4]The most elementary relationship and the foundation for all of the more complex logico-mathematical relationships is between two objects. When the child encounters two spoons of different size, for example, he may think of them as "the same," "different," "bigger than," or "two." These relationships exist neither *in* one spoon nor *in* the other. Relationships are literally created by the subject who puts the

inclusion task, there are more blocks than blue ones. The blocks are all "out there"—that is, observable in front of the child. However, they are not organized into the class of "all the blocks" composed of the subclasses "yellow blocks" and "blue blocks" until the child creates this hierarchical organization and introduces it among the objects. Another example of logico-mathematical knowledge is the conservation of number.[5] The two rows of objects are "out there" in front of the child, but he cannot deduce numerical equivalence until he can introduce this logico-mathematical relationship into the two sets. Once he has created this relationship, however, the equivalence of the two sets becomes obvious. The source of logico-mathematical knowledge is thus mainly in the subject, that is, in the way the subject *organizes* reality.

While Piaget insists on this distinction between the source of physical knowledge and that of logico-mathematical knowledge, he argues that the two are not entirely different because, in the psychological reality of the young child's experience, the two are inseparably linked. What must be analyzed to understand the constructive process is, therefore, the nature of "experience"—the relationship between physical experience and logico-mathematical experience.

Physical experience bears directly on objects and leads to knowledge which is derived from the objects themselves. The child obtains information from objects by empirical (or "simple") abstraction. In empirical abstraction, the child focuses on a certain aspect(s) of the object and ignores others. For example when he notices that a ball is round, he focuses on this property and, at that moment, ignores others such as weight and color. When he drops the ball and discovers that it bounces, he likewise focuses on this fact and ignores others, using, of course, his ability to organize to sort out his observations.

In the case of logico-mathematical experience, the knowledge the child gains from the experience is derived not from objects, but from his action bearing on the objects. For example, when he says that there are more blocks than blue blocks, he is getting this information by coordinating his action of putting into relationship "all the blocks" with his action on "all the blue blocks." When he says that there are more blue blocks (than yellow

---

objects into relationship, and if he did not put them into relationship, for him each object would remain separate and unrelated to the other. Since relationships are created by the subject, they cannot be judged "right" or "wrong" by empirical verification. The two spoons can thus be considered "the same," "different," or "two," depending on the subject's point of view.

[5]In this task, the experimenter typically makes a row of eight objects and asks the child to make a row for himself that has just as many. Then, one row is spread out, the other pushed together, and the child is asked whether the two rows have the same or one has more. Before about age five or six, children believe one row (usually the longer) has more, even when they count them correctly.

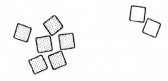

Figure 2.1. Bringing together the blocks that are the same, and separating those that are different.

ones), he is likewise coordinating his action on "all the blue blocks" with his action on "all the yellow blocks." When he figures out that $6 + 2 = 2 + 6$, he is also coordinating the action of putting 6 down first and then 2, with that of putting 2 down first and then 6. This knowledge thus stems from the child's own actions. The physical properties of the specific objects involved are irrelevant to logico-mathematical experiences. For example, the child can find out that $6 + 2 = 2 + 6$ with pebbles just as well as with marbles or blocks. By contrast, it is the physical properties of specific objects which are all-important in physical experience.

Logico-mathematical knowledge is constructed by "reflective abstraction" which is very different from empirical abstraction. While information about physical properties is abstracted from the objects themselves, in reflective abstraction, knowledge derives from the subject's action of introducing relationships into or among objects. When he is given six blue and two yellow blocks, for example, the child can act on them in a variety of ways, thereby introducing relationships. Following are three examples. First, he can bring together the ones that are the same and separate those that are different as shown in Figure 2.1. Here, the child introduces into each block the characteristic of being "the same" as the others that he grouped together, and "different" from those that he separated. Second, the child can order the blocks as shown in Figure 2.2. Here, he introduces into the first yellow block the characteristic of being "second" by virtue of the fact that he put one block before it. Into the second yellow block, he introduces the characteristic of being "sixth" by virtue of the fact that he put five blocks before it. Each object is thus enriched by the subject's action on it. These characteristics are abstracted not from the properties of the objects but from the subject's action of putting them into relationships. The specific colors of the blocks here are, therefore, irrelevant. The same organization could have been introduced into a collection of five spoons and two forks, etc. A third action of introducing relationships among the blocks is that of quantifying some or all of them, in which case each block acquires the characteristic of being "one." Figure 2.3 shows, for example, that the color of the blocks is irrelevant when each block becomes "one."

Figure 2.2. Ordering the blocks.

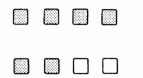

Figure 2.3. Making two groups that are quantitatively equivalent.

The term *action* requires clarification, as it has at least two different meanings in Piaget's terminology. The first meaning is the common one which we used in Chapter 1 to refer to manipulative actions on objects. There, action means to do something to (or with) the object, such as pushing it, pulling it, or putting it in water. The second meaning of action is harder to understand because the child can act on an object without even touching it. For example, when he looks at a block and notices it as a block, he can be said to be acting on it.[6] In the three examples we have just cited, physical manipulation is not an essential part of the child's action of putting the objects into relationships. In fact, physical manipulation eventually becomes unnecessary, and the child becomes able to sort, order, and quantify objects in his head without even touching them. At this point, the action is said to be internalized.

Action as a mental activity has two poles, or aspects—one which focuses on what is specific to the objects in question, and the other which concerns the general structuring of many specific experiences. For example, when the child looks at six blue blocks and two yellow ones and thinks about them as "blue ones and yellow ones," he is focusing on their specific properties on the one hand and, on the other hand, he is also activating a whole network of relationships. That is, to think of the blocks as blocks, he must distinguish their similarities and differences in relation to all other objects. In order to think of blueness, likewise, he must put this property in relation to all other colors. Only within such a network of relationships—a general framework—can the child recognize the blue and yellow blocks. In other words, although we have so far discussed physical and logico-mathematical experience separately, as if one could take place without the other, the two are in reality inseparable. There can be no physical experience without a logico-mathematical framework, and, for babies and young children, there can be no logico-mathematical experience without objects to put into relationships.

Having argued that mental action is necessary for the construction of both physical and logico-mathematical knowledge, we would now like to add a most important condition: namely, that physical manipulation is indispens-

---

[6]This conception reflects a basic difference between the empiricist conception of the term *stimulus* and Piaget's conception of the "object." Piaget insists that most stimuli do not stimulate the subject (the individual) because until the subject acts on an object, the object does not exist in the subject's mind.

able for mental action to become possible. Let us explain what we mean by taking the example of how a child comes to know a ball.

There is not much the child can find out about a ball if he does not act on it in the first sense of the term. It is only by dropping the ball on the floor, rolling it, rolling it down an incline, throwing it in the air, throwing it against the floor, throwing it against a carpeted floor, throwing it against the grass, throwing it against a wall, varying the force he applies, trying to catch it, chasing it down a stairway, kicking it, and so forth, that he discovers the properties of the ball. This is why in Chapter 1 we emphasized the importance of the child's action on objects and insisted that the child be able not only to produce a phenomenon by his own action but also to vary his action.

In Chapter 1 we also emphasized the observability of the object's reaction and the importance of the immediacy of this reaction. The child's observation of the object's reaction refers to action in the second sense. One pole of this action focuses on the specific bits of information which have their source outside the child, such as the fact of bouncing, bouncing higher, making a sound as it bounces, bouncing back at an angle, rolling, or rolling faster. The other pole concerns the general structuring aspect in the sense that the child can "read" observable facts from reality only by putting them into relationship with other facts he already knows. For example, the child can recognize a ball as a ball only by putting it into relationship with "things that are *not* balls." If he did not put each object into relationship with all other objects he knows, each object would, for him, remain a new object unrelated to anything else within his experience. To read the fact of "bouncing" from reality, too, the child has to put "bouncing" into relationship with "reactions which are different from bouncing." Otherwise, this bit of information remains isolated and unrelated to every other reaction of other objects. "Bouncing higher" and "rolling faster" are also relationships without which observable facts cannot be read from reality.

Our earlier statement that Piaget does not attribute two entirely different sources to physical and logico-mathematical knowledge should now be clear to the reader. The physical experience the child has gathered helps him to structure his logico-mathematical framework. The better this framework is structured, the more accurately and richly the child will be able to read facts from reality. In Part II, we will give many examples of classroom situations in which the teacher can see that young children are in certain situations either blind to physical facts or read them in inaccurate ways.

"Science Education" Contrasted with Physical-Knowledge Activities

In Chapter 1, we contrasted physical-knowledge activities with "science education." In light of the theoretical rationale for physical-knowledge activities, the differences between these and "science education" become clearer. Traditional science programs are based on the empiricist assumption that the child learns through the five senses (by looking at things, smelling them, hearing them, touching them, and tasting them) and through language (as he has things explained to him). Physical-knowledge activities, by contrast, are based on Piaget's constructivism—the theory which states that each child constructs his physical and logico-mathematical knowledge through his own actions on objects.

The importance of physical-knowledge activities was discussed by Piaget in a recent book on causality (Piaget and Garcia, 1971). He said:

> The child can certainly be interested in seriating for the sake of seriating, and classifying for the sake of classifying, etc., when the occasion presents itself. However, on the whole it is when he has events or phenomena to explain or goals to reach in an intriguing situation that operations are the most exercised. (p. 26)

> The functioning of intelligence (operations) . . . is all the more stimulated and developed as the problems presented by reality are more varied and more interesting. (p. 29)

> The structure involved is in fact a form, and as such is constructed by the subject's activity in order to structure a given content. (p. 30)

In an often quoted article entitled "The Having of Wonderful Ideas," Duckworth (1972) makes the same point in the following more general and down-to-earth manner:

> I think intelligence cannot develop without content. Making new connections depends on knowing enough about something in the first place to be able to think of other things to do, of other questions to ask, which demand the more complex connections in order to make sense of it all. The more ideas a person already has at his disposal, the more new ideas occur, and the more he can coordinate to build up still more complicated schemes. (p. 231)

In addition to the two sources of knowledge we have already discussed— namely objects and the subject himself—Piaget distinguished a third source: people. We now turn to this third aspect of knowledge.

Social Knowledge

Examples of social knowledge are that a glass is called "glass," that there is no school on Saturdays and Sundays, that December 25 is Christmas Day, and that one should not tell lies, steal things, cheat other people, or jump on tables. (It should be noted that while Piaget distinguished this aspect of knowledge in his works, particularly in *The Moral Judgment of the Child* [Piaget, 1932], he did not designate social knowledge with a specific term.)

Social knowledge is similar to physical knowledge in that it requires specific information from the external world. Without specific input, the child could not know that tables are not to jump on, that a particular object is called "glass," and that there is no school on Saturdays and Sundays.

While the ultimate source of physical knowledge is objects, the ultimate source of social knowledge is agreement among people. We prefer to make a distinction between knowledge agreed upon solely by convention, which we call "social (arbitrary) knowledge," and knowledge whose basis is the coordination of points of view about what is good or bad in matters concerning conduct, which Piaget called "moral judgment."

An example of social (arbitrary) knowledge is the fact that December 25 is Christmas Day. There is no inherent physical or logical reason why December 25 should be different from any other day of the year; neither is there any compelling reason why one should call a glass "glass" or dismiss school on Saturdays and Sundays. The criteria of truth for social (arbitrary) knowledge are thus decided upon by conventions that vary from one culture to the next.[7]

Morality, by contrast, is built by people as they regulate their interactions. Moral rules about such things as lying, stealing, and cheating were constructed and codified as people felt a necessity to regulate their actions for mutual benefit. Consensus in questions of morality is, therefore, not reached in the same way as consensus in social (arbitrary) knowledge. Moral rules thus resemble logico-mathematical knowledge in that they are built by the coordination of different points of view, and they are thus not arbitrary.

Moral development and the learning of social knowledge are very important aspects of an educational program based on Piaget's theory. However, since they are beyond the scope of this book,[8] we will limit our remarks concerning social knowledge to the following two points:

1. The logico-mathematical framework involved in the structuring of physical knowledge is the same logico-mathematical framework which is involved in the structuring of social knowledge.
2. In "science education" content is usually taught as if it were social knowledge.

As stated earlier, social knowledge is similar to physical knowledge in

---

[7]In social knowledge which is arbitrary, some conventions are completely arbitrary, while others are based on practical or physical considerations which are not completely arbitrary. Part of the convention of celebrating Christmas with presents and gay decorations, for example, is related to the fact that winter is a dreary time of the year. Eating dessert at the end of a meal and not using the spoon someone else has used are likewise not entirely arbitrary. The length of women's skirts, on the other hand, is completely arbitrary (except for the economic value of changing fashions).

[8]The book on group games which is in preparation will deal with moral development in greater depth.

that it requires specific information from the external world. Both are contents of knowledge, and each bit of specific content can make sense only in relation to every other bit. For example, the fact that there is no school on Saturdays and Sundays is specific information which can have meaning only in relation to every other day of the week. As we can see when children ask, "Do I go to school today?" days have to be structured into "school days" and "non-school days" with the same logico-mathematical framework that is involved in the reading of physical facts from reality. The fact that December 25 is Christmas Day is likewise understood only in relation to every other day of the year. Other examples of social facts which must be structured in order to be read from reality are that children can play with marbles in the house but not with basketballs, that spilling paint, milk, and water on the floor is frowned upon, that there are certain delicate objects which children are not allowed to touch, and that candy and gum are allowed only at certain times. Since the child has to structure a whole multitude of information from the external world (rules and events, for example), the more consistent and intelligible these phenomena are, the more they probably contribute to the child's structuring of a logico-mathematical framework.

Because educators have not made the distinction among the three ultimate sources of knowledge, and because they have not recognized the constructive process of learning, most science curricula in existence today call for teaching science as if it were social knowledge. Examples of this approach at the preschool level were given in Chapter 1 (crystals, condensation, electricity, and energy). In this social-knowledge approach, the teacher is like a funnel that collects knowledge and pours it into passive recipients. Since social knowledge can be acquired only from people, it is appropriate for the teacher to act as a source of this knowledge.[9] Phenomena taught in "science," however, belong to the realm of physical knowledge and should be taught in a different way. Physical knowledge can be constructed by the child only through acting on objects, and the teacher's role here must be to assist the child in this process rather than to serve as the source of knowledge.

Knowledge of Space and Time

Objects and events exist in space and time. However, space and time are not mere "containers" for objects and events. They are frameworks constructed by each subject as he tries to make sense out of changes in objects and events by putting them into spatiotemporal relationships.

---

[9]Moral judgment, however, cannot be taught in the same way as social (arbitrary) knowledge. The interested reader may refer to Kamii and DeVries (1977) for a brief discussion of moral development.

When young children are asked to imagine what the level of the water looks like in a tilted bottle wearing a tight-fitting, opaque cover, they make drawings such as the one shown in Figure 2.4 (Piaget and Inhelder, 1948). They draw the water level parallel to the bottom of the tilted bottle because their frame of reference is limited to the inside of the bottle. When they later have a larger framework which enables them to take account of what is exterior to the bottle (around the age of eight), they draw the water level parallel to the external frame of reference as shown in Figure 2.5. This is an example of the empirical facts which led Piaget to conclude that space is a framework constructed by each child as he coordinates spatial relationships into a coherent system.

For Piaget, time too is a framework constructed by each child. Let us consider the following example of the kind of experiments that led Piaget to this view. In this interview a large vessel was allowed to empty through an inverted Y-shaped transparent tube (see Figure 2.6). A single faucet controlled the flow of the water so that the child could see that the water started and stopped running simultaneously on both sides. To make the simultaneity of the stopping even more obvious, the experimenter sometimes pulled both bottles away from under the taps at the same time. The water was collected in small bottles or glasses of different shapes and dimensions. Below is the account of a typical four-year-old's answers to Piaget's questions:

> Per (4½): . . . Did we start (the water in both taps) at the same time? *Yes.* Did we stop at the same time on both sides? *No.* Didn't we take the bottles from under the taps at the same time? *No.* (wrong) (The experiment is repeated.) Did we stop them together? *Yes.* So did we stop them at the same time? *No, because this bottle* (the larger one) *is not full.* . . .
> (Piaget, 1946, p. 133)

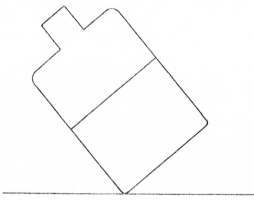

Figure 2.4. The level of water drawn by younger children.

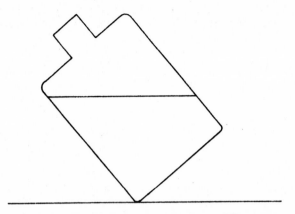

Figure 2.5. The level of water drawn by older children.

This is an example of how young children conceive time in terms of actions and/or the results of actions rather than in terms of a temporal framework common to a variety of actions. In this situation, they focus on the water levels at the end of the event. Thus, they are struck by the fact that the smaller bottle is filled up while the larger one is not, and conclude that the two taps did not stop at the same time! They have not constructed a framework in which the simultaneity, temporal order, duration of events, and final results can be coordinated in a coherent way.

The reader who is interested in finding out more about the child's

Figure 2.6. The apparatus used to make the water start and stop at the same time on both sides.

construction of a spatiotemporal framework is referred to Piaget (1946a, 1946b) and Piaget and Inhelder (1948a, 1948b, 1966). Suffice it to say here that physical-knowledge activities contribute to the child's structuring of space and time. As he anticipates and observes the movements which occur when he blows on a straw, releases a pendulum to hit a target, rolls a ball down an incline, shoots a marble, jumps on a lever, makes "wheels" with rollers, and tries to balance a mobile, he creates and coordinates spatial relationships. He also structures time in these activities and others such as drying collages, sifting dirt, stacking blocks and knocking them down with a ball, and making popcorn, Jello, crystals, ice, and candles. Causality, after all, involves phenomena which take place in space and time.

Physical Knowledge in Its Developmental Context

We have so far been discussing the important role of physical-knowledge activities in the origin of knowledge and intelligence. We would now like to discuss the importance of physical-knowledge activities from another angle by considering the developmental sweep from infancy to adolescence. This sweep can be summarized as follows: The young child focuses mainly on specific physical, observable content, particularly the result of his action. As he grows older, the balance between the physical and logico-mathematical aspects shifts, with the logico-mathematical aspect becoming increasingly detached from physical content. In adolescence and finally adulthood, the logico-mathematical aspect can become completely independent of content (as can be seen in "pure" mathematics), and the physical aspect becomes progressively more dependent on a logico-mathematical organization (as can be seen in physics). We elaborate this summary below.

From the very beginning, the infant's actions involve his social-biological relationships with people, especially his mother or caretaker, and his relationships with objects. The baby's actions on objects and people have two undifferentiated poles, one in which his attention is oriented toward the specificity of each object (such as the sound of a rattle) and one in which he is oriented toward what is general (such as shaking every other object and putting the rattle in relation with these). The first aspect of the action is the root of what will later become physical knowledge, and the second, the root of what will later become logico-mathematical knowledge.[10] During the sensory-motor period, the baby learns what happens when he pushes objects, pulls them, shakes them, and drops them.

[10]Since physical and logico-mathematical knowledge are in reality not differentiated during the sensory-motor period, this distinction is only theoretical. In discussing the sensory-motor period, it is only in light of the differentiation that later takes place that we can make this theoretical distinction.

During the preoperational period, the physical-material-observable and logico-mathematical aspects of actions continue to be undifferentiated,[11] with the child interested mainly in the results of his actions. When actions on objects change something observable in them, these changes are understood in physical-observable terms. For example, actions can modify the shape of a clay ball and the space occupied by a number of objects. Because these observable characteristics change, the child concludes that quantity has changed.

During the period of concrete operations, the logico-mathematical aspect becomes partially dissociated from the physical aspect of actions as a result of the internal coordination of the logico-mathematical aspect. The child coordinates relationships and structures them into operational systems which enable him to make logical deductions. As these systems become more powerful, the child becomes able to make deductions with a feeling of logical necessity rather than being limited to the observed results of actions. These operational systems appear first with respect to contents that are easy to structure. Thus the conservation of elementary number appears before the conservation of amount and weight of clay.

With the attainment of formal operations, the logico-mathematical pole becomes independent of content (as in "pure" mathematics), and the physical pole becomes increasingly more dependent on logico-mathematical structuring (as can be seen in physics). The same is true for the further elaboration of social knowledge. We will give a detailed example at the end of this chapter of how physical knowledge such as the notion of specific gravity can be elaborated only when formal operations are possible.

The above developmental sweep convinces us of the importance of physical-knowledge activities for preschool children because at this point in their development children are a) intrinsically and keenly interested in objects, and b) creating and coordinating the basic relationships which will later become structured into operational systems. Since later relationships are created by coordinating the ones that were created earlier, those that are established in early childhood are indispensable for the later construction of all knowledge. In short, we use physical-knowledge activities not only to enable children to build a foundation for physics and chemistry but also to stimulate them to construct a logical and spatiotemporal framework which

[11]While the physical and logico-mathematical aspects of actions are undifferentiated both during the sensory-motor and the preoperational periods, the nature of this undifferentiation is not the same. During the sensory-motor period, the infant is limited to the here-and-now, as he cannot represent objects that are absent, and he has no awareness of repeating or not repeating an action. During the preoperational period, in contrast, the young child's thought extends far beyond the here-and-now as he can represent objects that are not present, and can put into correspondence the variations in his actions and the variations in the results he produced.

will help them to structure many other contents. The use of objects is particularly good if children can observe the variations of the object's reactions in relation to variations in their own actions. In fact, actions on objects are so important that we are willing to speculate that without them children will not go far in developing their intelligence. (We would like to point out, however, that looking at something from different angles is also acting on an object and that carefully observing somebody else's action can, up to a point, replace one's own action on objects.)

Physical-knowledge activities are good also because they contribute to the development of certain attitudes necessary for intellectual development. If children learn by constructing their own knowledge from within, they have to be active, independent, alert, and curious, have initiative and confidence in their ability to figure things out for themselves, and speak their minds with conviction. Unlike "science education," physical knowledge activities foster these attitudes because children are not *shown* things or *told* what to do, nor do they have things *explained* with a barrage of words.

We have, in fact, found that certain physical-knowledge activities are particularly good for children who are constricted and fearful, and whose curiosity has been stifled. These children, for example, find security in making objects do what they want and seeing the regularity of their reaction. When a child rolls a ball down an incline toward a container, for example, the object reacts to the child's action with a certain regularity. Even failure is easy for the child to accept if his "mistake" is pointed out by an object. To be simply told by an adult that one is wrong is quite another thing!

"Intelligence," "Knowledge," and "Learning"

At the beginning of this chapter, we stated that physical-knowledge activities contribute to the development not only of the child's physical knowledge but also his intelligence in a general sense. We devote the remainder of this chapter to clarifying this statement.

When Piaget taught his course on intelligence, he began it by asking, "What is intelligence?" He then answered his own question by saying that intelligence is what enables us to adapt to new situations. He went on to point out that there are two aspects to any act of adaptation—our comprehension of the situation and the invention of a solution based on this understanding. Situations are never entirely new, and we understand them by assimilating what we observe to the totality of knowledge that we bring to each situation. The solution we invent can, therefore, never be more intelligent than our comprehension of the situation. Because our comprehension of the situation depends on the knowledge we bring to it, "intelligence" and "knowledge" for Piaget refer broadly to the same thing. This statement becomes clearer in light of the distinction Piaget makes between "knowledge" in a broad sense and "knowledge" in a narrow sense.

As Furth (1969) points out, if we told a four-year-old that "Washington is the capital of the United States," he would not understand what we mean. This is an example of "knowledge" in the narrow sense. The four-year-old does not understand this specific bit of knowledge because he does not have the general framework of "knowledge" in the broad sense of the term. Specific bits of knowledge are understood by assimilation into the totality of knowledge in the broad sense. The construction of knowledge in this broad sense depends on the construction of operational systems and a vast network of relationships. General knowledge about geographic and political organization cannot be built without a logical and spatiotemporal framework. Knowledge in the broad sense is thus not a collection of specific facts, but rather an organized network of ideas.

Although ten-year-olds can more or less understand that Washington is the capital of the United States, an 18-year-old who has lived several more years, read newspapers, watched TV, studied American history and civics, and made a senior trip to Washington can derive much richer meanings from the same statement. If asked to free associate to the word "Washington," he might say, "The White House, Capitol Hill, a square piece of land ten miles by ten miles," and so forth. If we ask *you* to free associate, you might say, "Budget cuts, bureaucracy, corruption, big-money interest, . . . " Note that, even in free association, nobody would say, "The price of eggs in China" or "Napoleon." These free associations illustrate Piaget's view that since knowledge is organized into a coherent structure, no concept can exist in isolation. Each idea is supported and colored by an entire network of other ideas.

To the extent that we know the relationship between London and England, Paris and France, and Moscow and the U.S.S.R., we have a richer understanding of the statement that Washington is the capital of the United States. This example illustrates how a larger frame of reference, and a well-structured one, enriches the bits of knowledge we had before, when our frame of reference was smaller and less well structured.

The fact that knowledge in the broad sense is not a collection of specific bits of knowledge implies that "learning," too, must be understood in a broad sense as well as in a narrow sense. Piaget's constructivism implies that it is better to put the accent on learning in the broad sense. In other words, learning cannot be devoid of specific input if young children are to learn anything, yet the question remains: What kinds of specific input contribute to learning in the broad sense of the term? We believe that physical-knowledge activities are good because they provide opportunities for the learning of specific bits of information in a way that contributes to learning in the broad sense of the term.

The kind of teaching described in Part II of this book may not resemble anything familiar to educators brought up with empiricist convictions about how learning takes place. But we believe, in light of Piaget's constructivism, that if we try to cram children's heads with a host of facts as empiricist educators try to do, we will have the short-term illusion of having taught a great deal when in fact we have contributed to the stifling of construction in the long run.

To illustrate the futility of specific teaching that ignores the importance of learning in the broad sense, it is useful to consider an example of a child taught by Siegfried Engelmann. To quote Engelmann, "I worked with seven kindergarten children on the logical structure of conservation problems, including specific gravity problems" (1971, p. 121).[12] Teaching "the logical structure of . . . specific gravity" meant to him teaching the following rule (among others): "If an object floats, it floats because it is lighter than a piece of water the same size. . . . If an object sinks in water, it sinks because it is heavier than a piece of water the same size (Kamii and Derman, 1971, p. 129)."[13] As far as the application of this rule was concerned, all four of the children taught by Engelmann used it often (during the post-test given by one of us). However, all the children also gave a multitude of other explanations commonly found among children of kindergarten age, without any awareness of the contradictions in what they were saying. This is what one of the children said.:

> The small candle will float "because it's light."
> The big candle will sink "because it's heavy."
> The small piece of soap will float "because it's lighter."
> An identical (small) piece of soap will sink "because it's heavier." (Kamii and Derman, 1971, p. 134)

We let the children verify their predictions on the first day by putting each object in water. On the next day, we questioned some of them again. With the big cake of Ivory soap (which floated the day before) and the little cake of soap (that sank), the following conversation took place with the child cited above:

Examiner: Did both of these sink yesterday?
    Child: Yes. *(Her memory was incorrect.)*
Examiner: Feel this big one and this little one in your hands.
    Child: *(Feeling the weight of the two pieces)* The big one feels heavier.
Examiner: Will both of them sink?

---

[12]This statement in itself seems peculiar in part because specific gravity problems are not conservation problems.

[13]We do not agree that the teaching of such a rule has anything to do with the teaching of logic. While Engelmann believed he was working on children's logical structure, he was in reality teaching specific gravity as content. In questions concerning specific gravity, what interested Piaget and Inhelder was whether or not children eliminate contradictions in their logic.

Child: I think the little one will sink, too. . . .
Examiner: Why?
Child: Because they are both soap.
Examiner: You put them in the water and see what happens.
Child: *(Finding out that the big one floated and the little one sank)*
I forgot yesterday!
Examiner: Remember you said the big one was heavier?
Child: The big one must be lighter, and the little one must be heavier. (Kamii and Derman, 1971, p. 140)

The child thus began by saying that the big cake of soap felt heavier than the small one. By the end of the quote, however, she was deducing that "The big one must be lighter, and the little one must be heavier" (because the big one is lighter than a piece of water the same size, and the little one is heavier than a piece of water the same size)! The child made these absurd statements precisely because she tried to use the specific bits of verbal knowledge that had been stuffed into her head. To show why we believe that this kind of teaching is not only useless but also harmful, we must discuss the long evolution of children's construction of the notion of specific gravity. As can be seen below, the explanation of why certain things sink while others float water is not possible until formal operations are possible.

In order to study children's explanations of sinking and floating, Inhelder and Piaget (1955, Chapter 2) devised the following task: They gave to the child a variety of objects (such as a candle, needle, plank of wood, and aluminum plate) and asked him to sort the objects into two piles—of things that float and things that sink. When this sorting was finished, they asked the child to explain why he put each object in a particular pile, and gave him one or more buckets of water to verify his predictions. If he did not do so spontaneously, the child was asked to give a general explanation that applied to all the objects.

Five protocols are presented below: one illustrating the preoperational stage, two illustrating the stage of concrete operations, and two illustrating the stage of formal operations. We hope the reader will note that (1) children put many things into a variety of relationships adults do not dream of, and (2) a coherent logico-mathematical framework is indeed necessary for children to construct physical knowledge.

The following protocol of a six-year-old who was asked to explain the reason for each prediction is filled with contradictions:[14]

---

[14]It must be remembered in reading the protocols about sinking and floating that the important thing to analyze is not the correctness of the child's physical knowledge about whether each object sinks or floats, but the consistency of his logic. Whether or not the child knows that a candle floats is thus beside the point. What interests us here is the logical inconsistency in saying that the candle sinks "because it's round" and the ball floats "because it's round too."

ELI (6;0): "That?" (candle).—"*It goes to the bottom.*"—"Why?"—
"*Because it's round.*"—"And that?" (ball).—"*It stays on top.*"—
"Why?"—"*Because it's round too.*". . . "And that needle?". . .—"*It
floats because it's light.*"—"And if you push?"—"*It will go under.*"—
"Why?"—"*Because it will be heavy.*" From *The Growth of Logical
Thinking from Childhood to Adolescence,* by Bärbel Inhelder and Jean
Piaget, translated by Anne Parsons and Stanley Milgram, (C) 1958 by
Basic Books, Inc., Publishers, New York.

For Eli, there is nothing funny about saying that a candle sinks "because it's
round" and a ball floats "because it's round too." Likewise, there is nothing
funny about saying that the needle floats because "it's light" and it will sink if
you push it down "because it will (then) be heavy."

In a more general way, Inhelder and Piaget summarize the kind of
sorting young children do and point out that this is in accord with the
inconsistency they generally show in classification tasks. Below is how the
young child often sorts the objects into two piles and explains his criteria:

In the pile of things that float:

A toy boat: Because it's a boat
A toy duck: Because a duck swims
A tiny pebble: Because it's small
Another pebble: Because it's flat
An aluminum plate: Because it's light
A wooden blade: Because it's thin

In the pile of things that sink:

A candle: Because it doesn't belong in water
A wooden plank: Because it's big
A wooden ball: Because it's heavy
A copper wire: Because it's long
A metal cover: Because it can be shoved

Evidently the young child thinks about only one object at a time, thus the
variety of criteria used to define each pile. Also, the positive criteria do not
necessarily have corresponding negatives in the other pile. For example, if
flatness and thinness are invoked to explain floating, not being flat and not
being thin must logically be invoked to explain sinking. But this logic is
lacking in the young child who, therefore, does not recognize the incoher-
ence in his discourse.

What operations besides classification must the child have to understand (or invent) specific gravity as the single explanation that applies to all
objects? While it is true that many heavy objects sink, there are those (such
as boats and wooden blocks) which float. It is likewise true that light objects
often float, but some (such as nails) sink. In other words, to understand
specific gravity, weight cannot remain absolute but must be relativized, or
put in relation with volume, as can be seen in Figure 2.7.

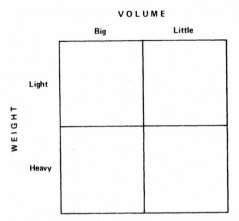

Figure 2.7. The relativization of the weight of each object involved in the child's construction of the notion of specific gravity.

This relativization of weight involves not merely the two dichotomies of light–heavy and big–little but also a seriation scheme within each dimension. Between "light" and "heavy" is a whole series of gradations. Between "big" and "little," too, is an infinity of relative differences. It is thus clear that without coherent systems of classification and seriation the child cannot possibly view the objects in terms of their relative weight.

Below is a protocol of a slightly older child who is in the early stage of concrete operations:

> DUF (7;6): "That ball?"—*"It stays on top. It's wood; it's light."*— "And this key?"—*"Goes down. It's iron; it's heavy."*—"Which is heavier, the key or the ball?"—*"The ball."*—"Why does the key sink?"— *"Because it is heavy."*—"And then the nail?"—*"It's light but it sinks anyway. It's iron, and iron always goes under."*

Duf neatly classifies the objects on the basis of only two criteria (weight and the material with which the object is made). He has clearly created the correspondences between wood-light-float and iron-heavy-sink. However, after saying that the ball is heavier than the key, he says that the key sinks "because it is heavy"! Nevertheless, when he says that the nail is light "but it sinks anyway," he is indicating that among the class of light objects, *some* sink. The structure of class inclusion which can be detected is illustrated in matrix form in Figure 2.8.

While Duf says that some light objects sink, he still feels a contradiction between this statement and the belief that when objects float, they float because they are light. He thus feels compelled to resolve this contradiction and, therefore, invokes the material with which the nail is made ("It's iron, and iron always goes under."). This is obviously an empirical generalization, not a single explanation that applies to all the objects.

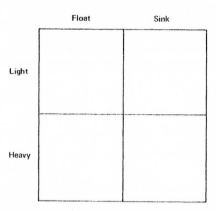

Figure 2.8. The structure of class inclusion seen in the sinking and floating task.

Interestingly, gross contradictions reappear in children's thought at a later level of concrete operations *because* they begin to take into account the dynamic interaction between the water and the objects. Let us take a look at the following protocol:

> BAR (9 years): (In the pile of objects that float, he had placed the ball, pieces of wood, corks, and an aluminum plate. In the pile of objects that sink, he has placed the keys, metal weights, needles, stones, large block of wood, and a piece of wax. He also created a third category: objects which may either float or sink, such as covers). . . . "Why do these things float?" (class 1)—*"Because they are quite light."*—"And the covers?"—*"They can go to the bottom because the water can come up over the top."*—"And why do these things sink?" (class 2).—*"Because they are heavy."*—"The big block of wood?"—*"It will go under."*— "Why?"—*"There is too much water for it to stay up."*—"And the needles?"—*"They are lighter."*—"So?"—*"If the wood were the same size as the needle, it would be lighter."*—"Put the candle in water. Why does it stay up?"—*"I don't know."*—"And the cover?"—*"It's iron, that's not too heavy and there is enough water to carry it."*—"And now?" (it sinks).—*"That's because the water got inside."*—"And put the wooden block in."—*"Ah! Because it's wood that is wide enough not to sink."*—"If it were a cube?"—*"I think that it would go under."*—"And if you push it under?"—*"I think it would come back up."*—"And if you push this plate?" (aluminum).—*"It would stay at the bottom."*—"Why?"— *"Because the water weighs on the plate."*—"Which is heavier, the plate or the wood?"—*"The piece of wood."*—"Then why does the plate stay at the bottom?*—*"Because it's a little lighter than wood, when there is water on top there is less resistance and it can stay down. The wood has resistance and it comes back up."*—"And if we begin again with this large piece of wood in the smallest bucket, will the same thing happen?"— *"No, it will come back up because the water isn't strong enough: there is not enough weight from the water."*

Bar still explains basically, in absolute terms, that things float because they are "light" and sink because they are "heavy." What is new in this protocol is that water begins to appear in the child's reasoning and interacts in a dynamic way with the objects. Thus, some objects (such as a cover, a large block of wood, and aluminum plate) which are not simple to classify are said to sink "because the water can come up over the top," "because the water got inside (the cover)," and "because the water weighs on the plate." The floating of the large, heavy block is explained in terms of its being "wide enough not to sink," and when he is asked to explain why the block springs back up after being pushed down to the bottom while the plate stays down, he invokes resistance—"The wood has resistance and it comes back up." Since the child thinks of water in terms of its action, he ends up saying that the block will come back up in the smallest bucket "because the water isn't strong enough: there is not enough weight from the water." There is thus a great deal of confusion in Bar's protocol, but the contradictions are due to the fact that he is taking into account the objects' dynamic interaction with water. Compared to Duf's protocol which is neat, static, and simplistic, Bar's is messy, dynamic, and rich.

One of the characteristics of formal operations is the combinatorial system which enables us to take into account all the possible hypotheses. Formal operations allow us systematically to formulate and test one hypothesis after another. During the concrete operational stage, as we saw in Bar's protocol, children generate all kinds of explanations, one after another, and juxtapose them without feeling any need to coordinate them into a single noncontradictory explanation. Just as the child in the preoperational stage can think about one object at a time successively in dichotomizing them into "things that float" and "things that sink," older children like Bar can think about one explanation after another without feeling the necessity of giving a single noncontradictory explanation.

Formal operations enable the child to eliminate inadequate hypotheses on the one hand, and generate more adequate ones on the other. Let us begin with the elimination of inadequate hypotheses in the following protocol.

> FRAN (12;1): (He is thinking about lightness as a hypothesis but goes on to say) *"The lightness has no effect. It depends on the sort of matter: for example, the wood can be heavy and it floats."* And for the cover: *"I thought of the surface."*—"The surface plays a role?"—*"Maybe, the surface that touches the water, but that doesn't mean anything."*

The child thus still thinks about weight, about the material with which the object is made, and about the surface as possible explanations but eliminates each one of these hypotheses. For this child, one counter-example, such as a heavy block which floats, is sufficient to reject the hypothesis of lightness as an explanation of floating.

Finally, we come to a child who has a single explanation which applies to all objects. Below is how he expresses specific gravity in his own words.

> MAL (12;2): *"The silver is heavy, that's why it sinks."*— . . . "The silver is heavier than that water?" (bucket).—*"No, you take the quantity of water for the size of the object; you take the same amount of water."*— "Can you prove that?"—*"Yes, with that bottle of water. If it were the same quantity of cork, it would float because the cork is less heavy than the same quantity of water."* And again: *"A bottle full of water goes to the bottom if it is full because it's completely filled without air, and that bottle stays at the surface if you only fill it halfway."* (Inhelder and Piaget, 1955, p. 38)

Mal never used the term "specific gravity" in the interview, but the idea of specific gravity is unmistakably present in what he says. Unlike the children taught by Engelmann, Mal is convinced of what he is saying and can think of supporting evidence. This indicates that his reasoning is not an isolated verbal rule, but reflects a whole network of ideas. We believe that it is when children can handle the ideas involved that the teaching of scientific terms and explanations can contribute to the construction of knowledge in a broad sense. Since all children have spontaneous beliefs, scientific concepts, as well as every other concept, must be taught in a way that meshes with the totality of knowledge they already have.

We stated earlier that the teaching of isolated bits of verbal knowledge as demonstrated by Engelmann is not only useless but also harmful. We say "harmful" for two reasons: Such teaching confuses the child because it is in opposition to his spontaneous beliefs, and it thus contributes to the development of attitudes that stifle the construction of his own knowledge. As we saw in the post-test after Engelmann's teaching experiment, it is not possible artificially to inject into children's minds material that erases what they honestly think. The stuffing of bits of knowledge foreign to the child's thinking confused the child who said, "The big one (piece of soap) must be lighter, and the little one (another piece of soap) must be heavier." When the child is taught adult ideas that contradict what he honestly thinks, he becomes unsure of himself and his own ability to figure things out. Rather than trying to figure things out for himself, the child may then become preoccupied with reading the teacher's face in order to say "the" right thing the adult wants to hear.

While many traditional, empiricist educators are not as extreme as Engelmann, it must be pointed out that most "science education" is based on the same empiricist assumptions about how children learn. In reviewing the activity on crystals cited at the beginning of Chapter 1, we note that the entire lesson is an example of the content approach that contradicts the way young children think. The behavioral objective—for the child to be able to define the word *crystal*—exemplifies the same verbalism inherent in the belief that science should be taught by social transmission of ready-made knowledge.

Even when proponents of a new "science education" program claim that it is "process oriented" and follows a "discovery method," their basic empiricist assumptions are still in contradiction with the important distinction Piaget makes between "discovery" and "invention." Columbus discovered America—it was already in existence; but man invented the automobile. This same distinction pertains to physical versus logico-mathematical knowledge, the former referring to the discovery of what is in the external world and the latter involving the creation of relationships, theories, and new objects. For the construction of scientific knowledge, the observation of empirical facts and the conceptualization of theories are both necessary. The teacher must, therefore, know what the child can learn by observation and what he cannot in order to avoid the danger of reducing all acquisition of new knowledge to "discovery."

By looking at what is meant by the "discovery method" in specific curriculum materials, one further finds that it usually means that the child is expected and even led to "discover" Fact X, Concept Y, or Law Z which the adult has in mind. Although lip service is thus paid to "discovery," the objectives and methods of these curricula actually serve to limit the child's initiative.

In conclusion, therefore, physical-knowledge activities are used not for the *in*struction or "discovery" of scientific knowledge, but for the child's *con*struction of knowledge in a broad sense.

Chapter 3

Objectives
and Principles
of Teaching

The principles of teaching can perhaps best be introduced in contrast with some principles for teaching "science" such as the following that can be found in early-education texts:

> Kevin was sawing a piece of wood with much vigor. He pulled out the saw and touched it. He drew back his finger and exclaimed, "Ouch!" He asked the teacher, "Why is it so hot?" She explained, "You rubbed the saw and wood together when you were sawing so fast. You made a lot of friction. That made the saw hot."
>
> Friction may not be a scientific concept that is high on nursery school priority lists, but Kevin discovered it that morning at the carpentry bench. He perceived a stimulus through his sense of touch. He reacted, asked a question, and received a knowledgeable answer from his teacher. This is the most effective order for preschool children's scientific education to follow. (Hildebrand, 1975, p. 231)

The principle of teaching advocated above reflects an empiricist view of learning and teaching. The "most effective order for preschool children's scientific education" is presented as beginning with the activation of the senses by an external stimulus. The perceptual reaction is then followed by a question and the teacher's "knowledgeable answer." As discussed in Chapter 2, Piaget's research leads to a rejection of this view of learning.

The above way of teaching is also contrary to Piaget's view because it is verbalistic. Aside from being a scientifically dubious explanation, the attempt to explain the heat by talking about friction is an example of giving the child a word that means nothing to him. When explanations are given, they should be in terms of what the child already knows and can understand, and "friction" does not correspond to anything he already knows. Meaningless verbalism like this is one of the things we try to avoid in physical-knowledge activities. Most preschool children seldom ask "why" questions about physical phenomena.[1] However, when they do ask for a causal explanation, they deserve an answer which is as close to their experience as possible. Such an answer to Kevin's question might have been: "When you rub things fast for a long time, they get hot. Let's rub the table top with our fingers and see if they get hot." This is more of a description than an explanation, but young children can understand empirical generalizations,[2] especially when they can produce the phenomenon by their own action.

Before going on to principles of teaching in physical-knowledge activities, we would like to discuss educational objectives conceptualized on the basis of Piaget's theory. It is out of the objectives that the principles of teaching flow. Let us first mention two objectives often given by others which are *not* aims in this book:

1. We do not aim to teach Piagetian tasks.
2. We do not aim to move children to the stage of concrete operations.

Unfortunately, these objectives are often the first ideas to occur to Piagetians who try to apply the theory to education. However, they are erroneously derived from Piaget's theory for the following reasons.

The stages of development revealed by the tasks are not the stages children go through in nature. For example, in life, children do not necessarily seriate little sticks before becoming capable of operational seriation. Sinclair (1971) points out that trying to teach Piagetian tasks is like trying to fertilize an entire field by fertilizing just a few soil samples. Another analogy might be that trying to teach Piagetian tasks is like trying to make the child more intelligent by teaching him to give correct answers on the Stanford-Binet Intelligence Scale. Even if we successfully teach the tasks to a child, he does not thereby attain the same general intellectual level as the child who solves them without specific training. When a child solves a task without instruction, his performance reflects a structure which consists of a whole network of interrelated actions. Learning a task is not the same as developing this entire network. Therefore, although earlier efforts by the senior author (Kamii, 1971, 1972a, 1972b, 1973a, 1973b; Kamii and Radin, 1967, 1970;

[1]As Piaget has pointed out, when the child asks "Why . . . ?" he often means something other than a request for a causal explanation. For example, "Why is it so hot?" may mean "Where did the hotness come from? It wasn't there before." The reader interested in Piaget's observations on children's "why" questions may want to read Piaget (1923, Chapter 6).

[2]In an empirical generalization, the child merely finds out that when he rubs the table top vigorously and fast, his finger *always* gets hot. It is much easier to generalize an "if X, always Y" relationship than to explain *why* the rubbing produces heat. The child likewise finds out early that if he turns on the switch, the light *always* goes on. Explaining why this happens is quite another story, even for adults.

Sonquist and Kamii, 1967; Sonquist, Kamii, and Derman, 1970) to apply Piaget's theory were conceptualized around each domain delineated by him, we now view such objectives as a misapplication of the theory.

While it is certainly desirable for children eventually to reach the stage of formal operations, and they inevitably pass through the stage of concrete operations on the way, this does not mean that we should aim to rush four-year-olds into concrete operations. Trying to move children to the stage of concrete operations reflects a confusion between the *results* of develop- ment and the *process* of development. The stages describe only in general terms the results of an underlying constructive process. It is this constructive process which is the most crucial aspect of Piaget's theory for educators.

Objectives

If we take seriously the basic notion that knowledge and morality develop through a process of construction from within the child, our objectives must be in accord with this constructivist theory of learning. Thus we discuss two sets of aims:

Socioemotional objectives:
For the child to

1. become increasingly more autonomous within a context of generally non- coercive relationships with adults
2. respect the feelings and rights of others and begin to co-operate (through decentering and coordinating different points of view)
3. be alert and curious and use initiative in pursuing curiosities, to have confidence in his ability to figure things out for himself, and to speak his mind with conviction.

Cognitive objectives:
For the child to

1. come up with a variety of ideas, problems and questions
2. put objects and events into relationships and notice similarities and differ- ences.

These objectives may seem just to reflect our own personal values, or what Kohlberg and Mayer (1972) call a "bag of virtues." We do happen to value autonomy, respect for the feelings of others, initiative, and self- confidence, but our personal opinions are not the basis for these educational objectives. We came to this conceptualization in light of Piaget's construc- tivism because these characteristics are necessary for construction to take place.

Socioemotional Objectives

The first objective, autonomy, is based mainly on research and theory discussed in *The Moral Judgment of the Child* (Piaget, 1932)[3] and *To Understand Is to Invent* (Piaget, 1972). In the first of these books, we see that Piaget was led to a theory of constructivism also in the moral realm. Unlike empiricists who believe that morality develops by "internalization" of values and rules from the outside, Piaget's research convinced him that morality, too, is constructed by each child from within. To understand what he means, we must understand the distinction between "autonomy" and "heteronomy."

Heteronomy is defined as being governed by others, whereas autonomy means being governed by oneself. The morality of heteronomy is characterized by obedience and conformity to external rules and/or the wishes of others. The morality of autonomy, on the other hand, is characterized by personal conviction about values and rules that are constructed by oneself. For example, the heteronomous pupil obeys the teacher out of fear of punishment or desire to be rewarded in some way. When the more autonomous pupil complies, it is not out of mere obedience, but out of a willingness to cooperate with a request he sees as reasonable and sensible. When he does not see any reason to comply, the more autonomous pupil resists and asks, "Why do I have to do that?"

Young children are all heteronomous, and many adults remain basically heteronomous all their lives. A child will continue to be heteronomous or become increasingly more autonomous, depending on the ways in which adults relate to him and try to influence him—especially in the early years. What keeps the child heteronomous is a preponderance of adult constraint. If the child's behavior is continually regulated externally, he has no opportunity to construct internal rules by which to govern himself. Coercion, punishment, and behavior modification are examples of constraints which tend to prevent children from developing autonomy. External rules can become the child's own only when he is given a chance to adopt them or construct them of his own free will. For example, when the child asks, "Why

[3]Of all of Piaget's books, this is the one which has the most basic message for parents and teachers. This is the first book which we recommend to our students and to readers interested in learning more about the educational implications of Piaget's work. It is especially useful in helping adults think through their basic attitudes toward children and develop a philosophy about the kind of relationships they want to try to establish with children. This book is a good place to begin studying Piaget's theory, not only because of its special relevance to education but also because it is relatively easy to read, in comparison with his later writing.

do I have to come inside?" many adults say, "Because I say so." However, some adults say something like "Because your lunch will get cold. Besides, I can't finish washing the dishes if you don't eat now." In terms of the child's possibilities for using his intelligence and cooperating, there is no comparison between these two kinds of responses. When the child is allowed to regulate his own behavior voluntarily without coercion, he can construct his own moral reasons for sharing a toy, not telling a lie, or keeping promises.

We do not mean to imply that the child should be given unlimited freedom. It is, of course, impossible to avoid adult constraint completely. As Piaget said:

> But in ordinary life it is impossible to avoid certain injunctions of which the purport does not immediately seem to have any sense from the child's point of view. Such are going to bed and having meals at given hours, not spoiling things, not touching the things on daddy's table, etc. (Piaget, 1932, p. 178)

However, to the extent that the adult encourages the child to think for himself, to that extent will his possibilities for becoming autonomous be enhanced. In an environment which minimizes coercion and is thus conducive to the development of autonomy, the child will come eventually to tell the truth because he wants to achieve mutual benefits (a relationship of mutual trust) that extend beyond immediate ones (avoiding punishment by telling a lie). Since the morally autonomous person does not blindly conform to existing rules, he will have the inner conviction to defy or attempt to change rules when he is convinced that they are unjust or immoral. A somewhat more detailed discussion of moral development may be found in Kamii and DeVries (1977).

For us, autonomy is the first and foremost objective because, as Piaget (1972) says, there can be no moral autonomy without intellectual autonomy, and vice versa. If the young child is constantly given moral rules ready made and is not allowed to question the adult, his experiences do not provide him with sufficient opportunities to develop an attitude of critically evaluating what the adult tells him. Constraint on moral behavior thus is a constraint on intellectual development. Conversely, if the child is constantly put into the intellectual straitjacket of having to give *the* right answer the teacher wants without questioning it, he cannot develop the freedom of mind to question the reasonableness of moral rules either. The child who thus does not have the freedom of mind to ask "Why?" in one area cannot be expected to exercise this freedom in the other area.

The second objective, respecting the feelings and rights of others and beginning to cooperate, is closely related to the first one. The first objective concerns the child's relationship with adults. The second one concerns the child's relationship with his peers as well. Peer interaction is of vital importance to what the child constructs in both the moral and intellectual realms. For example, it is by having a toy snatched away and eventually finding the advantages of negotiating with other children that the child figures out the desirability of sharing. It is also by coming in conflict with the desires of others in a group that he learns to see the value of voting. Likewise, by having others refuse to play with him when he cheats, he finds out the desirability of not cheating. In breaking a promise or telling a lie, too, he finds out that others lose confidence in him, and he may then construct rules about these temptations.

In the last chapter of *The Psychology of Intelligence* (1947), Piaget is especially insistent about the importance of social interaction for the development of children's logic. Without the reactions of others, the young child feels little need to be coherent in what he says. However, when others do not respond in the way he wants, he feels a need to make himself understood and to persuade them. For example, if he wants another child to play by his rule, he has to try to make sense so that the other person will accept his idea. In such situations, the child has to confront other points of view and coordinate them with his own. Such coordination, or construction of relationships, contributes to the development of coherent reasoning. Piaget thus argues that children must have many opportunities to confront the points of view of others. To cooperate, therefore, means for Piaget literally to co-operate, or operate together by considering others' perspectives in relation to one's own. By including co-operation as one of our educational objectives, we emphasize interactions in which children compare and coordinate different points of view. Even arguments are included in Piaget's definition of co-operation. (This is in contrast with certain uses of the term in which the "cooperative child" means a compliant child.)

The consideration of the other person's point of view is an example of what Piaget calls "decentering." All children begin by being egocentric, and all adults are egocentric to some extent. Most adults, however, have learned to decenter and to see events and ideas from many points of view. This decentering is essential for the child to develop socially and morally as well as intellectually. As we saw earlier, it is by becoming aware of other people's points of view that the child can construct the values of sharing, keeping promises, not telling lies, and so forth. As we saw in children's explanations of sinking and floating, it is also by seeing things from many points of view that children become able systematically to test a variety of hypotheses.

Our third objective is for the child to be alert and curious, and to use initiative in pursuing curiosities, to have confidence in his ability to figure things out for himself, and to speak his mind with conviction. If children are alert and curious and use initiative in pursuing curiosities, they are bound to construct knowledge and go on and on constructing it. This belief is in sharp contrast with the empiricist view, which has recently taken the form of "behavioral objectives" specifying precisely what bits of knowledge in the narrow sense children should have. We feel that young children will learn more if educators do not try to program them or specify exactly what they have to be able to do by the end of kindergarten, first grade, or second grade. In the day care center where we do research, for example, teachers put no pressure on four-year-olds to learn to read. Nevertheless, one four-year-old surprised her mother by asking how to spell "scrambled eggs," which she wanted for dinner. Upon looking at what the mother wrote, she asked, "How come there's no 'z' in 'eggs'?"

We have heard many parents and teachers remark that children are eager to learn when they first enter school but become passive and indifferent by the end of third grade, if not before. We feel that this is the result of coercive, empiricist teaching that attempts to mold children's minds and behavior. As Thomas Lickona (1974) put it, children sometimes exercise the last freedom left for them—the freedom not to learn. In contrast, when they are encouraged to use their initiative to pursue their own curiosities, they continue to be eager and active thinkers. This is why we believe that it is much better to put this educational objective ahead of the academic objectives of reading, writing, arithmetic, science, art, and music.

It is most important that teachers create an atmosphere in which children can speak their minds with conviction at all times. Muzzles are bad for the child's moral development as well as his intellectual development. If children do not question rules which make no sense to them, they cannot construct them for themselves and can only follow the will of others. Likewise, if they do not question ready-made knowledge which makes no sense to them, they cannot become critical constructors of their own knowledge. When children express their convictions, their ideas may seem childish and wrong to adults, but Piaget's research convinces us that they always have a good reason for thinking the way they do. For example, the child who believes that a leaf found on the ground will grow if planted has his own reason for this idea. If children are encouraged to speak their minds freely, exchange opinions with others, and put different points of view into relationship, they will eventually construct the truth as adults see the truth. Some will even go beyond to construct new truths.

Cognitive Objectives

Within the broad context of these socioemotional goals we can now begin to conceptualize cognitive objectives. Socioemotional objectives come first because unless these are realized, the child's construction of knowledge is hindered. If, on the other hand, the foregoing objectives are truly achieved, possibilities for cognitive development are maximized. Our first cognitive objective, for the child to come up with a variety of ideas, problems, and questions, was expressed by Eleanor Duckworth (1972) as "the having of wonderful ideas." This, too, is an objective which is in opposition to recitation of *the* right answer the adult wants to hear. Children work long and hard at problems and questions that *they* invent. And teachers who use these principles of teaching are frequently astonished at the difficult problems children set for themselves, problems they would never think of suggesting. Many examples of the variety of ideas, problems, and questions children come up with can be found in Part II of this book.

The second cognitive objective, putting objects and events into relationships and noticing similarities and differences, is a natural outgrowth of the first. When children invent their own problems, these invariably lead to the construction of relationships. We nevertheless state this objective to emphasize that the teacher must consciously encourage this important aspect of construction. Since we insisted at length in Chapter 2 on the importance of the construction of relationships, as well as the teaching of specific content in the context of learning in the broad sense, we will not belabor this point here.

The Relationship between These Objectives and Piaget's Descriptive and Explanatory Theory

Questions about the relationship between educational objectives and Piaget's work include the following: (1) Doesn't Piaget's theory concern only children's cognitive development? (2) What is the relationship between the two cognitive goals discussed above and the various books Piaget wrote on classification, number, space, time, and so on? and (3) What is the relationship between the two cognitive goals and the later learning of academic subjects?

With regard to the first question, Piaget has repeatedly said that although cognition and emotion can be discussed separately, in reality, one does not exist without the other. To cite an example which is particularly relevant to learning in school, he discussed the emotional block that most adults today have about mathematics (Piaget, 1972). He pointed out that this is the result of having undigestible, ready-made knowledge forced down the learner's throat, and went on to say that when the learner has an emotional block about something, further learning stops.

Piaget's view of the indissociable relationship between emotion and cognition is borne out by every teacher's observation. Whether a result of temporary conditions or more deep-seated problems, children's interest in learning is adversely affected by such feelings as insecurity, frustration, anger, and fear. Socioemotional difficulties beset all children from time to time, and the teacher at these times must be first concerned with these problems.

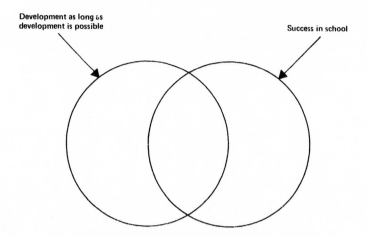

Figure 3.1. The relationship between the objective of success in school and development in light of Piaget's theory.

To answer the second question about the relationship between our dual cognitive objectives and the various domains studied by Piaget, we refer to the discussion in Chapter 2 of the logical and spatiotemporal framework through which the child organizes every bit of specific information. Although it was necessary for Piaget to study separately the child's development in classification, seriation, number, space, time, and so forth, he states that, in reality, all these aspects work together as an indivisible, coherent whole. As we saw in the quotes from Piaget and Garcia (1971) in Chapter 2, it is when the child has interesting events or phenomena to explain or goals to reach in intriguing situations that operations best develop. This is why we define our cognitive objectives in the way we do.

It follows automatically that if children come up with ideas, problems, and questions about specific content, and if they put objects and events into relationships, operations are bound to develop. Children will also go on thinking about fascinating content which will eventually take the academically "respectable" form of physics, mathematics, history, geography, and other subject matters.

This conceptualization of educational objectives does not coincide with the Head Start conception of preschool education for the purpose of preparing children to succeed in school. If the kind of overall objective we advocate were extrapolated to the elementary and secondary level, it would be "development as long as development is possible." The relationship between this objective and that of "success in school" is shown in Figure 3.1.

In the circle representing "success in school" the part that does not overlap with "development" includes all the "right" answers we memorized in school just to obey the teacher or to do well on an examination. All the adults we know admit to having memorized many words they did not understand or care about, just to remember them for exams. Without conforming to such arbitrary demands, students cannot be "successful" enough even to get to college.

In the circle representing "development as long as development is possible" the part that does not overlap with success in school includes critical thinking (which requires formal operations), moral autonomy, the desire to continue to learn after finishing school, and the creation of new knowledge. Recent research has shown that even among university students, that is, those who were successful enough to gain college admittance, formal operations are often lacking. The percentage of first-year college students with solid formal operations is 20 according to Schwebel (1975) and 25 according to McKinnon and Renner (1971). Those who were involved in the Watergate affair, too, were highly successful in school, but they stopped short of "development as long as development is possible."

In the intersection of the two circles we would place the academic subject matters taught in elementary and secondary schools which are an integral part of a person's development. For example, reading can be a very useful tool for development. However, it falls outside "development" when reading is taught as an isolated skill at the expense of thinking, without considering the possibile distaste which arbitrary demands can cause. Likewise, language and science, too, can be taught so as to enhance development or retard it. Paradoxically, preoccupation with the teaching of words in traditional education seems to result in low literacy and muddy thinking among many university students. If language and science were allowed to grow out of the way children honestly think, they would be more likely to bloom and bear fruit than when they are pasted onto the child by traditional curricula.

Principles of Teaching

Having clarified our objectives, we now turn to the principles of teaching which flow from these objectives. We will focus on principles that apply to the movement of objects and give a number of examples to enable the reader to generalize the principles to other activities. We have found the following questions uppermost in the minds of teachers with whom we have worked, and we deal with each in detail.

1. How do I plan a physical-knowledge activity?
2. How do I introduce it?
3. How do I interact with children during the activity?
4. What kind of follow-up is important?

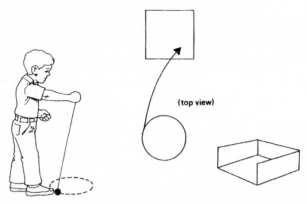

Figure 3.2. The twirling of an object on a string and making it land in a box.

Planning the Activity[4]

In planning activities, it is useful to keep in mind four ways, or levels, of acting on objects, each of which suggests a type of physical-knowledge activity. The following four ways are gleaned from Piaget's writings:

1. *Acting on objects and seeing how they react.* Babies put objects in their mouths, shake them, turn them over, and squeeze them, engaging in increasingly more finely tuned exploration. The first actions on objects are thus without any intention to produce a desired effect. Young children, too, act on objects without any particular effect in mind. This way of acting on objects suggests physical-knowledge activities of the type, "What can you do with these?" or "Think of whatever you can do with these that's interesting."

2. *Acting on objects to produce a desired effect.* By 10 to 12 months of age, babies begin to show intentions to produce an at least partly foreseen effect. When intentions appear, the exploratory behavior discussed above does not disappear, but a new way of acting on objects appears in addition— intentional behavior. At this time, for example, babies bang a spoon on the table *in order to* make a noise, and throw things out of the play pen *in order to* empty it and then scream for attention. At age four, children continue to engage both in exploratory behavior and in actions to produce desired effects. This way of acting on objects suggests physical-knowledge activities of the type, "Can you do X (such as blowing an object across the floor or knocking a doll down by releasing a pendulum)?"

3. *Becoming aware of how one produced the desired effect.* By the time they are four or five years of age, children are able to do many things at the level of practical intelligence, but they are not aware of *how* they pro-

---

[4]In Chapter 11 of this book we discuss in more detail how to select and develop physical-knowledge activities.

duced the desired result. For example, Piaget (1974) found that most four-year-olds could twirl an object on a string as shown in Figure 3.2 (dragging it lightly on the floor) and let it go just at the right moment to make it land in a box several feet away. When asked at what point in the ball's revolution they let go of the string, however, they were unable to give a correct description (at the position of 9 o'clock in a clockwise revolution, and at the position of 3 o'clock in a counterclockwise revolution). In fact, he found the following three levels of description:

Level 1:   Four- and five-year-olds said that they let it go right in front of themselves, at the position of 6 o'clock—the same point from which they would have thrown the ball into the box!

Level 2:   Seven- to nine-year-olds said that they let it go in front of themselves but at the position of 12 o'clock.

Level 3:   Around nine or ten years of age, children were able to describe accurately what they had actually done (releasing the string at the position of 9 o'clock).

Until age nine or ten, in other words, children did one thing but said something else when asked to describe how they produced the desired effect. This cognizance is a construction that is much harder and takes a longer time than common sense leads us to expect.

Let us describe another example that shows how easy it is for young children to *produce* certain results while it is extremely hard for them to *reflect* on the actions that produced these results. Piaget found that most five-year-olds could make a ping-pong ball go forward a certain distance and then return in boomerang fashion by giving it a strong rotary movement toward themselves while simultaneously pushing it away (see Photograph 3.1). (The ball slides forward, away from the child, until it loses its forward momentum and then reverses direction and rolls back toward the child.) Young children who had excellent mastery of this "trick," however, were not able to explain the event, or even give an approximately correct description. The following levels of description were found:

Level 1:   The child typically said, "You throw (push, slide) the ball and it comes back by itself." At this level, the child is not aware of exactly what he did, nor does he correctly "read" the movements of the ball.

Level 2:   The child typically said, "You push the ball forward and you pull back your fingers." However, when asked what that action did to the ball, the child said that the ball rotated in the same direction as it went forward. To explain the return of the ball, the child imagined a change in the sense of rotation, or else proposed that the forward impulse of the ball changes into a backward impulse, "rotating in all directions."

Level 3:   At this level, which is not reached until about age 11, the child understood that his action confers immediately two different movements on the ball—a forward movement and a rotation in the opposite direction—and that it is this rotation that is the reason for the ball's return. These children arrived at a complete coordination between the observation of their own action and that of the movements of the ball. First, it slides forward, they said, and when it has no more forward impulse, the rotation in the opposite direction makes it come back.

This third type of action on objects, namely, reflection on one's own action in relation to its result, would suggest physical-knowledge activities of the type "How did you do it?" and "How would you tell somebody else how to do it?" As indicated by the research discussed above, however, this type of activity is too hard for four-year-olds. Nevertheless it does suggest ways for the teacher to intervene occasionally in the course of an activity. The following level, explanation, is also inappropriate for four-year-olds. It is described below because it is important for the teacher to know the four-year-old within a developmental context and to know what *not* to do and why.

4. *Explaining causes.* If the correct *description* is not possible until many years after the production of the desired effect, an *explanation* is even more difficult. Explanations of most phenomena are, in fact, impossible for preschool children, as was demonstrated in the floating-sinking task described in Chapter 2. At this stage, children cannot possibly understand many "explanations" recommended in "science education," such as why rain comes out of the sky.

Many physical phenomena are impossible for adults to explain, too. The formation of crystals and magnetism are examples of such phenomena which can be explained only up to a point even by scientists. For the properties of objects, there are no adequate explanations. There is no explanation

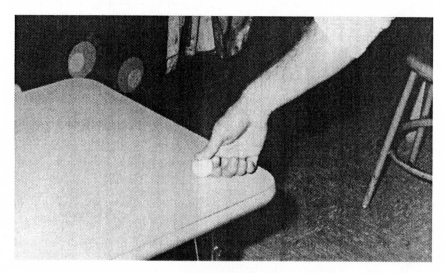

Photograph 3.1.

understandable to a child, for example, for the fact that sugar dissolves in water while sand does not.

Asking young children for an explanation produces answers of the type "The water went out because it wanted to," or "I let go here (6 o'clock) because if I let go here (another position), it won't go in." Answering the child when *he* asks a question is one thing. Asking him to explain physical phenomena is quite another thing and is generally fruitless.

The best activities for young children involve the first two of the above types of actions—acting on objects and seeing how they react, and acting on objects to produce a desired effect. The teacher who is not experienced in doing physical-knowledge activities may do well to start with the first type, using materials such as rollers (described in Chapters 4 and 5) with which children tend spontaneously to amuse themselves and pace themselves. The teacher can thus begin by observing how children play without the pressure of having the success of the activity depend on what he or she says next.

To illustrate how the different kinds of actions can be helpful in planning an activity, let us see what one teacher did with a blowing activity. The teacher, Ms. Fineberg, considered the first two types of activities. She dismissed the first because it would be boring to four- and five-year-olds to blow on things without a clear purpose. She thus decided on the second type of activity, and chose the effect of blowing things on water across the water table. She looked for a variety of junk objects in the room and decided on the following:

Straws	Mirror
Ping-pong balls	Unit block
Paper boat	Nerf ball
Cotton balls	Rubber band
4 different spoons	Plastic top to can
Paper cup	Plastic bowl
Pine cone	Wadded paper towel
A gourd	Styrofoam packing bits
2-pound coffee can	Lego block
Orange juice can	Crayon
Scissors	Round Tinker Toy
Chestnut	Cork
Paper punch	Checker
Ivory soap	

She planned to give a straw to each child and to suggest that he or she find the things which could be blown with it to the other side of the water table (Photograph 3.2). She also planned the following two possibilities to suggest, depending on how the activity went:

1. A race (by asking children to find the object that would get across the fastest)
2. A kind of hockey game in which two children on opposite sides of a water table blow on a ping-pong ball, each trying to make it touch the other side.

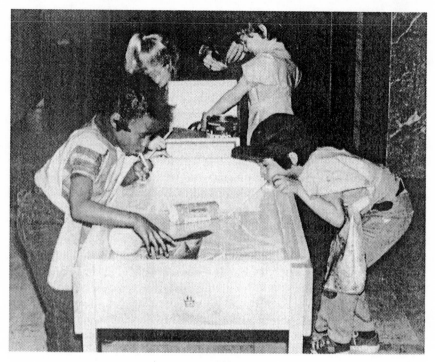

Photograph 3.2.

An important part of planning is for the teacher to play with the materials in order to get a "feel" for what the children will experience. Objects often do not behave in the way we imagine, and such experimenting sometimes leads to changes in the selection of materials. By experimenting with materials, teachers often come up with their own "wonderful ideas" to suggest at appropriate moments.

To summarize, we recommend the planning of one basic activity and several possible alternatives involving "acting on objects and seeing how they react" and "acting on objects to produce a desired effect." Good planning makes the difference between a flop and a successful activity, and it is a good idea even to make written plans because that often forces thinking through the activity in detail.

Beginning the Activity

Principle I: Introduce the activity in a way that maximizes children's initiative. Three ways to introduce an activity are: (1) by putting out material to which children will naturally gravitate, (2) by presenting the material and saying, "See whatever you can think of to do with these things," and (3) by proposing a specific problem such as in the blowing activity just described. Each of these is discussed below in terms of how the teacher can maximize children's initiative.

(1) *Put out material to which children will naturally gravitate.* In activities such as the pendulum (Chapter 8), children respond spontaneously when the teacher simply puts the intriguing material out in the classroom. Typically, upon first encountering a pendulum, the child tries a variety of actions such as swinging it, twirling it, pushing it, and telling a friend to come catch it. By observing how the child acts on the object, the teacher can judge when it may be appropriate to introduce an effect that children might be interested in producing.

(2) *Present the material and say, "See whatever you can think of to do with these things."* Rollers II (Chapter 5) is an example of an activity in which this type of introduction is effective. With this kind of introduction, the underlying message the child gets is that there are many interesting things one can do with the materials, and he will respond by eagerly tackling the materials in a number of ways. Also, this introduction can serve to free children of inhibitions about using the materials. It clearly communicates the expectation that they may do what they like. More spunky children get the message that they are expected to come up with "wonderful ideas" and have a lot of fun trying to impress everybody with their clever inventions.

This kind of beginning is especially appropriate when the materials are unfamiliar to the children. The more unfamiliar the material is, the more time the children should be given to examine it freely on their own before being asked, "Can you do X?" Otherwise, they feel pressured into doing what the teacher wants when they have ideas of their own they want to try.

(3) *Present the material and say, "Can you . . . ?"* When the materials are already familiar, as was the case in Ms. Fineberg's blowing activity, the teacher should suggest an idea immediately. Initiative is not hindered so long as children feel free to reject the teacher's suggestion.

For the development of children's initiative, it is better to ask *"Can you find something* that you can blow across to the other side of the water table?" than to ask *"Can you blow this block* to the other side?" The former leaves considerable room for the child's initiative, while the latter limits what he can do. In the first situation, the child is free to think about differences among a variety of objects and to make a selection on the basis of his own criterion. In the second situation, since the answer can only be "yes" or "no," the question invites little initiative.

Principle II: Begin with parallel play. Although interaction and cooperation among children are important objectives, it is better to begin physical-knowledge activities by providing each child with his own materials and encouraging parallel play. In these activities, young children want to *do* things with objects, and this initiative is exactly what we want to encourage. If the teacher has to insist that children take turns, they become restless and their initiative is thwarted. When, for example, only one ball is provided and children have to stand in line for a turn to aim at a target, half of the teacher's energy will be wasted reminding children to wait for their turn and consoling those who are unhappy. Therefore, it is better to set up materials for four or five children at a time (in a free-play situation where many other attractive activities are available) and encourage parallel play at first. When this principle of providing enough materials for several children at a time cannot be followed, as, for example, when there can be only one pendulum in the room, it is probably better to direct children to other activities and promise a turn later than to make them wait and watch others having a good time.

Beginning with parallel play in physical-knowledge activities does not mean that objectives of interaction and cooperation are abandoned. These are only temporarily set aside in the interest of encouraging children's initiative with objects. In fact, interaction and cooperation evolve more easily out of parallel play than out of "cooperation" imposed by the teacher from the beginning. In the blowing activity, children began by doing their own thing but soon showed off their feats, imitated each other, compared discoveries, and offered advice to one another. Another way to state this principle is: *Introduce the activity in such a way that cooperation is possible but not necessary.* [5]

Continuing the Activity

Once the activity gets going, we have found some do's and don'ts that make a difference in how well it proceeds. These are expressed in the following three principles concerning the elaboration of the activity.

Principle I: Figure out what the child is thinking and respond sparingly in his terms. If children build their physical and logico-mathematical knowledge by constructing it from within rather than by internalizing it from the environment, it follows that the teacher must interact with children in terms of how *they* are thinking. This means, first of all, that the teacher must be ready to drop her/his plan when the children do not take up the idea as their own. If, for example, the teacher suggests moving objects across the floor by blowing through a straw at them, and the group instead develops an interest in blowing through the straw to find the objects on which they can make a trace of vapor with their breath, it is better to follow their idea than to impose the teacher's agenda. Interrupting children's pursuit of their own

[5]Credit goes to Nicole Fortin, former Assistant at the University of Geneva, for conceptualizing this principle.

curiosity is bad from the standpoint of constructivism. Besides, the teacher can always try her suggestion later when children have exhausted their own ideas.

Figuring out what a child is thinking is the most challenging aspect of the kind of teaching advocated in this book. It is not always possible to know, of course, but careful observation can lead the teacher to educated guesses. For example, if a child blows harder and harder through the straw, trying to make an object move by blowing on it from the top, the teacher might hypothesize that, in this child's mind, force is what counts—not the direction of the airstream. Based on this guess he or she might say, "What happens when you blow on things from the top?" "Watch how Mary is blowing," or "Why don't you try lying down and blowing from the side?" It is truly an art to decide when to make which kind of suggestion and when to say nothing. Each such decision depends on a variety of considerations, for example, the child's ability to tolerate frustration and the flexibility of his thinking which enables him to decenter from one idea to another. Some children are easily frustrated and throw temper tantrums or leave the activity. Such children should, of course, be helped. With most children, however, it is best not to solve the problem for them, since the process of trying to figure things out is more important than the product, or the right answer.

Children often do things in physical-knowledge activities that the teacher does not anticipate. In the blowing activity cited in Chapter 1, for example, someone happened to make the popsicle stick jump. The teacher took advantage of this fortuitous event by asking, "Can you make anything else jump?" In the context of a classmate's discovery, this question served to intrigue other children, and they, too, tried to make other lightweight objects jump. This question was good also because it stimulated the children to put the popsicle stick into relationships. They blew on all kinds of objects from all angles with various amounts of force and concluded that the popsicle stick was the only object they could make jump.

As teachers begin to use physical-knowledge activities, they are often puzzled about what kinds of questions to ask children. In response, we refer again to the four ways of acting on objects, each of which suggests a particular kind of question. *Used sparingly and at the right moment* in situations like the one just described, a teacher's question can stimulate children to put objects and events into relationships. Let us consider these four types of questions.

1. "Acting on objects and seeing how they react" suggests questions which involve predictions, such as "What do you think will happen if you do X?"
2. "Acting on objects to produce a desired effect" suggests questions of the type "Can you do X?" and "Can you find anything else that you can do X with?"
3. "Becoming aware of how one produced the desired effect" suggests ques-

tions such as "How did you do X?" The teacher can also encourage comparisons by raising questions such as "Which way works better (or is easier)?" "How is so-and-so doing X differently?" and "Does it make any difference if you do X?"

4. "Explaining causes" suggests asking "Why does X happen?" or saying "I wonder why X happened."

If the teacher decides to ask a question, it should be timed so as to serve the child's construction of *his* knowledge. Often, when teachers are too centered on *their* ideas, they interrupt the child's thought with an intrusive barrage of questions which are far removed from the child's thought. (We have even seen a teacher interrupt a four-year-old's water play to ask what a funnel was called. When the child replied that he did not know, she made him say the word repeatedly. Needless to say, he stopped experimenting.)

The best questions for young children are the first three of the above four types because they connect well with natural interests in action. The teacher will probably use all three types of questions in a given activity. The fourth "why" type is best not asked, unless the teacher's purpose is to call the child's attention to something or to find out what he thinks.

In discussing teacher intervention thus far, we have focused mainly on what the teacher should or should not *say*. Since preschool children are, in general, more interested in action than in words, however, the teacher can very often be more effective by *doing* something than by talking. Three examples of what the teacher can do are the following:

(1) *Help the child with practical problems to facilitate experimentation and observation.* As children think of more and more things to do with materials, they sometimes invent ideas they cannot carry out alone. At such times, the teacher's help is necessary to enable a child to continue a line of experimentation. For example, in an activity with water, the teacher in Chapter 9 held tubes and bottles in place to facilitate observation when children did not have enough hands to hold everything they wanted in certain positions.

(2) *Offer materials to facilitate comparisons.* As children experiment, the teacher sometimes feels that the child might benefit from making certain comparisons. In Chapter 5 (Rollers II), for example, the teacher offered a large cardboard roller to a child who was experimenting with varying the fulcrum of his lever. In Chapter 10, a water activity, the teacher gave an intact container to the child who decided she wanted to try one without holes in it.

(3) *Model new possibilities.* When children's play becomes repetitive, or interest begins to lag, the teacher can often revitalize experimentation by simply modeling a new idea. In the rollers activity described in Chapter 4,

for example, when the teacher observed that children were drumming away on boxes for a long time, she quietly modeled a kneeling ride on a board across a track of rollers. Later, without saying a word, she also modeled a see-saw for children to imitate if they wanted to.

By emphasizing the importance of what the teacher does during an activity, we do not want to convey the impression that the teacher should continually intervene in children's play. All the interventions we have discussed should be used *sparingly* so as to encourage the *child's* initiative. Since an ill-chosen or ill-timed action may be less easy for the child to ignore than a verbal suggestion, the teacher should be particularly sensitive to the possibility of disrupting children's play. For example, in Chapter 9, the teacher thought she might open a new possibility by taking the cap off the funnel a child was using to pour water. The effect in this instance was to frustrate the child and stop her play.

In conclusion, when the child takes initiative, it is important to follow his train of thought and not interrupt. However, it is equally important for the teacher to be ready with ideas and possibilities to suggest when the child's initiative lags. Part of the teacher's job, after all, is to provide intriguing problems which children have not thought about before.

Principle II: Encourage children to interact with other children. When parallel play is well underway, the next goal for the teacher is to increase interindividual coordination and cooperation. The four types of questions delineated above are also helpful in this connection. Let us examine each one of them.

(1) *Prediction* ("What will happen if . . . ?). Certain questions of this type are particularly good because they elicit uncertainty and different predictions from different children. When Ms. Ellis asked the entire class what would happen if beans, blue water, styrofoam packing materials, and a Q-Tip were cooked together (example cited in Chapter 1), children had the opportunity to compare predictions. In situations like this, the teacher can write each child's prediction and say, "Let's see what happens." The objects then speak for themselves. An exchange of opinions sometimes heightens children's fascination with experimenting, but at other times it interrupts their train of thought. The timing of these questions is, therefore, an educated guess.

(2) *Producing a desired effect* ("Can you . . . ?). Children often do not need adult encouragement to imitate others. At times, however, they do not notice a feat worth emulating, and the teacher does well to call their attention by saying, "Look at what Johnny is doing. Can anybody else do that, too?"

Another way of encouraging interaction around producing a desired effect is by taking a difficult problem such as blowing a coffee can across the floor and asking who can do this (described in Chapter 1). Comparison and imitation can then be encouraged.

When they are encouraged to collaborate, four-year-olds display a surprising ability to play together. In an activity with rollers (Chapter 4), for example, two boys made a long track, put a board on it, and rode it together. After a while, one of them decided to put a chair on the board in order to make a "car," and told the other boy to give him a push. Everything seemed fine when the second boy started to push the chair, but the "car" broke down. The trouble was that the board was wide enough for the front legs of the chair but not for the back legs. The boys discussed what was wrong and how to remedy the situation.

(3) *Becoming aware of how one produced a desired effect* ("How did you do that?"). The process of telling others how to do something often makes us more aware of what we do automatically. This kind of interaction is, therefore, good both for the child who is shown how to do something and the one who shows how to produce a desired effect. The teacher can foster interaction by making remarks such as "I think Suzy wants you to show her how to blow to make the popsicle stick jump," or, to a child having difficulty, "Why don't you ask Jeff to show you?"

(4) *Explaining causes* ("Why . . . ?"). We stated earlier that most explanations are too hard for young children. Besides, four-year-olds are interested mainly in producing effects and not in explaining them. However, a "why" question that can be answered in relation to an action is something else. For example, "Why doesn't the block move?" can be answered, "Because I have to blow harder," or "Because it's too heavy." It can also be answered with another action to try to move it. An occasional question of this type can stimulate discussion and reflection.

In encouraging interaction among children by asking the above types of questions, it is important for the teacher to keep in mind that the objective is to foster an experimental attitude in a community of children and to encourage exchange of ideas and observations—not to arrive at the correct answer or even to reach a consensus. Such attitudes are fostered by the general atmosphere of a classroom, which is greatly influenced by the kind of interaction the teacher strives to promote.

Finally, group games can create a context which enhances not only social interactions but also the quality of children's play with objects. For example, marbles quickly become boring when the object is only to aim one at a pile of others. However, changed into a game, this activity acquires more purpose, challenge, and interest. It should be noted that four-year-olds do vary greatly in their ability to play an organized game. Therefore, the teacher will have to experiment to find out to what extent turning an activity into a game enhances or diminishes children's initiative.

Principle III: Integrate all aspects of development in physical-knowledge activities. During the course of a physical-knowledge activity, children do many things which go beyond physical knowledge in the strict sense of the term. Situations involving children's moral and language development arise continuously. Social knowledge often comes up, and children spontaneously engage in symbolization. The sorting and comparison of objects, as well as the recall and anticipation of their reactions, also go on all the time, and it is in these situations that children construct their logical and spatiotemporal framework.

During Rollers II (Chapter 5), for example, a child became so skillful that he could make a half-dozen objects fly high up in the air all at once. The teacher noticed that one of these was a hard, heavy roller from the duplicating machine. She quickly went over to the child and reminded him that the roller might hurt somebody. When the child agreed, he was decentering, anticipating a possible event, and also perhaps thinking about a moral issue. The teacher went on to suggest to the child that he put on his board only soft objects. This suggestion elicitated a sorting scheme (logico-mathematical knowledge), and the child went around looking for soft objects. (Although this particular child already knew these words, words such as "hard" and "soft," which are often found in preschool curricula, are best taught in this kind of meaningful, useful context rather than being learned only to please the teacher.)

In Rollers I (Chapter 4) one child stood the rollers on end and called out, "This is my candy store. Who wants to buy candy from me?" The activity thus involved symbolization, the social convention of selling and buying things with "money," and the balancing of rollers which did not always stand up easily (physical knowledge). Under the leadership of this child who seemed to have an endless supply of new ideas, the group also organized a "band," in which the rollers were used to beat on a "drum" (symbolized with a carton turned upside down).

A third example is a pendulum activity during which the string broke. When the teacher asked, "What do we have to do?" the children replied, "Tie a knot," and spent a good deal of time trying to make a solid knot (spatial reasoning). They then discovered that the pendulum became too short! When the teacher said, "What do we need to do now?" the children ended up discussing how long a piece they had to add (making an estimate, measuring, and language development).

These examples of children's initiative which go beyond the boundaries of physical knowledge emphasize the fact that knowledge of objects does not develop separately from other aspects of knowledge. Since it develops as a whole, the teacher should capitalize on opportunities to promote all aspects of development in physical-knowledge activities.

After an Activity

During the activity, children are busy doing things with objects. Teacher-initiated verbalization and discussion should, therefore, be kept brief. Afterwards, however, it is desirable for children to reflect upon what they did, what they found out, and how they produced a desired effect. One way of achieving this is in discussions after putting the materials away, or at snack time. The first and third types of questions are especially useful in promoting discussions. Examples are:

> What happened when you blew through two straws instead of one?
> What did you have to do to make the straw go straight?
> What happened when the string broke?
> What do you want to try next time?

Again, it must be emphasized that the important thing in these discussions is that children think honestly about what they did, what they observed, what other children noticed, and how they felt—not that they try to come up with the "right" answer an adult wants to hear. The focus here is on fostering children's awareness of their actions on objects and people and their alertness to how people feel and objects react.

In conclusion, the objectives and principles of teaching we derive from Piaget's theory are different from those found in sections on science in early-education texts. In these texts, the emphasis is on *observation, description,* and *explanation* as we saw in the examples of making crystals and explaining why a saw became hot. In contrast, Piaget's work leads us to emphasize the importance of the child's *actions* on objects, his *observation of the feedback* from objects, and his *organization* of this knowledge. These principles of teaching apply not only to the movement of objects but also to other planned activities such as cooking and to incidental situations such as when a child is about to spill milk.

The principles of teaching we have outlined in this chapter do not permit the reader to see how they are used in the fullness and complexity of a living context. In Part II, therefore, we present accounts of seven activities conducted with children by teachers who kept in mind not only these principles but also many other factors, including the children's personalities and their own.

PART II

Examples of Activities

Outside the context from which they were derived, the principles of teaching presented in Chapter 3 are only generalities of limited use. For example, to say to "figure out what is going on in the child's head and respond sparingly in his terms" is not very helpful without a specific description of **how** *a teacher figures out what to do. In Part II, therefore, we present seven activities from which we derived these principles of teaching.* **These activities are not intended as recipes or even models to copy**—*we have kept their number at a minimum in order to avoid conveying the idea that we are presenting a "method" or a "curriculum." What we hope to communicate is a way of thinking about teaching that can provide a basis for making decisions from moment to moment in the course of an activity as well as in planning and evaluation.*

The examples we present are activities we videotaped with three objectives in mind: (1) to test and evaluate the activity itself, (2) to conceptualize principles of teaching, and (3) to collect materials for teacher training. Because we wanted to focus on individuals, most of our examples involve small numbers of children. With only four or five children, it was possible to study what seemed to be going on in the child's head from moment to moment. Had we videotaped too many children, we could not have followed any single child in the depth necessary to conceptualize principles of teaching. We therefore caution the reader not to conclude that all physical-knowledge activities are only for isolated groups of four or five children. In Chapter 12 we discuss specifically how physical-knowledge activities can be integrated into an ongoing classroom program.

Each chapter in Part II was developed as follows. We planned the activity with the teacher (and sometimes one of us was the teacher who experimented in the classroom). This planning, incidentally, became an important part of teacher training in our research sites in that it gave the teacher a chance to think through and discuss materials, possible actions on objects, and the type of feedback children could get from the objects. It was also a valuable experience for us because the teacher invariably had creative and practical suggestions to make about what might or might not work.

At the appointed time, the teacher tried the activity, and the two of us took turns videotaping it. Afterwards, we discussed the tape with the teacher, keeping all three of the aforementioned purposes in mind. We evaluated the activity together with the teacher and compared views about the ways it went well or badly, how it might be improved, and whether or not it was worth further experimentation. We often asked teachers why they did what they did and thus discovered their perceptions and decision-making processes. With their intimate knowledge of each child, they almost always contributed interpretations which did not occur to us. We also discussed the mistakes they made, the most common one at first being talking and imposing too much, and not listening and observing enough to see the situation from a child's point of view. For teacher training, incidentally, we believe that the video machine is an invaluable tool. The tape enables teachers to critique their own teaching. Very often, the teacher needed no help in seeing what he or she did well or poorly.

In Chapters 4–10, accounts of selected activities are organized in the following way. We begin by discussing how we planned the activity and then give a chronological account of what individual children did and how the teacher reacted from moment to moment. (We hope we have communicated how much children can think and learn as they play. However, words are hopelessly inadequate to convey an accurate picture of children's thinking at the level of practical intelligence. Only a movie can show how children intelligently coordinated their hands, feet, and eyes, to achieve an objective. To separate what the teacher did and why, we indent the teacher's part. Our comments appear from time to time as notes to point out why we think a particular intervention was good or bad in a particular situation or how a child's action can be interpreted in light of Piaget's theory. Following the detailed account of each activity is an evaluation of the activity, a discussion of the surprises we had, and our thoughts on how the activity might be followed up.

We chose this format to enable the reader to study the activities from the teacher's point of view and get a feel for what it is like to teach according to the principles discussed in Chapter 3. We made a point of *leaving in the account mistakes teachers made because it is often by understanding what **not** to do that one understands better what one **should** do. We hope the following chapters make these principles sufficiently alive to guide the teacher in making moment-to-moment decisions in his/her own classroom. We would like to encourage teachers to take an experimental attitude and to expect to flounder at first. The kind of teaching we are advocating is an art, but an art based on a scientific theory, of knowing what to do and when, and what not to do and why.*

Chapter 4

Rollers I

In search of ideas for physical-knowledge activities, we looked through a children's book on simple machines. In this book we found out that, before the invention of the wheel, early man transported enormous stones over long distances by rolling them on logs. This historical fact struck us as being a particularly good source for the development of a physical-knowledge activity for two reasons: (1) it involves the movement of objects and clearly meets the four criteria of good activities discussed in Chapter 1; and (2) it suggests a constructivist approach to the teaching of physics to young children that would begin in a way that parallels the early history of technology.[1]

Planning the Activity

We decided that the activity would work better for young children if they first transported themselves rather than objects. We anticipated that specific actions children might perform to produce this effect were to:

Lie on the stomach on rollers and use one's hands to make oneself go (Photograph 4.1)
Put a board on rollers and then
Lie on it on the stomach (Photograph 4.2)
Kneel on the board and use one's hands (Photograph 4.3)
Sit on the board and use one's feet (Photograph 4.4)
Sit on the board and get somebody to push it (Photograph 4.5)
Stand on the board and ride it like a scooter (Photograph 4.6)

[1]As we noted in Chapter 1, there is a certain parallel between the development of human thought about such things as planets, gravity, and number, and the development of each child's knowledge. The explanations and problem-solving techniques of early man served Piaget as sources of his most original hypotheses. Early science and technology are likewise a gold mine of ideas and insights for the development of physical-knowledge activities.

Photograph 4.1.

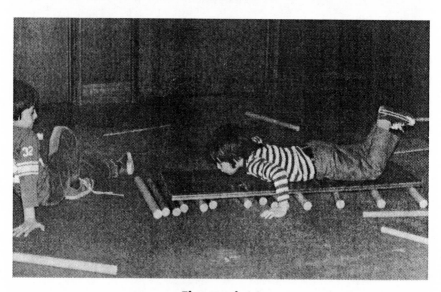

Photograph 4.2.

Photograph 4.3.

Photograph 4.4.

Photograph 4.5.

Photograph 4.6.

With these ideas in mind, we went to the lumber yard to have dowel rods cut into 10- to 16-inch lengths and came back with the following rollers:

Diameter (in inches)	Number of rollers
1.5	30
1.25	15
1	30
0.5	15

We wanted larger rollers two to three inches in diameter, but could find only the above sizes. The reason for providing rollers varying in diameter was to make it possible for children to compare the different rides that fat and skinny rollers give.

In addition, we scrounged up two cartons (large enough for a child to sit in) and four boards ranging in length from two to six feet. We put these on rollers to play with them and were pleased with the way they moved easily across rollers placed parallel to one another.

The teacher's objectives for the first day were:

1. To find out if children would be interested in acting on these objects to transport themselves; more specifically, she wanted to find out if children might become interested in figuring out how to get a smooth and fast ride.
2. To observe what children did spontaneously with the materials, in order to get ideas about activities that would be completely different from that of transporting themselves across the room.

Thus, although she had a definite plan in mind, she decided to introduce the material to a group of four children by saying, "See whatever you can think of to do with these things (alternative (2) of how to introduce an activity)."

Trying the Activity

The teacher went to the backyard during outdoor play time and asked for four volunteers who wanted to play inside with rollers. Only three children volunteered:[2] Barbara (4 years old), Mark (4 years old), and Brian (5 years old). During the course of the activity, however, two other four-year-olds, Joyce and Bruce, joined in after trips to the bathroom when they saw the others playing.

> The teacher introduced the materials by dumping them all out on the carpet and asking, "What can you do with these? What can you think of that would be interesting to do?"

Barbara immediately said, "I know," picked up a fat roller, aimed it toward

[2]The names of all the children in this book (except in Chapter 5) are pseudonyms to protect their privacy.

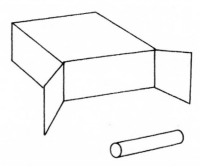

Figure 4.1. Barbara's game of rolling rollers into a carton.

the overturned carton which had contained the rollers (see Figure 4.1), and successfully rolled it in. She repeated this game four times and then exchanged her roller for a skinny one. She tried rolling the skinny stick into the carton twice, but each time it got stopped by the edge of the carton. Barbara then put the skinny roller back and got another fat one, saying, "This one's better."

> The teacher noted that Barbara had compared the way in which a fat roller rolls well into the carton with the way in which a skinny one gets stuck under exactly the same circumstances (cognitive objective 2).

The first idea that occurred to Mark was to get inside one of the large cartons and curl up in its bottom. Brian picked up two rollers and began beating a rhythm on the side of the same carton.

> The teacher let this drumming continue for a good while, but since this was an activity that the children engaged in all the time, she decided to suggest to Brian the activity she had planned. She was apprehensive about introducing her idea too soon, but seeing that Mark was still in the carton, she decided to go ahead by gently suggesting to Brian, "Maybe Mark wants us to give him a ride in this."

Brian thought this was a good idea and started to push the box with all his might. The carton barely moved.

> The teacher felt uneasy about perhaps being too directive, but since Brian had noticed that the carton was too heavy to push, she decided that this might be the right moment to put the rollers under it so that the boys would observe the difference the rollers made. Saying, "That's hard to push, but I have an idea that might be easier. Can I try it out?" she arranged the rollers under, in front of, and in back of the

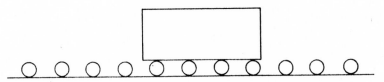

Figure 4.2. The teacher's arrangement of the carton on rollers.

carton as shown in Figure 4.2. She then gave Mark a ride (an action for children to imitate if they wanted to).

Barbara joined the boys, and everybody clamored for a ride . . . and one more . . . and one more, back and forth.

> After giving each a ride, the teacher suggested that the children take over. She wanted them to play independently of her as soon as possible and to interact among themselves (Principle II under "Continuing the Activity"). She also wanted them to find out about giving a push as well as getting one.

The carton often ended up on the carpet as the children zoomed across without the foresight to stop it before it reached the end of the line of rollers. Mark grabbed a turn by jumping in the carton without putting it back on the rollers! He waited for a ride until Barbara told him to get out and put the box back on the rollers! Brian put the carton on the rollers at the end of the track before getting into it, but then sat in the back of the box which was unsupported. The box ended up off the track, tilted on a single roller as shown in Figure 4.3. At first, Brian had no idea why the box slid only a little when Mark pushed. Gradually, in the course of several similar experiences, he figured out where to put his weight in the box as well as how to place the carton in relation to the rollers. While the two boys continued to give each other rides, Barbara picked up the sticks that were not being used, and began to arrange them as shown in Figure 4.4 using more than half of the entire carpeted area.

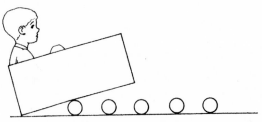

Figure 4.3. The way in which Brian got stuck.

Figure 4.4. Barbara's arrangement of large rollers.

The teacher observed that Barbara not only *imitated* the idea of putting the carton on rollers but also *invented* a way of giving herself a long ride by curving the track. She also noticed that Barbara was using only the largest sized rollers. She decided to "help" Barbara by handing her rollers of all four sizes in order to see how Barbara would react and give her a possibly useful opportunity to think about the relationship between the size of the rollers and their function in relation to the box.

Barbara accepted the big rollers, but when the teacher handed two skinny ones to her, she contemptuously refused by shouting, "Not that one! Not the skinny ones!" When she had exhausted all the larger rollers, she put a carton on them at the beginning of her semi-circular arrangement and said, "Teacher, push me," as she lay down in the carton.

The teacher complied, wondering what would happen at the curve (Principle I under "Continuing the Activity"). To her surprise, the carton turned a little bit on the semi-circular arrangement just as Barbara had planned. However, it soon derailed without completing the turn, and ended up on the carpet. The teacher said, "We're stuck. What shall we do now?" (Obviously, she was trying to make use of every problem situation as an opportunity for thinking.)

Barbara got out of the box saying, "We don't need the box, Teacher. We can *walk* on the rollers." She then got the skinny rollers and arranged them on the inside of the semi-circle as shown in Figure 4.5. When she finished arranging all the skinny sticks, Barbara said, "Teacher, let's have a race. *We* walk on the *in*side (referring to herself and Joyce, a good friend who had joined her in the meantime), and *you* walk on the *out*side, and whoever gets to the end first wins."

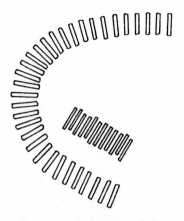

Figure 4.5. Barbara's addition of skinny rollers.

The teacher wanted to make sure she understood what Barbara meant; so she said, "I don't get it. You mean *I* go *all* the way around on the *fat* rollers, and you two walk on the skinny ones?"

"Yeah," said Barbara and repeated the rule she had just made up.

The teacher saw that for Barbara it was obviously not necessary to go the same distance to have a race!

Barbara went on to say, "OK? Let's try it," and started walking on her rollers.

It was clear to the teacher that in Barbara's mind it was not necessary for the three participants to start at the same time either![3] She (the teacher) started walking on the big rollers while Barbara continued to

[3] Four-year-olds' ways of playing games are hilarious, as they are not yet able to compete in them. For example, if we ask a group of four-year-olds, immediately after a race, "Who won?" almost all the children say, "I did." The reason for this phenomenon is that, to them, winning means "to do successfully what one is supposed to do." It is in this context that we can understand why it seems unimportant to young children to run the same distance or start running at the same time. Barbara is an unusually sophisticated four-year-old in that she correctly uses the term "to beat somebody." Nevertheless, neither the equality of the distance nor the simultaneity of the departure has occurred to her as having any importance in this situation. For further reading on how young children play competitive games, the reader is referred to Chapter 1 of Piaget's *The Moral Judgment of the Child* (1932) and to our forthcoming book on *Group Games*.

walk on her skinny ones, and Joyce followed right behind Barbara.
(The teacher was sure that it would be not only useless but also harmful
to insist on other rules at this point.)

When Barbara got to the end of her line of skinny rollers (with Joyce tagging
right behind), Barbara yelled, "We beat you, Teacher! Now, *you* have to
walk on the *little* ones and *we* have to walk on the *big* ones."

The teacher went to the beginning of the short line as Barbara had
suggested, and asked, "Is it all right for me to start walking now?"

Barbara replied, "Yeah," as she started at the beginning of her long line.
Again there was no concern over whether or not the two started at the same
time. Joyce followed Barbara as usual. Just before the teacher got to the end
of her line, Barbara said to Joyce, "She's gonna' beat us."

The teacher got to the end of her path and said, "I won! I won!"

The two girls seemed to pay no attention to the teacher as they went on to
the end of their line. Then their interest shifted to balancing themselves on
two rollers.

The teacher decided not to dwell on who won since this would have
been pointless. Besides, she did not want to interfere in the play the
children were initiating next (Principle I under "Continuing the Activity").

Bruce had joined Brian and Mark in the meantime, and all three had been
giving rides to each other. When they heard Barbara and Joyce scream as
they lost balance, they joined the girls and all five children walked on rollers
and balanced on them. Some screamed as they fell down, and the rollers
became scattered all over the room.

The teacher wondered whether or not she should do something to calm
the children down at this moment, but decided not to, as they were not
really out of control but just noisy.

Barbara dragged out a board and shouted, "Let's put all the rollers on this,"
as she began to arrange them as shown in Figure 4.6. Joyce and Bruce
helped Barbara, but the other two ignored her. When there was a good pile

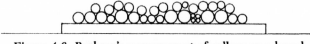

Figure 4.6. Barbara's arrangement of rollers on a board.

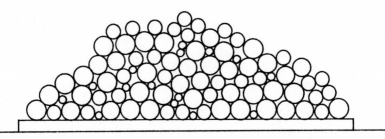

Figure 4.7. The way the rollers looked when they were all placed on the board.

of rollers on the board, Barbara began to walk on it, screeching as they rolled away from under her feet. Joyce and Bruce imitated, and the three laughed and giggled with great amusement as they piled the rollers back on the board and walked on them several times.

Mark came around and without a word started to swipe some rollers from Barbara, Bruce, and Joyce. The two girls shouted, "Teacher, Teacher, he's taking our rollers!"

The teacher immediately said that since Barbara, Bruce and Joyce were playing with the rollers first, Mark could not take them without getting their permission.[4]

When Mark pouted, Barbara suggested, "You can have a turn if you help us put *all* the rollers on this board." She got everybody, all four children, to help pile every roller in the room on her board as shown in Figure 4.7.

The teacher thought, "What a politician Barbara will make!"

As Barbara got ready to step into her huge pile of rollers, she announced, "Watch what I do!" As soon as she took her grand first step into the pile, the other children imitated her and waded into it. They walked on every spot that had more than a few rollers and scattered them all over the room once more, kicking some of them.

[4]In this situation, the teacher's intervention was not an abrupt imposition of adult authority. This activity took place in May, and all the children had lived since September with the rule that the snatching of toys was not allowed. Children should not be forced to share their toys, and, for the sake of moral development, it is better to establish the rule that if A wants the toy that B is playing with, B should give it to A *only when he (B) has finished* playing with the toy. It is very bad for children's moral development to have the rule of sharing imposed on them. Such a ready-made adult rule makes no sense to children and in fact prolongs their heteronomy, as well as encourages the snatching of toys. (If an attempt to take somebody else's toy is followed by the adult's preaching of sharing, children quickly learn to take advantage of such a convenient rule!) For the development of children's initiative, too, we feel that each child should be allowed to play with the toy *he* chose and keep it until *he* chooses something else.

The teacher was getting uneasy about the rambunctiousness of the activity but was reluctant to stop such initiative, especially when it involved so much collaboration. However, when the children seemed to be merely strewing things around, she decided she must take action. Quietly, she suggested that things were getting too noisy and asked individual children if they would like to build another road.

While the rest of the group gradually went back to riding in the carton, Barbara picked up two sticks and started hitting one against the other. She then busily dragged a carton up close and started beating it like a drum. Joyce and Brian joined in this drumming, and in no time at all the whole group was standing around two cartons beating on them like a well organized orchestra. There were the following three patterns:

$$1111111 \ \ 1111111 \ \ 1111111 \ \ 1111111$$

$$1 \ 1 \ 1 \ 1 \ 1 \ 1 \ 1 \ 1 \ 1 \ 1 \ 1 \ 1 \ 1 \ 1 \ 1$$

$$1 \ 1 \ 111 \ 1 \ 1 \ 111 \ 1 \ 1 \ 111 \ 1 \ 1 \ 111$$

This concert went on for a long time (Principle III of how to continue the activity). After a while, in anticipation of the children's tiring of this activity, the teacher, without saying anything, arranged all the fattest rollers into a conspicuously long line, put a board on them, and started riding it on her knees from one end of the carpet to the other (Figure 4.8).

Barbara was the first one to notice the teacher. She left her orchestra without a word, picked up a board for herself, and quickly copied the teacher's kneeling ride. The other children soon noticed the fun Barbara and the teacher were having; so they also abandoned the orchestra. All four were soon following one another in a rolling parade over the track. Then Brian shouted, "Everybody get out of my way!" When they cleared the track, he zoomed across the room, riding his board like a scooter.

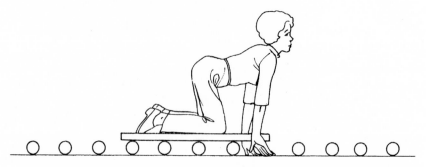

Figure 4.8. The conspicuously long track the teacher made for herself.

Figure 4.9. The teacher rocking herself on a board which is on a roller.

The teacher said, "That was a long ride, Brian. What other way can you ride that board?"[5]

Brian got on both knees and used his hands to push himself. Barbara shouted, "I'm on my stomach." Joyce put a carton on her board, got in the carton, and shouted, "Push me, Teacher, push me." A variety of rides continued for a long time.

To give another idea to the children, the teacher put a board on one roller as shown in Figure 4.9, sat sideways on it without saying anything, and started making a seesaw by leaning alternately down on one end of the board with one hand, and then on the other end with the other hand.

Barbara was the only one to notice the new idea, and immediately wanted to try it. However she put four rollers under a short board, and it was too stable and would not work. Barbara was not aware of this until she invited Mark to sit on the other end and discovered that the board would not move. She told Mark to get up, and he became interested in something else and wandered away. Barbara immediately focused on the rollers as the source of the problem and swept two of the rollers away. She then sat on one end of the board and saw that it went down. As the board went down, one of the rollers was jarred out of position, and Barbara finally concluded that a single roller made the best seesaw. But she needed a partner; so she ran to the house area for a doll. She put the doll on the opposite end of the board and happily rocked up and down, shifting her weight alternately by pushing down one end of the

[5]Encouraging children in this way to achieve the same effect in a number of ways is very different from the type of teaching in which there is only one correct answer to each question. Whether the teacher's timing of this comment was good is not easy to judge. Sometimes children's reactions will give the answer.

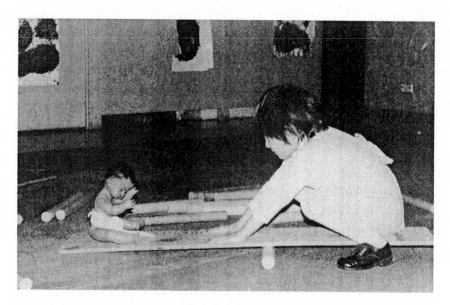

Photograph 4.7.

board or the other as can be seen in Photograph 4.7. Later, Barbara got Joyce to seesaw with her. Repairing a broken track, Mark arranged a whole bunch of fat rollers, one right next to another as shown in Figure 4.10, put a board on them, and went back and forth on it on his stomach. Joyce started to arrange some sticks as shown in the same figure and asked the teacher to help collect some rollers.

> The teacher noticed that Joyce was arranging her rollers on a collision course with Mark but decided not to point this out so that Joyce would find out for herself what she had done. As she handed rollers of all sizes to Joyce, she observed that Joyce was accepting all of them without paying any attention at all to their sizes. She, too, was arranging them without any interval in between, revealing that in her mind it was important not to have any empty space between the rollers.

Mark complained, "Teacher, why do you give all of them to Joyce?"

The teacher answered, "Because Joyce asked me to help her. Besides, who has more rollers now?" (Mark had more.)

Mark claimed that Joyce had more, but when the teacher asked, "How do you know she has more?" he only said, " 'Cause I only have . . . mmmmm . . ."

The teacher wondered whether to pursue quantification by pressing Mark to prove that Joyce had more. She decided to drop the issue here because such a request would interfere with the play with rollers. Besides, neither Mark nor Joyce was advanced enough in their quantification to benefit from such a request, and Mark seemed to have become satisfied once more.

Sure enough, Joyce's board ran into Mark's track, messed it up, and the two began an argument about who should not be there.

After this was resolved, Mark and Brian pushed one another on a board across the track, and then Brian had the idea of making a "car" by putting a chair on the board. He dragged a small chair in from the other room and placed it on the board, not noticing that although the front legs of the chair rested on the board, the back legs (which were farther apart) rested on a roller. He sat in the chair and asked for a push. Mark tried, but the "car" broke down because the back legs of the chair ended up on the floor. They then took the chair off, readjusted the board and tried it again, and seemed very puzzled that the back legs fell off again but the front ones did not.

The teacher was surprised that the children would dream up such a clever idea and even more surprised that they could not see that there was no use trying.

Barbara in the meantime made a small track, put a small board on it, and made two dolls sit on it for a ride. One of them fell down, and Barbara balanced her more securely in a sitting position.

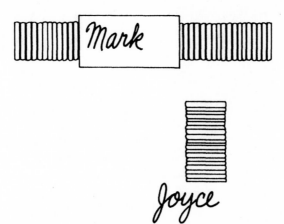

Figure 4.10. The tracks made by Mark and Joyce with no empty space between the rollers.

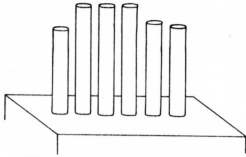

Figure 4.11. Barbara's candy store.

Barbara then thought of playing "store" and stood some rollers on end (Figure 4.11), calling them "candy" and announcing, "This is my candy store. Who wants to buy candy from me?" (She had trouble getting some of them to stay up.)

At this moment, the rest of the children came back into the room for a story before lunch, and the activity therefore had to come to an abrupt end.

Evaluation

a. As indicated by the length and intensity of their involvement during an entire hour, the children clearly enjoyed the activity. It inspired their interest in riding a variety of boards on a variety of rollers in all the different ways we had anticipated. Contrary to anticipation, no one seemed interested in figuring out how to get a smooth ride or a fast one.
b. The material turned out to be much richer in possibilities than we expected. In addition to being used as wheels, the sticks were used in the following ways:

> To roll into a box (Barbara)
> To hit to make music (everybody)
> To walk on, trying not to lose one's balance (everybody) and to have a "race" (Barbara and Joyce)
> To pile up and step into (everybody)
> To seesaw on (Barbara and Joyce)
> To compare quantities (Mark and Joyce)
> To make a "car" (Mark and Brian)
> To balance on end (Barbara)
> To symbolize "candy" and "candy store" (Barbara)

We were thus impressed once more that a good material is one that lends itself to many different activities rather than serving only one purpose.
c. The activity also seemed to be open-ended enough to provide for a wide

range of individual differences. Barbara was by far the most inventive child, but her higher-level play in no way interfered with the play of other children at their own level.

d. The activity also proved to be good in that cooperation was possible but not necessary (Principle II under "Beginning the Activity"). Thus, children freely pursued individual curiosities, but there were many instances of voluntary cooperation, including two instances of conflicts that had to be resolved. Among the instances of cooperation:

> Children gave one another rides in the box, taking turns
> Barbara pointed out to Mark that he had to get out of the box and put it on the rollers
> Brian, in collaboration with other children, figured out how to put his weight in the box and place it on the rollers
> Barbara and Joyce raced with the teacher
> Children piled rollers together
> Children coordinated their rhythms in an orchestra
> Barbara and Joyce seesawed
> Joyce and Mark came in conflict about the number of rollers and whose track had to be moved when they collided
> Mark came in conflict with Barbara, Bruce, and Joyce by stealing rollers

The Surprises

a. All the children imitated the teacher's track which was made with rollers placed a least five inches apart. When they made their own tracks, however, all the children except Barbara "imitated" the teacher by putting the rollers right next to each other, without any space between them—as if the board could not go from one roller to the next if there were space between them! Less advanced children such as Joyce even used rollers of many different sizes under their boards (Figure 4.12), totally unaware of the relationship between board and rollers.

b. The teacher never expected anybody to think of riding on a semi-circular track or riding on a chair atop a board. She marvelled at the freshness of the young mind in which many effects are not yet considered impossible to produce. The teacher was thus pleased that the activity permitted trying out ideas she would never have thought of suggesting.

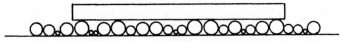

Figure 4.12. The way in which Joyce carefully arranged rollers of various diameters to make a track.

Photograph 4.8.

Follow-Up

Alternative (2) of how to begin the activity ("Do whatever you can think
of to do with these things") seems by far the best way to continue this
activity, because the material offers a variety of possibilities and thus allows
children to exercise their own inventiveness. Some will ride boards in different ways and others will invent new things to do that would never occur to
us. We list some additional ways in which this activity can be developed.[6]
a. Riding a board on rollers
   (1) Children make "two wheelers" and "four wheelers" as shown in Photo-
       graph 4.8, and push themselves alternately to the left and to the right,
       observing how the board moves in relation to the rollers, and how the
       rollers move (or do not move) in relation to the floor, and so forth. (See
       Chapter 5 for a description of how children pursued this idea.)

[6]The following discussion is based on what we learned in subsequent observations.

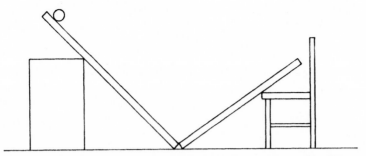

Figure 4.13. Inclines made by children to play "catch" with rollers.

(2) They sometimes make a very long track for their carton, get into it, and pretend that it is a boat (with two rollers serving as "oars").

(3) For much older children, a race might be good, with each team having a board and six rollers of their choice which quickly must be replaced under the forward edge of the board as it advances toward the goal.

b. Other possibilities with rollers

(1) Some children play a bowling game, standing rollers on end to serve as pins, and using one as the ball. Left to their own, they often stand farther and farther away from the target, thereby making the task more and more difficult for themselves. Such self-invented problems often result in the children's working surprisingly long and enthusiastically.

(2) With chairs, boxes, and boards, children make various inclines such as the ones shown in Figure 4.13. One or two children position themselves by the chair to catch the rollers that come rolling up the ramp on the other side. They also experiment with how hard they have to push different sized rollers from the bottom in order to make them go all the way up the incline, but not over the top.

c. Moving from rollers to wheels

(1) Putting clamp-on wheels on blocks and riding them like roller skates.

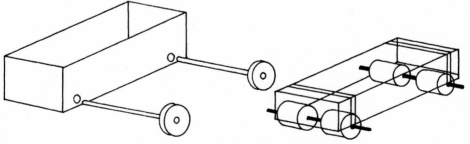

Figure 4.14. Examples of shoe-box wagons.

Creative Playthings used to make clamp-on wheels; ours unfortunately broke when children rode the blocks.

(2) Playing with a wheelbarrow. A wheelbarrow may facilitate the observation of a wheel, since it has only one.

(3) Making a shoe-box wagon. Examples are shown in Figure 4.14. This activity is appropriate for older children, but we include it to show how children can be encouraged to reinvent the wheel and figure out how to make better wheels.

Chapter 5

Rollers II[1]

After the initial rollers activity, the children had many other opportunities to play with this material. In the course of this play one day, Ricky discovered a lever effect as he walked on a board placed on a roller. He then stomped harder and harder on the end that went down, trying to make a sponge fly higher and higher in the air. The teacher recognized this as an excellent physical-knowledge problem. She thought about how she might extend Ricky's experimentation and inspire other children also to experiment with levers.

Planning the Activity

The teacher decided to add thicker rollers to the rollers described in Chapter 4 and a variety of soft objects which could be catapulted into the air. The materials thus provided were

> 90 wooden dowel rods, 10 to 16 inches long, varying in diameter from 0.5 to 1.5 inches
> 30 hollow, cardboard cylinders, 4 inches in diameter (discarded from an IBM duplicating machine)
> 3 rubber balls
> 2 sponges

[1]This chapter is an account of the activity shown in the film, "Playing with Rollers: A Pre-School Teacher Uses Piaget's Theory" (Kamii, DeVries, Ellis, and Zaritsky, 1975), which is no longer available for distribution. We would like to acknowledge the assistance of Colleen Blobaum and Maureen Ellis in writing this chapter.

2 paper balls (made from crumpled newspaper)
6 boards, three to six feet long, 10 to 36 inches wide
2 plastic laundry baskets
1 heavy cardboard cylinder 18 inches in diameter.

The teacher planned to put out the rollers and boards and encourage children to think of what they could do with the materials (alternative (2) of how to introduce an activity). She expected that a situation would arise when she could suggest the idea of levers in a way that would flow naturally into a child's spontaneous play. She planned to have the balls and sponges ready to offer the children in case they were interested in making them fly up from the lever.

Trying the Activity

During free play, the teacher asked the following four children if they would like to play outside the classroom with the rollers and boards:

Jeff	(5 years old)
Jennifer L.	(5 years old)
Jennifer M.	(4 years old)
Ricky	(5 years old).

The teacher went on to say that some men would be making a movie of them playing and that there would be some bright lights. "You don't have to do anything special or different," she assured them, "because the men really just want to see children playing with rollers and boards."

All four children were enthusiastic about the teacher's suggestion as she had expected.

When everybody was in the area prepared for the filming, the teacher introduced the activity by saying, "You see whatever you can think of to do with these things."

Immediately, Jennifer M. responded with "I can think of something."

"You can think of something?" echoed the teacher.

"Yeah, something rolling," Jennifer said gesturing with her hand to indicate that she was going to build something that would move back and forth.

The teacher pointed out the boxes containing the rollers, saying, "There are two different kinds of rollers here—this kind (pointing to the carton of wooden rollers) and this kind (pointing to the carton of cardboard cylinders)—and all kinds of boards."

The children busily began to select the rollers they wanted to use. Jeff took one small roller and placed it under a narrow board. He glanced up, and seeing that Ricky placed *two* rollers under a narrow board, he went to get another roller for himself. Ricky told him, "No, they're not there. They're over here." He was referring to the large wooden rollers because he was convinced that they were the best to use. He followed Jeff back to his board to insist, "I didn't get them from over there." Jeff at this time was not concerned with the size of the rollers and just kept on working to arrange the two small ones under his board.

To make her "something rolling," Jennifer M. put about 15 large cardboard cylinders in a long row.

By this time Jeff had placed two different-sized rollers under his board. He stood sideways on it with his legs spread wide apart and shifted his weight from side to side, moving back and forth across the rollers (see Photograph 5.1).

Wondering if any of the other children would be interested in doing what Jeff was doing, the teacher decided to draw their attention to him. She said, "Look at Jeff. He's really moving!"

Photograph 5.1.

Jennifer L. watched Jeff for a moment, then imitated him, placing two rollers on the floor about two feet apart with a narrow board on top. For a while she stood teetering on the board, working hard to keep her balance.

Since Jeff's two rollers were not the same size, his board was not perfectly horizontal, and it began sliding toward the lower end as he stood on it. To correct this, he shifted his weight to the higher side, but all of a sudden he lost his balance, and the board flew out from under him. He landed on the floor, laughed, and got up to try again. He rearranged the materials, then stood on the board with his feet spread wide apart. He shifted his right foot closer to his left one, lost his balance, and again landed on the floor.

Meanwhile, Ricky had placed three rollers underneath his board—a medium-sized one at each end, and a small one in the middle. He stood on his board sideways, his legs spread wide apart, and moved it back and forth across the rollers by shifting his weight from side to side. As he rolled, he exclaimed, "Look at me! I'm really rolling! You know what? I'm really rolling!" Then he inched his right foot toward his left, and lost his balance. "Whoa!" he yelled as he kept himself from falling by stepping off the board onto the floor.

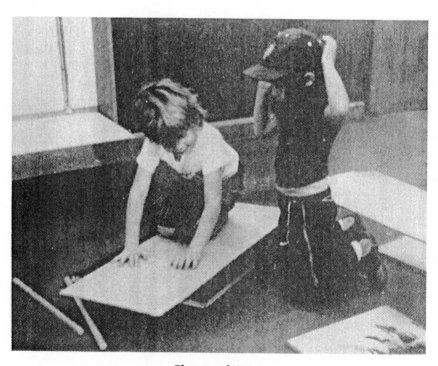

Photograph 5.2.

Jeff decided to abandon his narrow board and gathered four rollers (two small and two medium-sized, apparently without noticing the size difference) and a wide board. He arranged the rollers on the floor about four to six inches apart. Ricky seemed to get the same idea at the same time. He announced, "Now you know what I'm gonna do? I'm gonna do a four wheeler. Wanna do four wheels, Jeffery?" "Four?" Jeff asked. "A four wheeler, yeah," replied Ricky. "That's what I'm doing," Jeff said. "Come on," urged Ricky. He pointed to Jeff's wide board and said, "You know what those are? They're heavy. These are heavy. I'm not using any of those."

"You're not using any of which?" asked the teacher hoping to clarify Ricky's suggestion for Jeff. Ricky did not answer her question and Jeff did not hear it; so nobody understood what Ricky meant.

Apparently thinking that Ricky was suggesting he exchange his rollers for different ones, Jeff picked up his four, put them back into their box, and grabbed five others indiscriminately. (Three of these were larger than those he had been using and two were medium-sized, but he did not seem to notice this aspect either.)

Meanwhile the two girls worked together on their construction of boards and rollers. Jennifer M. put a roller under one end of a wide, heavy board, and Jennifer L. brought over more rollers, saying, "Want me to help you?" Jennifer M. answered, "O.K., you do some of it. You do that," pointing to the other end of the board. Together they lifted the end of the board, and placed a small roller underneath. "Now we need one more, right?" "Right," answered Jennifer M. as Jennifer L. put a third roller under the middle of the board. Jennifer L. suggested putting another board on top of the first one and Jennifer M. agreed. Jennifer L. put it on and said, "Get on it, and go like this," as she knelt on the boards and rocked back and forth over the rollers (see Photograph 5.2). "No, no," Jennifer M. objected. "Put two of *these* here." She put two small rollers on top of the boards, one near either end. Completing the pattern of rollers-board, Jennifer L. added, "And then another cardboard (referring to a thin board)." As Jennifer L. was reaching for the board, Jennifer M. continued her own train of thought, "And then I'm gonna take . . . No, not another cardboard! Take this (IBM cylinder). Put one here." She put the IBM cylinder near one of the two small rollers, and Jennifer L. immediately took another cylinder and placed it next to the small roller at the other end (see Photograph 5.3). (Throughout this interaction, both girls were concerned with the symmetry of their construction. Each time something was placed on one end of the board, either Jennifer M. or Jennifer L. would then duplicate it on the other end.)

When the objects began to roll off the board, the children tried three

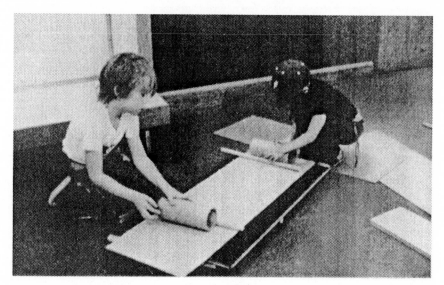

Photograph 5.3.

solutions—putting the rollers nearer the center of the board, reversing the positions of the small roller and large cylinder, and putting the rollers back on the board, near the end. But nothing seemed to work. Jennifer L. leaned back, resting her head on her arm, and studied the situation. Suddenly she had an idea. "Hey, how about we put it through here?" she exclaimed as she put the dowel inside the cylinder (see Figure 5.1). "There," she said with satisfaction and offered to help Jennifer M. fix the one near her (Jennifer M.), but Jennifer M. refused the offer and did it herself.

Jennifer M. then jumped on top of the boards. "Me, too!" said Jennifer L. as she joined her (see Photograph 5.4). Both girls giggled with pleasure as the boards slid around. The boards slipped off the rollers after only a few seconds, and, attracted by the action on the other side of the room, the two girls walked over to see what Ricky and Jeff were doing.

Jeff was kneeling on top of a wide board with one roller under its middle. In seesaw fashion, he rocked back and forth.

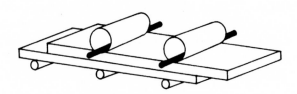

Figure 5.1.

When the teacher saw that Jeff had thus made the essentials of a lever and seemed already to be thinking about a somewhat related action, she thought this might be a good time to suggest her idea of making things fly up in the air. (She was, of course, prepared to withdraw this suggestion if Jeff was not interested.) She brought over a lid of a shoe box containing the paper balls, rubber balls, and sponges, and, holding a rubber ball on the end of Jeff's board, she asked, "Jeff, do you think you can make this ball go up in the air?"

"Yeah," replied Jeff, taking the ball. The other children crowded around with interest.

"Do you want to try something?" the teacher asked them.

Ricky selected a sponge, and Jennifer L., a paper ball. Ricky immediately thought of using his long, narrow board (with two rollers under it near each end) as a lever. He placed the sponge on one end, and jumped on the other. The sponge flew into the air about four or five feet.

"Woo-oo, look at that!" exclaimed the teacher.

Jeff glanced at Ricky's sponge in the air. Then he placed his ball on the high end of his board and jumped hard on the down end as the ball rolled down. This had the effect of making the ball bounce only a few inches into the air

Photograph 5.4.

and then off the board. As he went after his ball, Jeff watched Ricky move both of his rollers next to each other under one end of his board. Then Jeff returned to his own board. Knowing from his previous attempt that the ball would roll off the board if he let go, Jeff tried another idea. While standing on the down end of the board, he bent over to place the ball on it in the exact center. Still bending over, he jumped just as he released the ball. The effect was no more satisfying than the first.

Meanwhile Ricky had arranged his two rollers so that they were together under one end of his board. He placed his sponge on the end of the board that was up (see Photograph 5.5). Flexing his knees slightly as if readying himself to jump on the other end, he noticed that the end on which he was about to jump rested on the floor. Ricky paused, looked at the sponge, and moved it quickly to the low end.[2] After waiting a moment for Jeff to move out of his way, Ricky leaped on the board, and the sponge flew up about four or five feet into the air.

Ricky felt that Jeff was too close to him; so he asked Jeff to move his materials farther away. He then asked Jeff if he could "use the ball for a second."

> Since Jeff was intensely involved in trying to get the ball to stay on the board, the teacher told Ricky that she had another ball and went to get it.

At this point, Jeff's board had one roller underneath, about one-third of the distance from the up end. While kneeling on the down end of the board, Jeff placed his ball on it a little closer to him than the roller, then stood up quickly. This caused his board to slip out from under him and he landed on the floor on his knees. With a surprised grin he picked himself up. He put the board back on the roller as before and stepped on the down end holding the ball in his hand. As he could not make the ball stay on the board, he dropped it on the board just as he jumped. However, he could not synchronize the two actions, and the ball only bounced off the board. He tried again, with the same result.

---

[2]This portion of Ricky's play illustrates Piaget's view that complex relationships are not constructed all at once but that young children begin by putting two elements into a relationship. When Ricky thought about *jumping* on the board, he knew that he had to jump on the end that was up. The two elements in this relationship were the action of jumping and the up end of the board. When he thought about *placing the object* on the board, he figured that if the object was to go up, he had to put it on the end that was up. Ricky was thus able to think about each of these relationships separately, but he was unable to think about both at the same time. Therefore, when he placed the sponge on the board, he did not see any contradiction in his thinking. It was only when he got ready to jump on the board that the first relationship reoccurred to him and he realized that the sponge had to be moved to the down end.

Photograph 5.5.

The portion of the film which followed was destroyed through improper processing. According to the teacher, the two girls built a long "road" by spacing the large wooden dowels about four inches apart across the floor. They placed two boards on top of the rollers and a large cardboard box (the one which held the dowels) on top of a board. By sitting in the box (their "rowboat") and pushing against the floor with a dowel in each hand, they were able to move across the floor on the "river." Meantime, Jeff became increasingly frustrated as he watched Ricky's objects fly up much better than his. The teacher suggested to Jeff that he ask Ricky for help. In helping Jeff, Ricky got a long, narrow board like his own and actually built the lever for him. This helped Jeff only temporarily because each time he jumped, he had to rebuild the lever. The film resumes at this point as Jeff continues to have trouble building the lever.

The teacher noticed that the main problem Jeff had in rebuilding the lever was in the placement of the rollers for the fulcrum. He either placed them near the ends of the board so that they rolled out from under it or near the middle but spread about six inches apart so that the board was horizontal. Because Jeff was again becoming frustrated by being unable to make his lever work, the teacher decided to move the

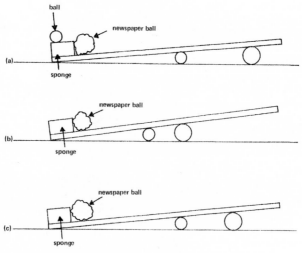

Figure 5.2.

rollers closer together nearer the end of the board and asked, "What would happen, Jeff, if you put the rollers *there*?"

[Note: Ordinarily, we would consider such an action on the part of the teacher as the imposition of a solution, but in this instance, it seemed necessary to prevent Jeff from becoming completely frustrated.]

At first, Jeff said, "No-o-o," and began to move his rollers back to the middle. But he changed his mind and decided to try the teacher's suggestion.

The teacher, therefore, asked again, "What do you think would happen?" Jeff did not respond. He picked up a sponge and the ball instead and focused on how to make the ball stay on the board. First, he put it on top of the sponge, but it rolled off. He briefly rotated the sponge, but decided that didn't help either. Finally, he placed the ball in front of the sponge, which was at the low end of the board, and thus succeeded in preventing the ball from rolling off.

"Oh, that's an idea," commented the teacher.

Jeff jumped on the up end of the board and seemed pleased to see the objects fly about three feet into the air.

Next, Jeff put one roller under the center of the board, and moved the other nearer an end (see Figure 5.2a). On the opposite end, he placed the sponge, managed to get the rubber ball to stay on it by pressing it down into the sponge,[3] and placed the paper ball in front of both. Then he readjusted

---

[3]The reader may wish to refer to Karmiloff-Smith and Inhelder (1975) regarding the significance of young children's pressing down of objects to make them stay in place.

his rollers by moving one of them toward the center (see Figure 5.2b), then back again to a position between the center and the end of the board (see Figure 5.2c). Intently absorbed in the task, he did not notice the ball roll off the sponge. He jumped on the board, and both the sponge and the paper ball flew up. The paper ball happened to come down right in front of him, and he quickly caught it. He beamed with surprise and pleasure, and glanced around as if to see if anyone was watching.

Meanwhile, Jennifer L. had taken the huge (18-inch diameter) cylinder and laid a narrow board across it. She said she was making a teeter-totter, and asked Jennifer M. to get on the other end (see Photograph 5.6). However, Jennifer M. was busy with her own idea. She had laid one of the wide boards across a roller and told the teacher that when she stepped on one side, "it goes *up*, but when I step on this (the other) side, it goes *down*." Jennifer L. then tried to walk on the huge cylinder as she rolled it. She was able to take two or three steps backward before losing her balance.

Jeff called to the teacher, "Maureen, you wanna see this?"

"Yeah. What are you doing different?" she replied.

The board was set up as before, with the paper ball on the down end. Jeff jumped on it, then answered, "You have to try to catch it," as he caught the paper ball.

Photograph 5.6.

The teacher responded, "Oh, you have to try to catch it when it comes up, huh?" She noted that in trying to reproduce what had happened accidentally Jeff had set himself a new problem which provided a new incentive for figuring out how to make the lever work.

Then Ricky called the teacher's attention to what he was doing. Under his board, the rollers were placed as previously—both near his end. On the down end he had placed a rubber ball, a sponge, and a newspaper ball, all in a row. He jumped on the up end of the board, and all three objects flew spectacularly into the air, about six or seven feet. He ducked his head to avoid getting hit by the objects as they came down. Jeff continued to catch the ball. Ricky went over to see what Jeff was doing, then returned to his lever. He arranged on the down end of his board a sponge and two rubber balls and covered them all with a shoe box. Then he jumped on the up end, and again ducked his head to protect himself from the flying objects.

In rebuilding his lever after a jump, Jeff picked up the paper ball and started to place it on the up end of the board. He quickly checked himself and put it instead on the down end.[4]

On the other side of the room, Ricky was still experimenting with putting various objects on his lever. He stood a cylinder upright on it, put a rubber ball inside the cylinder and a sponge on top.

Noticing what Ricky was doing, and realizing that the cylinder might hurt someone, the teacher hurried over and asked, "Ricky, what do you think will happen when that flies up in the air?"

Before the question was completed, Ricky had already jumped on the board and sent the objects flying. Ricky ducked his head and covered it with his arm as he answered the question belatedly: "Hit somebody's head."

The teacher picked up the sponge and said, "See, these are real soft. If this hits me on the head, it won't hurt. But if *this* hits me on the head (picking up the IBM cylinder) *that*'ll hurt."

"What about this?" asked Ricky, holding up the rubber ball.

"I don't think that'll hurt too much," replied the teacher. "So I don't think we should use this," she said, indicating the cylinder.

[4]This action illustrates well the nature of the constructive process. Relationships are not created once and for all but, instead, by being coordinated only some of the time at first.

Ricky placed the sponge on one end of his board (which was flat on the floor), a rubber ball on top of the sponge, and a paper ball in front of the sponge. He looked around the room and asked, "Where's that white ball?"

> The teacher did not hear Ricky's question but could see that he was looking for something to use as the fulcrum. She thought he might be interested in trying a larger fulcrum and asked, "Does it work just as well if you use these big ones (indicating the IBM cylinders)?"

"I don't know," answered Ricky, still looking for the white ball.

"Do you want to try?" asked the teacher.

"No," replied Ricky. He spotted the white ball by the box of rollers, went to get it, and also picked out a short roller from the box.

> In retrospect, the teacher realized that she was suggesting that Ricky use the cylinders which she had just told him not to use! It was clear in her mind that she meant not to use them *on* the board, but that it was all right to use them underneath. She wondered if Ricky understood what she meant.

Ricky slid the short roller under his board as a fulcrum.

"Hmmm, a little one," commented the teacher.

He added the white rubber ball in front of the paper ball on his board, and jumped on the up end. Again, he ducked his head as the objects flew high into the air.

> The teacher saw that, since he was always ducking his head, Ricky could not observe where the objects went. She decided to get him to focus on the feedback from the flying objects and asked, "Can you make them come high enough to catch them? How can you make them come up just high enough to catch them?"

Ricky shrugged. He picked up both rubber balls. He readjusted the short roller under the board and placed the sponge next to it. Then he took a larger roller and placed it next to the sponge (see Photograph 5.7). Ricky piled a paper ball and two rubber balls on the lever and sent them flying, again ducking his head and turning away as they fell.

Photograph 5.7.

In another attempt to focus Ricky's attention on the feedback from the objects, the teacher asked him how high he thought the sponge would go.

Ricky indicated a spot about eight inches above the board. Jeff called for the teacher to come and see something.

She replied, "Well, first I want to see how high a sponge goes, O.K.?"

Ricky jumped on the board and the sponge flew about six feet into the air. This time Ricky watched as the sponge flew up rather than ducking his head.

"Does a sponge go as high as a paper ball?" asked the teacher.

"I don't know," Ricky answered.

"Do you want to see?" the teacher asked offering the paper ball to him.

"I want to use the *ball* under here," said Ricky, who was busy placing the rubber ball under the board between two rollers (see Figure 5.3).

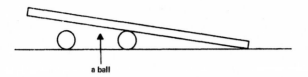

Figure 5.3.

"Oh, a *ball* under there. That's another idea," the teacher said. Finally decentering to Ricky's interest, she decided to shift her remarks to what interested *him*.

Jeff came over to see what Ricky was doing, and Jennifer M. called to the teacher to come and see what she was doing.[5]

The teacher replied, "I will in a minute, Jen, O.K.? I just want to see something."

Ricky put the sponge on the board and tried unsuccessfully to get the second rubber ball to stay on top of it. Finally, he put the ball in front of the sponge to prevent it from rolling off the board.

To Jeff, who was watching with interest, the teacher commented, "He put a *ball* under there," pointing to Ricky's fulcrum.

Ricky then jumped on the high end of the board, and watched as the ball and the sponge flew six or seven feet into the air.

"Was that any better?" asked the teacher.

"I don't know. The ball came out," said Ricky, indicating that he was interested in the ball as the fulcrum. He placed the board on the rollers again (one long and one short).

Thinking that Ricky was still interested in seeing what effect different objects had when used as the fulcrum, the teacher asked, "What about these (holding up an IBM cylinder)? Did you try these already?"

"No," said Ricky. He placed it under the board, in front of the other two rollers. He then removed the short roller and placed it *on* the board in front of the sponge. He placed a rubber ball in front of the short roller, and the long wooden roller in front of the ball (see Figure 5.4).

[5]It was unusual for the children to call for so much of the teacher's attention. She felt that this was because the children thought the camera was following her.

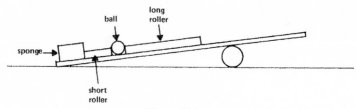

Figure 5.4.

Again with safety in mind, the teacher tried to get Ricky to anticipate the danger of flying rollers. She asked, "Ricky, what do you think's gonna happen when those wooden things fly up in the air?"

With a somewhat sheepish look, Ricky answered, "I don't know," as he removed the rollers from the board.

The teacher nodded and confirmed casually, "They might hit somebody."

Jenifer L., who was still rolling on the huge cylinder, called, "Maureen!"

"I see you're still practicing," answered the teacher. "Are you getting further and further?"

"Yeah," answered Jennifer.

In the meantime, Ricky replaced the wooden objects with balls. He put the paper ball on the board in front of the rubber ball which was in front of the sponge, but accidentally knocked it off as he reached for a second rubber ball. He tried to put the second rubber ball *on* the sponge, but quickly moved it to the board in front of the first ball because it would not stay on the sponge. After placing the paper ball in front of both rubber balls as shown in Figure 5.5, he got another IBM cylinder and tried to slide it under the board to the left of the cylinder that was holding it. There was not enough room for it; so he gave up on the idea and jumped (see Photograph 5.8).

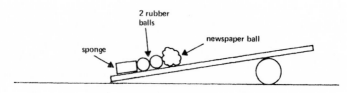

Figure 5.5.

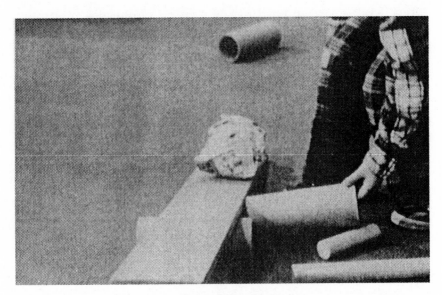

Photograph 5.8.

The teacher noticed Jennifer M. wandering around looking for something to do. "What happened to your rowboat, Jennifer?" she asked.

"I fell out of it," replied Jennifer with amusement.

"You fell out of it?" laughed the teacher.

"It fell sideways," Jennifer explained.

"Would these make a good rowboat?" the teacher asked as she walked over to the two plastic laundry baskets. "Why don't you make the 'road,' and then you can take a ride on it."

"Yeah, I tried it," Jennifer said as she picked up one of the baskets. "Can you help me?" she continued.

Trying to find out why Jennifer was unsuccessful before, the teacher asked, "Well, what happened when you made the road?"

Just then, Jennifer L. came running over to join the road building, and when the teacher asked if she (Jennifer L.) was going to help make a "road-river," Jennifer M. knew that the teacher was now going to shift her attention to building with them.

This activity seemed to be especially good for constructing relationships among objects and for inspiring new ideas. Because the materials were open-ended, children were able to play with them in different ways, each child at his/her own level.

The Surprises

The teacher was surprised at the difficulty the children had in building the lever and in figuring out how to keep the ball from rolling off the board.

Follow-Up

a. The best follow-up for this activity would be more of the same.
b. According to the teacher, it was especially difficult to figure out what was going on in a child's head from moment to moment in this activity because each of the children had different problems that she had not encountered before. The teacher felt that the next time she did the activity, she would stay with each child a longer time in order to follow the sequence of ideas instead of moving about rather randomly from child to child.

Chapter 6

Target Ball

Planning the Activity

We wanted to develop an aiming game with balls and the action of throwing. Since the use of a single target such as a block would be too hard and probably boring, we decided to suggest that children make a construction of many objects to knock down. Building such a target is in itself a good physical-knowledge activity involving the balancing of objects (a particular instance of the movement of objects). We also thought that children might be inspired to compare the ease or difficulty of knocking down different constructions. In addition, throwing the ball at the top, bottom, or other parts of the construction would give children an opportunity to compare the effects of throwing the ball at different places. With these objectives and plan in mind, the teacher collected the following materials:

> A ball for each child
> About three dozen each of
> > juice cans (48-oz. size)
> > heavy cardboard cylinders (discarded from IBM duplicating machine)
> > milk-carton blocks (Tops were cut from one-gallon cartons, and one carton was fitted into another to make blocks.)

We decided to use alternative (3) of how to introduce an activity, and to propose to the children right from the beginning the idea of aiming the ball at the objects. We made this decision because we thought children might otherwise get involved in a building activity which would be awkward to interrupt. We also decided, in accordance with Principle II of how to begin the activity, that each child should build his own target to hit rather than being pushed into cooperative play. As we stated in Chapter 3, a good activity is one in which cooperation is possible but not necessary.

The teacher placed the materials in an area outside the classroom. At the end of group time, he asked for volunteers who would like to play a game of knocking down some things with a ball. The children who participated in this activity were:

Sandy (3 years, 8 months)
John (4 years, 5 months)
Jack (3 years, 6 months)
Bobby (3 years, 10 months).

The teacher showed the children the pile of neatly stacked objects. Giving each a ball, he said, "Let's sit down and talk about this game." The children sat in a cross-legged semi-circle around the teacher who continued, "There are lots of things here to play with. All these things are here for you to use, and you can take as many as you want. The idea of the game is to take the ball and knock these things over. You can bring as many of these things as you want over there (indicating an open area), and throw your ball to try and knock them down."

Sandy said, "I can knock them down easily!"

The teacher replied, "Why don't you put them the way you think you can knock them down the easiest?" The teacher then identified a target

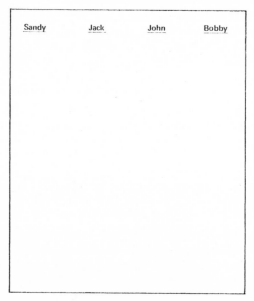

Figure 6.1. The areas defined by the teacher for each child to construct his target.

area for each child as shown in Figure 6.1. As they began to look over the materials, he said, "Think about what you want to use. You can take one or a lot of them." Then he sat back to watch what the children would do.

Because the activity evolved very differently from those described in Chapters 4 and 5, we deviate from the format used there. In those chapters, it was appropriate to describe how the teacher observed and interacted with a group of children. In this chapter, however, since each child "did his own thing" in parallel play for 30 minutes, it seems best to describe separately what each child did. In fact, this is an example of an activity that went all by itself without much need for teacher intervention because each child was thoroughly absorbed in following his own ideas.

We will start with Sandy, who was positioned at the left as shown in Figure 6.1, and proceed toward the right with an account of each child. The first and third children, Sandy and John, played as the teacher expected. They started out with fairly simple, low structures and gradually elaborated them into tall, wide, and complex ones which took a long time to build. Jack, the child who played between Sandy and John, did something completely different—he used only one can the whole time and aimed more than 64 shots at it during the 30-minute period. The last child, Bobby, whose motor coordination was not well developed, tended to make low constructions with a few objects spread in a line or in a clump. The wide constructions he made often enabled him to hit *something*, and he frequently hit the target with the ball still in his hand.

As can be seen in the following account, the teacher's interventions were minimal. The teacher could well have gotten the activity started, left it, and returned occasionally to see how it was going.

Sandy

Sandy picked up a couple of cylinders, wandered around, then took them back and exchanged them for a block. She put it against the wall and got another to add alongside it. Swinging her arm and saying "One, two, three," she aimed her ball at the blocks, but it hit the wall above her target. As she chased and caught her ball, she stopped to watch John stack a can on a block. Deciding to try that, too, she ran to get a can and a cylinder, and put one on top of each block. From a distance of about three feet, she threw the ball and knocked the cylinder off. She then threw again, bouncing the ball on the floor. The rebound missed. Throwing once more, she hit the can but not hard enough to make it fall. Finally, she hit it hard enough to knock it over. She threw again, but missed. Then, coming right up to the blocks, she bounced the ball right on top of them, but they only wobbled (because they

Photograph 6.1.

were braced against the wall). She went over to talk to the teacher, then returned and, using brute force, knocked over the blocks with the ball held in her hand.

She then exchanged the can and cylinder for two more blocks and built a tower four blocks tall, away from the wall.

The teacher noticed that Sandy had figured out the undesirability of making a target right against the wall.

Sandy threw her ball with an underhanded toss at close range, and the tower toppled with a crash.

The teacher exclaimed, "Oh, look what Sandy did!"

Sandy gathered cans, more blocks, and cylinders and took a long time building the complex construction shown in Photograph 6.1. The last block on top of a can kept falling off, and she had to try several times to find a way to make it stay on.

The teacher commented, "I wonder if Sandy is going to be able to knock all those down." Noticing that Jack was watching, he asked, "What do you think, Jack?" but got no response.

Sandy threw from a distance of about three feet, missed, then threw again, this time making everything except the base tumble down. Beginning to rebuild, Sandy said, "Mine's going to be real easy to knock down."

The teacher asked, "Why is it going to be easy?"

"Because it's made out of blocks," Sandy responded.

[*Note: This is an example of the general futility of asking "why" questions. Here it did not seem to stimulate the child's thought and did not provide the teacher with any useful information either. The teacher asked the question because some response seemed called for, and he did not know what else to say. In retrospect, he thought that it might have been better to make a comment more related to Sandy's action. For example, he might have responded, "How can you stack them to make it easy?" Such a comment does not require a response, and keeps the conversation open.*[1]]

Sandy then took a long time carefully building another elaborate structure similar to the one in Photograph 6.1, and said, "Look!" About that time, a stray ball thrown by Jack knocked down most of it. Uncomplaining, Sandy set about rebuilding.

The teacher had to tell Bobby, who was attracted by the excitement, not to aim at Sandy's things, but to knock his own down.

With great care and concentration, Sandy built several more elaborate structures similar to the first one, occasionally having difficulty with balancing objects the way she wanted them. Each time she was satisfied with what she had built, she knocked it down by throwing the ball at close range. Once she knocked it down with her hands.

Thinking that Sandy might like the challenge of a new problem, the teacher asked, "Sandy, can you make yours as tall as you are?"

"No," Sandy answered.

The teacher decided that the question was not a good one since Sandy rejected it.

---

[1]The wording of the teacher's verbal response may or may not make any real difference in terms of its effect on the child. More research is needed to clarify this point.

Sandy began a new construction, had several things fall over before she was finished, and was interrupted by Jack's ball which bounced into her area. She threw it to him, and it went past him. As the teacher started to help find Jack's ball which had disappeared behind a screen, Sandy followed. She dropped her ball, and there was then some confusion over which ball was hers and which was Bobby's. Finally, Sandy returned to her area, and built a tower of five cylinders. She jumped up and down, shouting for the teacher to look at her tower.

> [*Note: The way in which she built this tower was interesting. She carefully looked for and chose only the rollers from a sea of blocks that had tumbled down all over the floor. This is an example of the type of situation we prefer to mere sorting activities in which children are told to sort things for the sake of sorting them. Children spontaneously sort things when they have their own reason for doing so.*]

The teacher was surprised to see that Sandy had built this tower. Wondering if it was his earlier suggestion that inspired this construction, he remarked, "Wow, look at how tall Sandy's is! It's as tall as she is. I wonder if she can knock that down."

Sandy put her nose against the tower and seemed to be measuring herself against it. Then she took her ball in hand and whacked the tower in the center. Everything toppled.

"Oh, Sandy! Did you *throw* the ball that time?" the teacher asked.

"No, I didn't want to," Sandy replied. "I'm going to make one as tall as me again." She rebuilt the tower and put her nose against it again.

> Thinking that this tower was a more difficult target to hit since it was so narrow, the teacher tried to encourage Sandy by saying, "Sandy, let me see if you can *throw* it and knock it over."
>
> [*Note: Here the teacher suggested that the child do something for him. The reason offered is for the teacher's benefit, not the child's. It might have been better for the teacher to say, "Is it harder to throw it and knock it over?" In this particular case, Sandy was fortunately independent enough to resist the teacher's pressure.*]

As Jack watched and imitated her gestures, Sandy elaborately wound up and whacked the tower in the middle again, with the ball she was holding in her hand. She then rebuilt it again, stopping only to help John find his ball. Then, counting to five as she wound up, she whacked the tower again.

Photograph 6.2.

Using the blocks once more, she began to build another structure as Jack watched. She asked him to help her, and Jack obliged by placing one block on her construction. After she built the structure shown in Photograph 6.2, Sandy added one more block, and the whole thing collapsed.

The activity soon came to an end as the teacher warned, "We have to start cleaning up in five minutes because it will be lunch time."

Jack

Jack (who played with only one can for half an hour) set his can about 1½ feet from the wall and stood back a minute, watching as the teacher helped the other children identify their areas. He energetically wound up and took a few practice swings but did not let go of the ball. He then wandered over to Bobby's area and dropped his ball into one of Bobby's upright cylinders. He picked the cylinder up, retrieved his ball, and balanced it a moment on top of a can. Then he hopped over to look at John's bunch of cans.

The teacher said, "Jack, which is your space? Where are you going to be throwing?"

Jack returned to his area and for a few minutes aimlessly twirled around a little and watched as the other children ran back and forth getting materials. Seeing Sandy throw her ball and knock her building down, Jack was inspired to throw his. He knocked his can over on the first attempt.

"Good shot, Jack," applauded the teacher.

Jack immediately retrieved his ball, set the can upright, and aimed again, swinging the ball in both hands. He missed, and his ball bounced against the wall and into John's territory. Figure 6.2 shows how Jack aimed 64 times. First, he varied his distance from the can. Then, after the ball's accidental ricochet off the wall knocked over the can (throw 8), he attempted to repeat this interesting accident, and intentionally aimed at the wall instead of the can (throws 9–20). After two unsuccessful attempts in throws 9 and 10, he moved himself close to the can, still aiming at the wall. Finally, saying to the teacher, "Watch this," he moved himself and the can inches away from the wall, still aiming at the wall rather than directly at the can (throws 19–20). (A couple of times during this sequence he paused to draw with his hand the path from the wall to the can which he wanted the ball to follow. Then he tried moving the can, first far, then very near the wall.)

The teacher thought about Chapter 1 of Inhelder and Piaget (1955) and remembered that the problem of angles of incidence is not possible for the child to solve before adolescence. However, he felt that this experimentation was excellent, since the problem in this situation was truly Jack's own.

Finally, giving up the idea of reproducing the ricochet effect, Jack moved the can farther from the wall (about four feet), and aimed four times from a distance of two or three feet (throws 21–24). Apparently finding this too easy, he moved back a couple more feet and aimed a series of shots at the can (throws 25–32). After one more close shot (throw 33), Jack thought of aiming from the other side of the can. He stood with his back to the wall, threw, missed, and chased the ball (throw 34). Catching it about eight feet away, he tried throwing it from that distance, and succeeded in knocking the can over (throw 35). After missing twice (throws 36–37), he moved closer (about five feet from the can (throw 38). Beginning to tire of aiming, twice he just threw the ball in the air and followed its bouncing, jerking his head up and down with each successive bounce. One bounce happened to hit the wall and rebound on the can, knocking it over.

The teacher commented, "Oh, you got a ricochet there, Jack!"

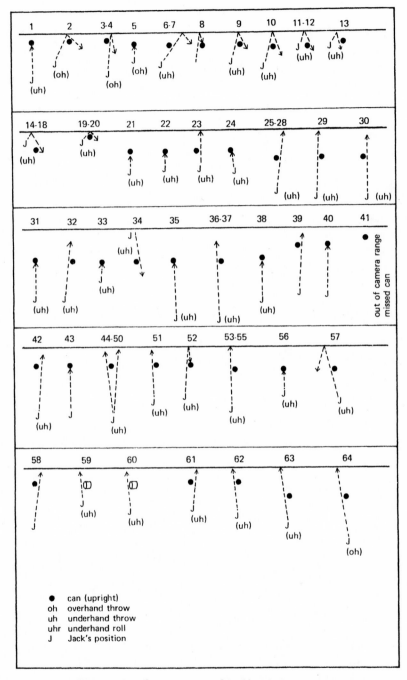

Figure 6.2. The sequence of Jack's 64 aims at one can.

Jack moved the can farther away, threw a few times (throws 39–41), then threw again and accidentally toppled Sandy's tall, elaborate construction.

The teacher laughed at Jack's surprise and exclaimed, "Oh, Jack, you knocked Sandy's down!"

A few throws later, Jack's ball landed in the middle of John's materials. John was just then talking about "doing a ricochet, like Jack's." Jack got his ball, walked away, then returned and balanced John's ball on top of a can. He backed up, watched John building, and then added a can sideways across the two columns of cans John had built. When John threw his ball at his structure, Jack followed suit. He missed, and John protested, "Stop!"

The teacher intervened, saying, "Jack, don't throw at John's. If you want to build a big one like that, build your own, O.K.?"

Jack returned to his own activity, aiming at the single can from about eight feet for quite a while. Finally, he turned the can on its side and aimed from about two feet, unsuccessfully (throw 59). After missing a couple of throws, he righted the can and aimed from about three feet. Wandering intermittently, he aimed a few more times. Then, losing interest in his can, he watched Sandy build a tower. She appealed, "Help me." Jack picked up a block, put it on the tower Sandy had started, then watched as she finished it. He was taking aim at it when Sandy added another block and the whole thing collapsed.

John

Our description of what John did will be brief, since his actions were similar to Sandy's. John began by struggling to carry five cans all at once to his designated space—a feat in itself! He added three more cans and two blocks and then, with some uncertainty, arranged a can on top of a block (see Photograph 6.3). He stood rather far away (about 10 feet), aimed, and missed several times. He rolled the ball much of the time, sometimes standing close to the target, and kept throwing until every object was knocked over.

John's second construction included a three-tiered section consisting of two stacked cans with a carton on top. After missing his target, John added a block on top of it, threw, and knocked off the top three objects. Then he built four more constructions, increasingly tall and more varied in arrangement. He was always absorbed thoughtfully in the construction itself, and always persisted in knocking over every object before beginning a new arrangement.

Overhearing the teacher comment on Jack's "ricochet," John said, "I'm making a ricochet."

Photograph 6.3.

Wondering whether John understood the word he had picked up, the teacher asked, "What is a ricochet, John?"

John replied, "Like Jack's. He speeded his ball. Watch out for my ricochet!" John then proceeded to make a more elaborate tower (see Photograph 6.4).

[*Note: John obviously did not understand the correct meaning of the term "ricochet." The teacher did not try to teach the word, as this would have disrupted the physical-knowledge activity. The occasional introduction of a big word like "ricochet" is good provided (a) it is not done too often, and (b) the teacher does not expect the children to understand its meaning. In this situation, three out of the four children liked the way the word sounded and repeatedly used it.*]

The teacher exclaimed, "See how tall John's is!"

John then said, "This is the Sears Tower. I'm gonna knock all the people down." With five throws, he succeeded in bringing down the last of the tower. He then built another structure which he said was "spooky," and knocked it down.

Bobby

Bobby put two cylinders down in his spot and watched the other children who were busily getting materials.

Photograph 6.4.

The teacher prompted, "Bobby, which ones are you going to use?"

Bobby pointed to the cans and made five trips in a rather babyish gait to the pile of materials, each time returning with one can or one carton. Then he ambled over to John's spot, looked at his collection, and helped himself to a can.

"Bobby, where is your space?" the teacher prompted again.

"Here," Bobby replied, moving back to his area. After placing the last can on the milk carton, he had the arrangement shown in Photograph 6.5, and

Photograph 6.5.

called out excitedly, "Look at mine! Look at mine!" He held the ball up, awkwardly shifted his feet and twisted his body several times before he called "Ready! Set! Go!" and threw the ball. It bounced over and behind the carton. Clutching his pants (which he was trying to keep up) in his left hand, Bobby retrieved the ball, aimed with similar contortions, and missed again. Standing closer and saying, "Here I go!" he finally knocked down one of the cans in the middle of the linear arrangement. After two more misses, he succeeded in knocking two cans over with one throw. Aiming with great deliberateness, he swung the ball toward a can and knocked it down by hitting it with the ball in his hand. Moving back a little, he threw the ball and again missed his target by a large margin. After chasing his ball, he noticed what John was doing and stopped to watch him take aim and knock down a rather elaborate structure which collapsed with a big noise. After a total of 16 tries, each one preceded by a loud "Ready, set, go!" Bobby finally knocked over all the objects shown in Photograph 6.5. He started to rebuild close to John.

The teacher said, "Let's move yours over here (back to the original space). You're getting too close to John." He noticed that Bobby had a good deal of difficulty with motor coordination and that when he suc-ceeded in hitting objects from a distance, this was largely by accident.

Bobby then built a three-tiered structure (see Photograph 6.6).

The teacher asked, "Bob, do you think that's going to be hard to knock over or easy to knock over?"

[*Note: A better question might have been, "Can you build it so it's easy to knock down?"*]

Photograph 6.6.

"Easy to knock over," replied Bobby. After missing from a distance, he stepped closer, missed again, and finally, in rapid-fire order, knocked them all over with the ball still in his hand, yelling "Ready, set, go!" with each strike.

Stacking one can on a carton, he called out, "Here I go, teacher!" Standing very close, he threw the ball as he shouted "Go!" The can fell over, and Bobby rolled on the floor in triumph.

Then he built a new structure by stacking a can, a carton, and another can, and arranging three single cans around this tower. His attention was caught as Sandy's big structure collapsed and the teacher applauded with an excited exclamation. Then, yelling "Go!" he aimed at his structure and missed several times. Meanwhile, Jack accidentally knocked over Sandy's tower. Bobby heard the teacher laughingly say, "Oh, Jack, you knocked Sandy's down!" Bobby grabbed his ball and ran over to join the fun. Yelling "Go!" he hit one of Sandy's fallen blocks with the ball in his hand.

The teacher intervened, saying, "Oh, Bob, you knock your *own* down. Sandy's building something *she* wants to knock down."

Bobby returned to his area and watched the others a moment.

The teacher said, "Bobby's doing something interesting. I wonder if that's going to be easy to knock down."

Bobby responded, "Look at my big one!"

The teacher affirmed, "Bobby has a big one now, too."

Bobby rapidly repeated, over and over, "Ready, set, go!" as he vigorously hit each object in his arrangement, one right after another, ball in hand again.

The teacher noted that Bobby seemed to be trying to achieve an effect like the other children whose elaborate structures often collapsed all at once.

Panting after chasing his ball, Bobby swung so hard at the last can with his ball in hand that he hurt himself. Surprised, he paused to rub his hand.

The teacher asked, "Are you O.K., Bob?"

Bobby nodded.

"Why don't you try throwing the ball instead of your hand?" the teacher suggested.

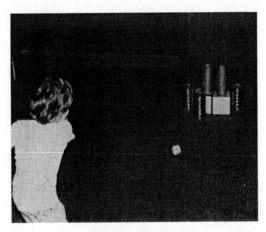

Photograph 6.7.

Recovered, Bobby yelled "Go!" and let go of the ball. He then decided to rebuild, and put a can and cylinder side by side on top of an overturned block. He arranged single cans around these. Aiming at close range, he knocked the can off. Excitedly, he yelled, "Did it! I did it! I did it!" Then, ball in hand, he rapidly knocked over the remaining objects, shouting "Go, go, go-go, go!" as he hit each one. After looking around, he built the structure shown in Photograph 6.7.

The teacher noticed Bobby's latest effort and decided to try to encourage him to release the ball. "Hey, Bob, that's a nice thing you've built. Do you think you could stand back here (about six feet away) and still knock it over?"

Bobby followed the teacher's suggestion, said his usual "Ready, set, go," and threw the ball, knocking over a can. He paused to look when John's structure collapsed with a bang, then ran to demolish his own structure, ball in hand once more, yelling "Go!" repeatedly.

Wanting Bobby to build in a more elaborate way, the teacher said, "Bobby, let me see how high you can build yours. See how high Sandy's is? See if you can build a tall one."

[*Note: In retrospect, the teacher realized that this was an inappropriate imposition. Bobby had his own reasons for building the low structures he was building, and there was no reason for him to build his like anybody else's.*]

Somehow, Bobby picked up Sandy's ball.

The teacher saw a ball lying in Bobby's area and said, "Here's a ball. Whose is it?"

Bobby replied, "That's mine," dropping Sandy's ball.

"How can you tell?" asked the teacher curiously.

Bobby shoved his ball in front of Sandy and persuasively pleaded, "See, Sandy, this is *mine*," as if this were a proof! Sandy returned to her space, and Bobby watched the other children for a few moments.

The teacher asked, "Bobby, how tall can you make yours?"

Bobby then built the structure shown in Photograph 6.8.

The teacher wondered if this wide structure was Bobby's attempt to make sure he hit *something* when he threw the ball. He asked, "Can you stand back here?"

[*Note: This was again an imposition. The teacher's request was too difficult for Bobby.*]

Obligingly, Bobby threw his ball from about six feet away, missed, then watched as John talked about building his "Sears Tower." He threw the ball several times and knocked over a can and a block. After watching John make his Sears Tower collapse, Bobby walked up to his own structure and swatted hard at the remaining objects, with resounding thuds, saying, "Go! Go! Go!" After scattering the objects, he announced to the teacher. "I'm going to sit down."

Evaluation

a.   The construction of a target proved a great success. All the children except Jack were thoroughly occupied in figuring out how to make an interesting target. All three were eager to demolish their targets with a ball, though not always by throwing it. By the end of the activity, the three were making more elaborate structures than at the beginning.

b.   Organizing the activity in the form of parallel play was good. It permitted a wide range of individual differences and creativity while encouraging a good deal of imitation and observation of what others were doing. For example, Sandy got an idea from seeing John stack a can on a block, and proceeded to stack many objects on her own. The parallel organization of the activity permitted all the children to vary what they

Photograph 6.8.

were trying to do. Sometimes they focused more on the construction itself, and sometimes on aiming the ball. Many experiments were pursued, including varying the distance and angle of aiming the ball, and using the ball in various ways (overhanded and underhanded, rolling and hitting directly, and trying to hit on the rebound).

c.   It is difficult to say whether the children were thinking in terms of different structures or of different spots to hit them. It is probably unrealistic to imagine that the children had either factor in mind, especially on this first encounter with the material. Such comparisons cannot be made until children have enough experience to enable them to know that different types of structures react differently, and that strikes at different points produce different results. The children's interest on the first day was simply in building and knocking down (or, in Jack's case, knocking down from different places).

The Surprises

a.   The biggest surprise was Jack's satisfaction with aiming at a single target. Contrary to expectation, he was not bored, but found many challenges in aiming in different ways at his lone can. He even tried to reproduce a ricochet effect. It was very sophisticated of Jack to see that it was possible to knock over the can by aiming at the wall. When children are thus encouraged to come up with their own ideas and problems (cognitive objective *1*), they sometimes invent very difficult ones and work at them for a long time. There is a big difference between a child's choosing to aim at a single target and *being told* to aim at a single target.

b.   We were surprised to see Bobby's solution to the problem of not being able to hit a target by throwing a ball. His solution was to hit the target with the ball in his hand. Sandy, too, did the same thing from time to time, thereby complying with the rule to knock things down *with a ball*!

Follow-Up

The activity went so well, and children were still so intensely engaged in building and/or aiming, that the short-term follow-up is simply more of the same activity. In addition, the following variations and long-term follow-up were planned:

a.   Using bean bags instead of balls
Since bean bags will not bounce or roll and are heavier than balls, children may be more likely to notice where the bag hits the structure. (Bean bags will also be easier for Bobby to aim.)

b.   More cooperative play
A natural shift toward more cooperation can be facilitated by encouraging children to offer help and advice to one another or to build targets together, and by suggesting a group game involving aiming at the target. For example, children might build various targets and then aim to see whose falls down first. They might also want to construct a single target at which they would take turns aiming.

Chapter 7

Inclines

As evidenced by the popularity of slides on playgrounds, young children are naturally interested in inclines. At our University day care center, one of the most used pieces of equipment is a wide slide made with the top of a large discarded table (Photograph 7.1). Children slide down in a variety of ways and make toy cars and trucks, blocks, dolls, and other objects roll or slide down. They also like to climb up this side; and find that this is easier in tennis shoes than in shoes with leather soles.

Another day care center we know has a small, grass-covered hill which inspires many different uses. Children love to ride down the hill on tricycles, sometimes sailing down with both feet in the air as the pedals seem to move all by themselves! Wagons become more in demand because children can ride down the hill without depending on anybody to give them a push. Races with toy cars also take place on this hill. Here, the teacher has many opportunities to get children to think about the variables that make the cars go faster and better (by encouraging children to try the cars, for example, on the bumpy grass, on dirt, and on a board placed on the hill). Even running up and down the hill involves a different kind of effort than running on a flat surface, and those physical experiences contribute to the child's knowledge of inclines. Skiing and sledding, of course, are other excellent activities involving the elementary physics of inclines in which children's practical intelligence develops.

The activity described in this chapter was inspired by the above observations of children's spontaneous interest in inclines. Inclines seemed particularly rich in potential because they enable a child to make an object move by letting go, without applying any force to it. The behavior of a ball on an incline is determined solely by the characteristics of the objects. An incline,

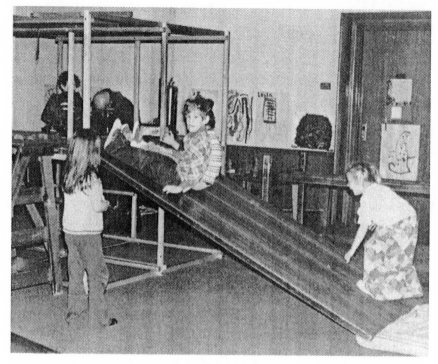

Photograph 7.1.

therefore, gives to the child a special occasion to observe the interactions among objects as well as to structure spatial relationships.

Planning the Activity

We decided that, to be interesting, an incline activity would have to take the form of producing a desired effect. The child would try either to *hold* a container at the right place in order to catch a ball that rolls down or to *let go* of a ball at the right place on the incline in order to make it land in a container. Objectives for the children that first day were formulated.

1. They could try to figure out where to hold the container when the ball is released from different spots and when the characteristics of the incline change. The changes we could think of were the following:

Turning the incline in various directions on the table
Asking children to put the container on the floor to catch the ball rather than holding it at table level

Photograph 7.2.

Making an incline on an incline (as shown in Photograph 7.2)[1]
Tilting the incline (as shown in Photograph 7.3)

2. They could compare the shape and size of various containers to figure out which one is best for catching a given ball (or which one is best for catching all the balls). With these objectives in mind, we collected the following materials:

3 tennis balls in a can
Small rubber balls (1¼ inches in diameter)
Marbles
Ball bearings (3/4 inch in diameter)
2 coffee cans (2-lb. size)
2 cottage-cheese containers (1-lb. size)
2 plastic jars (smaller than cottage-cheese container)
Triangular hollow blocks
A small wooden plank

[1]Photographs 7.2, 7.3, and 7.4 were taken on a different occasion for purposes of illustration. They, therefore, do not correspond to the details of the activity described in this chapter.

Photograph 7.3.

We planned to begin the activity by suggesting that children try to catch the ball with a container of their choice (alternative (3) of how to introduce the activity). As soon as possible, we thought the teacher should withdraw from the game, encouraging the children to continue the activity without her. Later, we thought she might vary the characteristics of the incline as listed under our first objective.

Trying the Activity

During outdoor play time we asked for four volunteers to go inside and play with balls and marbles. Barbara, Jerome, Joyce, and Mark, all four-year-olds, volunteered:

When the four children came into the room and saw the inclines (hollow triangular blocks on two tables), Barbara immediately asked, "What are we gonna do now?"

The teacher held a tennis ball at the top of the incline and said, "I thought you might like to catch balls in a different way today. Would you like to pick one of these containers and see if you can catch this ball with it?"

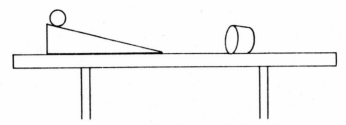

Figure 7.1. Mark's first attempt at placing a container.

The children each took a container and Mark held his cottage-cheese container on top of the table about 4 inches away from the foot of the incline as shown in Figure 7.1.

> The teacher released the ball, and it hit the edge of the container in such a way that everybody expected it to settle in the can. However, surprisingly, the ball was deflected to the side of the container and landed on the floor. The teacher asked (somewhat gratuitously), "How can you change it so it will catch next time?"

Mark moved the container closer, and held it firmly right up against the foot of the incline. After he succeeded in catching the ball, the other children clamored to get a turn. None of them had any trouble catching the ball. Barbara soon said, "Let *me* do it," asking to play the teacher's role.

> The teacher was glad for this volunteer, since she wanted children to play at both aiming and catching anyway. She yielded her spot to Barbara, put two more triangular hollow blocks next to the first one as shown in Figure 7.2, and continued to roll balls, this time with both hands so that two children could play with her simultaneously.
>   Noting that nobody had any difficulty catching the ball at the foot of the incline, she asked, "Where else can you hold the can to catch the ball?" (hoping that the children would hold their cans farther away).

No response from anybody! The children went right on playing in the same way as before.

> The teacher then decided that her question was stupid because the children had no reason to hold their containers anywhere else when they were successful in achieving their desired effect! She, therefore,

Figure 7.2.

suggested, "Do you think you can catch it if you hold the can at the edge of the table?"

The children did move their cans back to the edge of the table and, after some initial difficulty, became very skillful at catching the ball. However, Mark and Joyce from time to time moved their containers closer and closer to the foot of the incline itself.

After a while, Jerome got bored and decided to tease the teacher by holding his container at the edge of the table right up until the moment everybody expected the ball to roll into it. Then, at the very last moment, he removed the container, and everybody laughed.

> The teacher observed that this trick involved a lot of thinking. (Jerome had to exercise precise spatiotemporal reasoning to know the last possible moment at which to withdraw the can.) Picking up on the idea of a trick, she said, "That was a good trick. I think I'll try to trick *you* and start the ball from a different spot."

Jerome pulled the same trick with a dead-pan expression, and ended up bursting into laughter.

> After several repetitions, the teacher felt she needed to do something new and different. She therefore suggested, "How about coming here and holding the ball for Barbara to catch?" When Jerome did not respond to this idea, she decided to try changing the rule of the game to "This time, see if you can hold your ball catcher on the floor and catch the ball." (In retrospect, the teacher wished she had tried to

capitalize on Jerome's inventiveness and humor rather than trying to counteract it. For example, she might have said, "Can you think of a different way to trick me?")

Jerome had his can at an angle as shown in Figure 7.3. (The angle was exactly the same as when he was trying to catch the ball at the edge of the table and at the foot of the incline.)

The teacher was surprised at Jerome's generalization. Trying to make him more conscious of what he was doing, she asked, in a disbelieving tone, "Can you catch it like that?"

Jerome said, "Yeah," and when the ball bounced on the container and ended up on the floor, he was surprised. He quickly changed the position of the container, making it stand up. The ball went in on the second attempt.

After a while when the teacher again felt that more variation was needed to sustain the children's interest, she got a small wooden plank and a tennis ball. She used the plank as an incline, moving it around the table to vary the direction of the ball's rolling. When children began succeeding easily, the teacher decided this was the right moment to ask, "Is there a can that catches this ball more easily? Which can is the best to catch this ball on the floor with?"

Joyce responded by running to get the tennis ball can—obviously thinking that the best can for a tennis ball is the can it came in! She was subsequently surprised that the ball always hit the edge of the can and rolled off to the floor.

Barbara was holding a jar just large enough to hold the tennis ball.

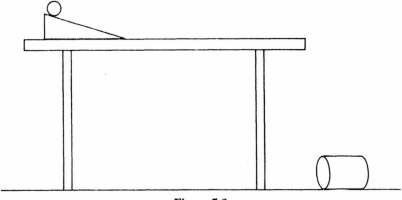

Figure 7.3.

When the teacher asked, "Which catcher is the best to catch the ball on the floor with?" Barbara noticed a second jar lying on the floor and picked it up. She held the two jars side by side at the edge of the table (as if to say, "Two jars are better than one," and "It is easier to catch the ball at the edge of the table than on the floor.").

> The teacher noted that the children seemed generally not aware of the desirability of using a large can. When she asked repeatedly, "Is that really the very best one to use?" only Barbara changed her mind and finally used a big coffee can. The rest seemed perfectly happy with any container that was bigger than the ball they were trying to catch.

Joyce noticed the jar of marbles, decided to try using them, and dumped them out on the floor.

> The teacher wanted at some point to switch from tennis balls to marbles anyway; so she followed Joyce's initiative and offered to hold a marble on the incline. "See if you can hold your ball catcher at the edge of the table to catch this one," the teacher said. (The tennis ball always rolled on the same path, but the marble's path was affected by the smallest, imperceptible factors. The teacher had worried that these variations in the marble's path might confuse the children. She had even wondered about the desirability of using the marbles at all and considered limiting the activity to the big balls only. In the end, however, she decided that the variations in the marble's path were part of the physical world that the children lived in, and that it would be best to let them have a chance to notice these variations. Besides, she decided that the unpredictability of the marble's path might cause them to think about the desirability of using a big can).
>
> The teacher held a marble in each hand so that Joyce and Barbara both could catch one. She released the marbles at the same time.

After each attempt to catch the marble, the children began to shout, "Aah!" whenever they were successful. This "Aaah!" soon became part of a ritual in which Joyce and Barbara placed the containers in position, told the teacher they were ready, watched the marble roll down, and shouted "Aaah!" if they were successful and "Nyah!" if they were unsuccessful.

> Barbara said, "Teacher, you need more marbles. I already have two," showing the two she had caught and collected in her jar.

> When the teacher watched the videotape later, she realized that Barbara was proposing the game of keeping the marbles in the container to see who could collect more. At the moment, however, she was too preoccupied to decenter to what Barbara was trying to say. Instead of

picking up on this idea, the teacher proposed a completely different game. She said, "Now, *I* want a turn to hold the cans. See if you can roll the marbles into these cans." She held a coffee can in each hand at the edge of the table and waited.

Joyce and Barbara responded to the teacher's suggestion, and Barbara's marble went in, but Joyce's did not.

The teacher exclaimed, "Oops! Try again." She noted that Barbara released her marble from the middle of the incline closer to the can, while Joyce released it from its top edge (as far away from the can as was possible).

The two children repeated exactly the same thing they had done before. Joyce plaintively said, "Mine never goes in," but seemed not to notice that Barbara gave her marble an advantage.

Since this did not seem to be going anywhere, the teacher shifted, saying, "I'm going to do something else now," and used the plank on the block to make an incline on an incline (see Photograph 7.2). She took two small rubber balls for the children to catch.

Joyce and Barbara had some difficulty at first but less than the teacher had expected.

After a while, when this became too easy, the teacher tilted the two inclines as illustrated by Photograph 7.4, saying teasingly, "I'm going to do something else again. I want to see if I can fool you." She let the same rubber balls roll as shown in the photograph.

Both Joyce and Barbara missed the ball, as they both expected it to take the usual path parallel to the side of the incline. On the second trial, Barbara corrected her prediction and caught the ball. Joyce, however, continued for at least six tries to make her prediction as if the incline had not been tilted.

The teacher observed that Joyce seemed to realize only that the ball never went into her can. She did not seem to be reading which way the ball was rolling in relation to the sides of the incline. Since she was very frustrated over her lack of success and was not shifting to other efforts, the teacher decided to suggest that Joyce just watch for a while to see how the ball rolled.

Finally, Joyce seemed to notice that the ball rolled diagonally on the incline, and moved her container to catch it. While the teacher was playing with

Photograph 7.4.

Joyce and Barbara, Mark and Jerome were pursuing many interests, such as rolling two balls into two cans with both hands at the same time. Jerome experimented with a marble, a very light plank, and a tennis ball can as shown in Figure 7.4. When he put the marble on the plank as shown in the figure, he was surprised that the plank fell over. He then came up with the question of where to put the marble without making the plank fall over. It took a lot of trial and error before he found out.

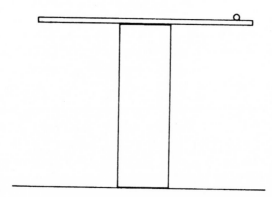

Figure 7.4 Jerome's experiment in quest of a place to put the marble without making the plank fall over.

Photograph 7.5.

Evaluation

a.　The activity seemed especially good for the coordination of spatiotemporal relationships, and the children had great fun making predictions and testing them as the teacher introduced the variations listed under objective *1*. However, the teacher felt that interest would have lagged had she not been so active in introducing these variations. She concluded that the activity as conducted was a bit too sterile for four-year-olds and would probably be better with younger children. This was borne out when the activity was tried with the three-year-olds shown in Photograph 7.5.[2]

b.　The children had little interest in comparing the shape and size of various containers (objective *2*). They generally seemed not to notice that a big container made it easier to catch the ball. The activity

[2]One of the teachers at Circle Children's Center who read this chapter expressed strong reservations about the appropriateness of this activity for four-year-olds. She felt the activity was too artificial, too much like a test, and too divorced from natural play. She pointed out that the activity was essentially teacher-directed because of children's short-lived interests, and suggested that it is better for the teacher to relate to more natural experiences with inclines such as those mentioned at the beginning of the chapter. We agree with this view in large measure. However, we have included this chapter as a way of illustrating how an activity can be evaluated and improved. Target Ball (Chapter 6) was an example of an activity that required no pushing by the teacher. Inclines (Chapter 7) is an example at the other extreme that seemed to require her direction every inch of the way.

seemed to present no real need for children to think about such comparisons.

The Surprises

The teacher was surprised that the children were so indifferent to the size of the containers. She had expected the larger containers to be in more demand. When the teacher tried to focus Barbara's attention on a comparison of containers, she found that Barbara thought only of using two jars together instead of a bigger one!

Follow-Up

Since the teacher felt that the activity quickly became too easy for four-year-olds and, therefore, boring without the continual introduction of variations, she felt the need to invent ways to make it more interesting. Three possibilities are the following:

a. Varying the shape of the incline
    When round boards (such as pizza plates) and irregularly shaped boards are used, children have to predict and "read" a fall line that is not parallel to the side of the incline.

Photograph 7.6.

b. Using a troughed incline

Tom Gleeson, one of the teachers at Circle Children's Center, used the troughed incline and the target made of an overturned box with openings of different sizes cut in the side, both shown in Photograph 7.6. This activity encouraged children to compare the following:

the steepness of the incline in relation to the distance of the ball's travel
the distance to the target in relation to the likelihood of the ball's entering the hole
the size of the ball in relation to the size of the hole
the different ways ping-pong and golf balls behave.

When Mr. Gleeson tried the activity, the children eagerly played with different balls and turned the box (thereby varying the size of the hole at which they aimed). They also varied the steepness of the incline (even standing it upright) and adjusted its direction. Some children preferred to have the target hole very close (at the very base of their incline, for example) to be sure of success. Others preferred to maintain a distance of four or five feet and kept trying to work at a different problem. One child found out that sometimes balls would go through the target and out the other side, but that sometimes they would go through one opening and get stuck because they were too big to go out the other side. She also explained that one ball small enough to come out the other side did not come out because a big one blocked the passage inside the box.

c. A game

Children can keep what they catch and see how many they can collect (as suggested by Barbara in the above account). They may be interested in comparing who got more.

Chapter 8

The Pendulum

On an incline, a ball rolls simply by being released. A pendulum likewise moves when it is released from a point away from its equilibrium position. In other words, these are both situations in which the object moves without needing a push. When the movement of an object is thus determined by the point of release and the characteristics of objects in relation to one another, the child has a unique opportunity to structure spatial and logical relationships. For example, he might notice that the bob of the pendulum always goes too far to the left of the target under certain circumstances, and too far to the right under other circumstances. Because of these possibilities for action and observation, we decided to focus on a pendulum activity.

Planning the Activity

As in the case of Target Ball (Chapter 6) and Inclines (Chapter 7), we felt that, in order to be interesting, the activity would have to take the form of producing a desired effect, such as knocking an object over. We then decided on objectives for the children for the first day. We hoped they would

1. think about where to hold the bob before releasing it to knock down the target
2. think about where to position the target when the bob is already held in a given position, ready to be released.

With these objectives in mind, we collected the following materials:

a piece of No. 36 cotton string
a wooden block (2-3/4" × 2-3/4" × 1-3/8")
a rubber doll that can stand erect

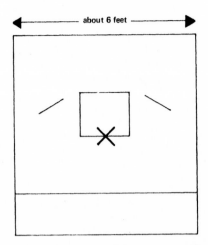

Figure 8.1. The way in which the teacher taped the floor with masking tape (the "X" marks the position of the bob at rest).

The general procedure we planned was to begin by making a pendulum during free play so that the children who gravitated toward it could observe how the pendulum is made. After letting the children play freely with it, the teacher would put the doll at various spots on the floor for the children to aim at (objective 1). From time to time, we felt that the teacher should ask for a turn to play with the pendulum, and ask the children where to put the doll so that the bob would hit it when released from a specific point (objective 2).

Trying the Activity

When we arrived in the classroom, we discovered that the teacher had taped the floor with masking tape as shown in Figure 8.1. She put a chair on a table, climbed on top, tied the string to a light fixture on the ceiling, removed the chair and table, and let the string hang down. A dozen children congregated and asked the teacher what she was doing. The teacher answered, "I'm making a pendulum for you to play with. Do you know what a pendulum is? You will see in a minute. . . ." She then tied the block, square side up, to the free end of the string in such a way that it almost touched the floor.

[*Note: The center of the block in its resting position is shown in Figure 8.1 with an "X" (which was not marked on the floor). After the activity, we decided that this "X" should have been taped on the floor—a point we will discuss in the evaluation of this activity.*)]

As soon as the teacher finished making the pendulum, the children started to play with it. They hit the bob and watched it swing back and forth, grabbed and released it, pushed it, and caught it again. The children in this account are:

Barbara (4 years old)
Margaret (3 years old)
Brian (4 years old)
Keith (4 years old).

Barbara characteristically took charge and told Margaret and Brian to stand on the other side of the rectangle (taped on the floor) to catch the block. When one of them caught the block, Barbara commanded, "Throw it to *me!*" Keith tried to join in at Barbara's side, but she told him to go to the other side where Margaret and Brian were. The children who were excluded by Barbara wandered away or stood around, not sure what to do next. The four children thus played spontaneously with the pendulum for a while, pushing or throwing the bob for somebody else to catch as directed by Barbara. The teacher told the other children, one by one, that there was not room for everybody to have a turn now. She suggested they find something else to do and come back if they wanted a turn later. The children accepted the teacher's request, knowing that she always kept her promises.

The teacher noticed that most of the time the children *pushed* or *threw* the block. They were thus using the same actions on the pendulum that they used to make balls and other objects move. The teacher wondered how she might get them to see the possibility of *letting go* of the pendulum without pushing it.

When she felt that the children were getting a little tired of this free play, she put the doll down as shown by the "o" in Figure 8.2, facing in the direction shown by the arrow. She said to Margaret, the three-

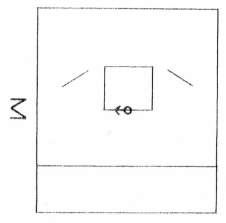

Figure 8.2. The placement of a doll.

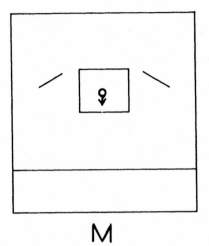

M

Figure 8.3.

year-old who was holding the block, "Can you hit this man, Margaret?" (Her reason for putting the doll there, just below the point of suspension, was to make the task easy at the beginning. For the time being, the teacher wanted Margaret just to get the idea of hitting the doll and knocking it down with the pendulum.)[1]

Margaret went from one side to the adjacent side of the rectangle shown with an "M" in Figure 8.2 and *threw* the block toward the doll. She missed her target by about five inches. When the block swung back to her, she tried to catch it, but it moved faster than she did. It swung back toward the doll, almost hitting it. Margaret let the block swing, and watched until its third swing knocked the doll down. She jumped up and down, laughing.

The teacher wanted Margaret to try aiming at a different spot; so she put the doll at "o" in Figure 8.3, facing in the direction shown by the arrow. She said, "What if I put him over here?" (The teacher had noticed that, on her first attempt, Margaret had gone out of her way to put herself in a face-to-face relationship with the doll, and she thought that it would be better if Margaret changed her position in reaction to the doll rather than in reaction to a direct suggestion from the teacher.)

[*Note: There were two aspects to the teacher's changing of the doll's position from that shown in Figure 8.2 to that shown in Figure 8.3. One*

---

[1]It should be noted here that many teachers have objected on socioemotional grounds to encouraging children to hit a doll. It probably would have been better to use a different object.

was the direction the doll was facing, and the other was its position in relation to the trajectory of the pendulum. Changing the direction the doll faced was good, but leaving the doll in the path of the pendulum's trajectory was not. Had the doll been placed farther from the bob's rest position, the child would have had a reason to figure out something rather than waiting for the pendulum to knock the doll down.]

Margaret again walked over to the side facing the doll as shown with an "M" in Figure 8.3 and *pushed* the block toward the doll. She missed the target again by about five inches. With an expectant expression, she again watched the pendulum swing back and forth. On its third swing toward the doll, the pendulum knocked it down. Margaret jumped up and down, laughing heartily.

By this time, the teacher could see that Margaret had figured out how to succeed by throwing or pushing the block and merely waiting for the desired outcome. Therefore, she changed the doll's position to the "o" shown in Figure 8.4 so that Margaret could no longer succeed by merely waiting.

[Note: This was an unfortunate spot because it was a very difficult one for the pendulum to reach from where Margaret was. A better position would have been the one indicated by "Y" which would have been easier to figure out in relation to where Margaret stood. Since Margaret seemed guided by the direction the doll was facing and the doll was already facing her, she could not be expected to think about walking

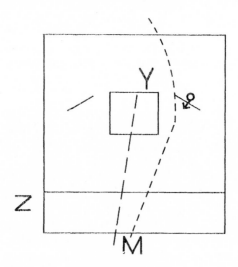

Figure 8.4.

*around to the position indicated by "Z" from which she could have
succeeded in knocking the doll down.*]

Margaret stood at the same place as before and *threw* the block toward the
doll. It moved as shown by the dotted curve in Figure 8.4. Just as before, she
waited expectantly for the pendulum to knock the doll down. As the pendulum slowed into an oval farther and farther from the doll, Margaret looked
puzzled. As if she still hoped that it might hit the doll, she watched until the
pendulum slowed to a very small circle. With a rather disgusted expression,
Margaret grabbed the block and stood at the same place as before. She raised
the block to her right shoulder and threw it toward the doll. She missed the
doll, and when the block came back to her, she made a half-hearted attempt
to catch it, but did not succeed.

The teacher exclaimed, "Catch the block, Margaret!" in an attempt to
get Margaret to try again to anticipate the pendulum's trajectory.

Margaret caught the block with both hands, then took it in her left hand,
and, extending her arm as far as it would go, *threw* it toward the doll.
Margaret's feet were thus at about the same place as before, but throwing
the block with her left hand made it come much closer to hitting the doll.

As the block began its backward swing, Margaret did not appear ready
to make the effort to catch it; so the teacher exclaimed, "Catch it,
Margaret, catch it!"

[*Note: In this situation, when Margaret was spontaneously letting the
pendulum swing on its own and watching, it was inappropriate for the
teacher to push the child into trying to catch the bob. The child's being
active sometimes means that he or she simply studies objects' movements.*]

Margaret caught the block, then held it in both hands in front of her
stomach, and pushed it toward the doll. She saw the block did not go toward
the doll as she expected. When it swung back to her, she caught it, and with
an impatient expression, walked over to the doll, picked it up, and plunked it
down at "o" in Figure 8.3. (She had apparently concluded by empirical
generalization by this time that the pendulum had a tendency to go toward
this point.) Holding the block in front of her stomach exactly as before, she
gave it a slight push toward the doll. It hit the doll squarely on its stomach,
and Margaret jumped up and down, patting her own stomach and shouting,
"I did it! I did it!"

The teacher exclaimed, "Wow, you sure hit him that time! Can I have a

turn now (as she caught the block)?" She asked Margaret for a turn as
an equal in order to reduce the effect of her adult authority and to
encourage the child's development of autonomy. She was hoping that a
demonstration of the action of *letting go* of the block would inspire
Margaret to imitate.

Barbara, who had been watching while jumping on a board attached to a
second board with strong springs, shouted, "Can I have a turn, Teacher? I
want a turn." (Brian and Keith had disappeared in the meantime, looking for
something else to do.)

"Yes, after Margaret is through," the teacher said as she positioned
herself where Margaret had been. She held the block in both hands
and said to Margaret, "Would you like to put the doll where I can hit it
if I let go of the block from here?"

Margaret stood the doll in the middle of the square where she had succeeded
in hitting it before (Figure 8.3). She ran to the side of the teacher and looked
at the doll as if she were sighting it for an aim.

The teacher asked, "If I let go of the block from here, do you think I
can hit the man?"

Thoughtfully, Margaret replied, "Yeah."

The teacher held the block still in both hands and said to Margaret,
"See, I'm just going to let go of it without pushing it." She slowly
released the block, narrowly missed the doll, and caught the block on
the upswing.

Margaret ran to the doll and moved it in the path the pendulum had followed. She ran back to the teacher and took the block from her, saying, "*I'll
show you how to do it.*" She then held the block in both hands, just like the
teacher, but *pushed* it again and missed her target.

The teacher wanted to try demonstrating again the idea of letting go.
Therefore, she said, "Can *I* have a turn again?" and positioned herself
as shown with a "T" in Figure 8.5. As she held the block in both hands,
she said, "I'm going to let go of it from here. I'm not going to push it
like you did. See, this is pushing (demonstrates), and this is just letting
go of it (demonstrates). Can you put the doll where I can hit it from
here without pushing the block?"

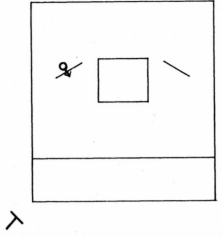

Figure 8.5.

Margaret put it as indicated by the "o" in Figure 8.5.

"O.K.? Can I hit it if I just let go of it?" asked the teacher.

Margaret said, "Yeah," with confidence.

> The teacher knew that she would miss the target, but she released the block so that Margaret could find out from the object the outcome of her prediction.

Margaret saw that the block went in a completely different direction from what she had expected. She then took the block in both hands, told the teacher to move, and stood where the teacher had been. Saying, "I know how to do it," she carefully aimed the block and gave it a strong push toward the doll. The block traveled as shown by the dotted curve in Figure 8.6. Margaret stared in surprised disbelief. She then said, "I'll show you how," moved the doll to her favorite position (Figure 8.3), and stood in exactly the same place as before. She pushed the block and it hit the doll. She ran to the doll, stood it up again, and repeated her action, knocking the doll down again.

> The teacher noted that Margaret had figured out one successful combination of positions for the doll and herself. She thought that it might help Margaret notice how the pendulum worked if she put the doll at "o" in Figure 8.7, too far for the pendulum to reach.

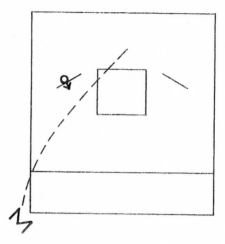

Figure 8.6.

Barbara was getting more and more impatient and demanded, "I want a turn, Teacher. I want a turn."

The teacher said, "O.K., in just a minute, Barbara," and turned to Margaret, saying, "Do you think you can hit him here?"

Margaret pushed the block toward the doll as usual and saw that she missed it. She then pushed the block harder and saw that it still did not go far enough. She pushed it even harder the third time. By this time Barbara was angry and shouted, *"Teacher,* I want a turn! *I want a turn, you fathead!"*

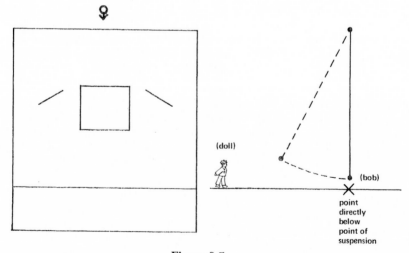

Figure 8.7.

The teacher turned to Barbara and said, "Yes, I know, Barbara. Do you think Margaret will hit the man?"

It was obvious to Barbara that the teacher was thoroughly absorbed in what Margaret was doing and was hardly paying any attention to her. So Barbara got even louder and more agitated when she answered, "NO, YOU BIG HEAD!

[Note: It would have been better in this situation for the teacher to recognize Barbara's frustration more clearly and appeal to Margaret to help figure out a solution. This would also have helped prepare Margaret for the impending loss of her turn.]

Margaret went on with her sixth, seventh, and eighth attempts, pushing the block harder and harder—in fact, as hard as she could.

The teacher turned to Barbara and asked, "Why do you think Margaret doesn't hit the doll?"

Barbara's resentful answer was " 'Cause she's too little." (Barbara knew she was older and bigger than Margaret.)

The teacher asked Barbara, "Do you think you are big enough to hit it?" Barbara answered, "Yeah," with an air of disgust. Margaret went on playing, moving the doll again to her favorite position (the one shown in Figure 8.3).

The teacher said, "Oh, Margaret, why did you move him up?" (She asked this question not to find Margaret's reason, but to help her become conscious of what she was doing.)

As she ran back to her original position, Margaret answered, " 'Cause I don't want him way over there"—a typical answer teachers get from three- or four-year-olds in response to a "why" question. On the second attempt, Margaret hit the doll. Barbara was getting still more angry and began pounding on the table, singing and shouting, "Old MacDonald had a farm, ee-ai-ee-ai-oh!"

The teacher moved the doll back to the other side of the rectangle (as shown in Figure 8.7), saying to Barbara, "Do you think you can hit him over here?"

Barbara answered, "Yeah, and *you* better give *me* a turn!"

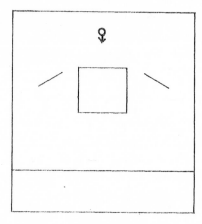

Figure 8.8.

The teacher said to Margaret, "You had a *long* turn, Margaret. Now, let's give Barbara a turn and see if *she* can hit the man over there."

Barbara skipped over to the block and took it away from Margaret. Margaret was taken by surprise and began to cry.

The teacher had assumed that Margaret realized she would have to give Barbara a turn soon. However, in retrospect, she realized the need to prepare Margaret specifically for giving up her turn. For example, Margaret could have been helped to anticipate this event if the teacher had suggested, "Three more tries, and then Barbara wants a turn." Holding Margaret in her arms, the teacher comforted her, explaining that Barbara had been waiting a *long, long* time while Margaret had a turn, and so on.

Margaret howled and stamped her feet as she cried. The teacher gently pulled Margaret onto her lap and suggested, "Let's watch Barbara and see if she's really big enough to hit the man. Margaret began to recover from her upset as she watched Barbara. Barbara pushed the block with confidence but saw that it did not reach the doll. She pushed a second time, and a third time, each time with more force than before. Seeing that pushing the block harder did not change the result, Barbara ran to the doll and brought it closer (as can be seen in Figure 8.8).

The teacher laughed and said casually, "Why did you do that, Barbara? I thought you were big enough to hit him where he was." (She wanted

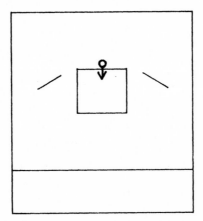

Figure 8.9.

Barbara to become conscious of the difference between her previous idea and what she found out from the object.)[2]

Barbara ignored the teacher and aimed at the doll again. Giving a slight push to the block, she missed the target. The same action was repeated three times, with the same amount of force each time. Then, concluding that the doll was still too far for the pendulum to reach, Barbara moved the doll still closer to the position shown in Figure 8.3. In the three attempts that followed, she gave a slight push to the bob and missed the target by only an inch or two. On the fourth try, she hit the doll.

The teacher asked, "Now, where do you want to stand him?" hoping to suggest that Barbara try some other place.

Barbara stood the doll as shown in Figure 8.9 and tried twice to hit it by letting go of the pendulum without pushing it.

In order to help Barbara become conscious of what she had done, the teacher commented, "Oh, Barbara found out that she could just let go of the block. She doesn't have to push it." (Barbara's quick shift into

[2]One teacher who read this account got the impression that the teacher was taunting Barbara. She thought the teacher should have said something more sympathetic, such as, "See, it really *is* hard to do." To us, however, the teacher's comment sounded friendly in tone and not negative in light of Barbara's reaction. This is an example of the inadequacy of words to convey an affective context.

The Pendulum

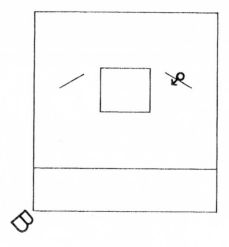

Figure 8.10.

letting go of the block caused the teacher to reflect upon her unsuccessful demonstration with Margaret. She wondered why Barbara shifted so quickly into releasing the block while Margaret never did. She suddenly felt that she should not have insisted on Margaret's letting go of the pendulum when she went on pushing it.)

Several children ran across the taped area at this point. One of them unintentionally kicked the doll.

The teacher said consolingly to Barbara, "They didn't do it on purpose. We'll have to ask them to be more careful." She took this opportunity to move the doll to the position shown in Figure 8.10, saying, "What if I put him over here?"

Barbara immediately moved to the left, indicated by the "B," and knocked the doll down on her second try.

The teacher then moved the doll to "o" in Figure 8.11.

Barbara did not move this time. She stood in the same place as before, aimed at the doll, and gave the block a hard push. It traveled as indicated by the solid arrow in Figure 8.11.

The teacher was surprised that Barbara did not move immediately to the right, in the same way that she had corrected her position in Figure 8.10.

Barbara tried from the same position once again. She then moved to the middle of the rectangle (indicated by "Y" in Figure 8.11) and pushed the block toward the doll, achieving the trajectory indicated by the dotted arrow in the figure. Barbara was surprised, but her puzzled look suddenly changed into one of insight. She quickly moved to point "Z" in the right-hand corner of the rectangle and tried a dozen times from there, each time missing the target by only one or two inches. Finally, she succeeded in hitting the doll.

(The teacher told herself that this was another example of how young children learn. The fact that they immediately can put objects into a certain correct relationship at one point in time (Figure 8.10) does not imply that they will be able to do the same thing the next time. Old "errors" keep reappearing before they are modified and disappear from observable behavior.) She saw that Brian (a four-year-old) had returned to the activity, saying he wanted a turn; so she appealed to Barbara, "How about giving Brian a turn now? You had a long turn already."

Without any fuss or reluctance, Barbara said, "O.K.," and went to a chair to take her place as a spectator.

Saying, "That's very nice of you, Barbara," the teacher put the doll down in the position shown in Figure 8.3.

Brian positioned himself in the same spot that Margaret had chosen (the "M" in Figure 8.3), holding the pendulum by the string, and when he gently let go of the string, the block hit the doll on the very first attempt. He beamed.

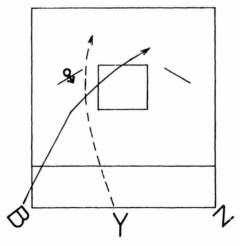

Figure 8.11.

The teacher, along with all the other spectators, expressed admiration of Brian's success on the very first try. The teacher went on to say, "Now, put him where *you* want to hit him." (She said this mainly because she could not figure out what might be an appropriate task for Brian. She was also curious about whether he would continue to hold the string rather than the block.)

Brian put the doll slightly farther from where it had been before. This time, however, it took him ten tries before he finally hit it. Each time he caught the pendulum by the string, he held the string at a different spot and released it without giving much thought to where or how he held it. He generally missed the target narrowly and did not seem to notice that the exact spot from which he released the string made a difference in the path of the pendulum.

The teacher purposely refrained from pointing out this relationship to Brian, as she felt it would be better for him to do things *his* way. Besides, she knew that he was emotionally in good shape and not likely to be crushed by missing the target repeatedly.

After Brian finally hit the doll, he stood it as shown in Figure 8.10. He then positioned himself as Barbara had and hit the doll on the fifth attempt, continuing to hold only the string (and not the block).

The teacher moved the doll to the opposite side as shown in Figure 8.11.

Brian immediately positioned himself correctly. This time it took seven attempts to hit the doll.

The teacher asked for a turn and positioned herself as shown by "T" in Figure 8.12, holding the block in both hands. She said, "Brian, can you put the doll where I can hit him if I let go right here?"

Brian put the doll at "o."

The teacher asked, "If I let go of this block, will I hit the man from here?" (Her voice was neutral and did not suggest to Brian that he might be wrong.)

Without a word, Brian picked up the doll and moved it to "d."

The teacher released the block, and it came within three inches of the doll. She repeated the same thing a second time.

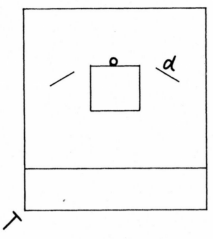

Figure 8.12

Brian walked to the doll and moved it in the path of the block.

The teacher succeeded in hitting the doll. She then put it on the other side of the rectangle as shown in Figure 8.7, too far for the pendulum to reach.

As usual, Brian held the pendulum by the string and either released it or gave it a push. Trying about 20 times, he did not seem to be at all aware that the problem was impossible.

Because Brian seemed not to be giving much thought to what he was doing, the teacher decided to focus his attention on the block. She asked him, "Do you think *I* can hit the man with the block?"

Brian nodded and offered the block. He sat near the doll, and when he saw that the block missed the doll, he immediately moved it into the block's path.

The teacher asked, "Can't the block reach it way back there?" She hoped he would reflect on what he had just done.

Brian did not answer, but looked at the teacher, waiting for her to release the block.

The teacher knew it was no use insisting on a verbal answer from Brian. She let go of the block, and the doll fell over. She then positioned herself in the same way as in Figure 8.12 and asked Brian if he could "stand the doll where I *won't* hit him."

Brian held the doll in the position shown in Figure 8.7. (He thus gave to the teacher the answer he did not give verbally. He obviously had figured out that this was an impossible spot for the pendulum to reach.)

> [*Note: The request to "stand the doll where I* won't *hit him" was an excellent one. One of the ways of coming to know what a pendulum does is by coming to know what it does not do.*]

As Brian tried to make the doll stand, it kept falling over. He bent the rubber figure in several different ways before he finally succeeded in making it stand alone. With a sigh of satisfaction, he moved back and looked expectantly at the teacher.

> The teacher noted Brian's persistence in figuring out how to make the doll stand. She asked, "Is that where I *won't* hit the doll?"

Brian nodded. As the teacher was just about to release the block, Margaret decided to sit in a different chair and walked across the taped area, totally unaware that she might be hit on the head by the block.

> The teacher exclaimed, "Margaret, it's *dangerous* to walk where the block is swinging! You might get hit on the head by this block if you don't get out of its way."

Margaret got out of the way, but her slow response convinced the teacher that she did so only because she was told to, and not because she could anticipate the impact.

> The teacher released the block, and it sailed over the doll's head.

Brian beamed and said, "See, I told you."

Evaluation

a. The activity seemed to appeal to both three- and four-year-olds, and to enable each child to play in his own way at his own level. The three-year-old always pushed or threw the bob, as she was too egocentric to objectify the pendulum. For her, the pendulum moved mainly because *she* gave it a push. The four-year-olds, by contrast, understood that the pendulum moves by itself if released away from the point of equilibrium, and that its trajectory depends on where it is released.

b. Objectives *1* and *2* both seemed appropriate to get children to make predictions and test them.

The Surprises

a.   We were surprised that none of the children could predict after one or two observations that the task shown in Figure 8.7 was impossible. Margaret seemed to proceed on the assumption that the harder one pushes, the farther the block goes. Barbara needed four attempts before making an empirical generalization, and Brian tried 20 times in his unfocused way. We were also surprised that none of the children ever looked at the point on the light fixture from which the pendulum was suspended. The children's frame of reference was thus limited to what was happening on and near the floor. In other words, they were trying to knock the doll down by systematizing the regularity of a limited part of the pendulum's action.

b.   The teacher was also surprised by the variety of methods the children used. As stated above, Margaret tended to push the pendulum and wait for the desired effect. When she could not make the pendulum do what she wanted, she typically moved the *target* rather than herself. Brian held the string instead of holding the block. His gross reasoning was always correct, but he never focused on details. For example, when the target was moved to the right of center, he immediately moved to the left, and when the target was moved to the left of center, he immediately moved to the right. Once he positioned himself, however, he paid little attention to what he was doing and nonchalantly repeated the same unsuccessful action many times. Barbara was the only one who did about what the teacher expected, releasing the pendulum most of the time rather than pushing it, and moving herself most of the time rather than moving the target.

Follow-Up

a.   The teacher realized that she had made two big mistakes that first day. One was starting out by putting the doll on "X," and the other was the taping of the floor. Both efforts were intended to help the children act on the objects successfully, but they actually prevented them from thinking and moving freely. For example, all three children felt constrained to stay outside the big rectangle in spite of the fact that the teacher never stated such a rule. The rectangle also seemed to suggest to the children that they stand in the middle of a side or at a corner. The teacher, therefore, decided to do the same activity in the near future without the taped rectangles. Instead, she planned to tape two lines at right angles passing through the "X" in Figure 8.1 Then she planned to vary the position of the doll all over the floor. (In trying to draw Figures 8.4, 8.6, and 8.11, we were surprised to discover how hard it was even for adults to "read" reality. The pendulum swung fast and by the time we tried to draw its trajectory, we were not sure of what we had just seen. Two lines at right angles passing through "x" were helpful to us in "reading" the path of the pendulum.)

b.   We decided to make an activity out of Margaret's inability to anticipate that the block might hit *her*. This game would be like Dodge Ball, in which the children try to avoid getting hit while two or more children try to hit them with a soft ball as the bob.

c.   We also decided to have children make and play with much smaller pendulums, so that they might put into relationship the point of suspension, the length of the string, and the areas in which the bob can or cannot travel.

Chapter 9

Water Play I

KATHLEEN GRUBER

Water play is a regular part of most preschool programs. I have noticed that young children enjoy the water table in a variety of ways. Some use it to begin their exploration of the classroom by playing near, but not with, other children. It can be a safe spot from which to survey the unfamiliar classroom environment. Sometimes children stand for long periods of time with their hands in the water while their attention is riveted on other activities in the classroom.

Symbolic play at the water table most often involves "cooking," bathing dolls, or spanking "naughty babies" who nevertheless continue to "pee" with abandon. This play is sometimes well elaborated and cooperative.

Some children enjoy repetitive pouring, filling, and emptying containers. They may blow bubbles or pour for some time. It may be that this repetitive play continues partially because of the soothing quality of water or because it provides an acceptable way to mess, but it may also be that children repeat actions because they cannot develop their play any further.

In hopes of sparking more lively investigations with water, teachers sometimes supply children with a variety of objects such as cups, bottles, and pitchers. These materials do not seem to enrich the play appreciably, since pouring, filling, and emptying are the only actions elicited and children's interest in the new equipment lasts only for a short while. Suggesting actions or asking questions such as, "If you pour the water from this cup into that bottle, will the bottle be full?" stimulates children to try it and see, but these interventions do not produce the anticipated extension of play. The kinds of experimentation and thinking that we want to encourage are apparently rather difficult for young children to initiate and sustain.

These observations led me to ask if and how water play could be

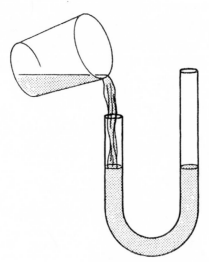

Figure 9.1

improved by choosing better materials and interacting more effectively with children as they played. The present chapter is an attempt to answer this question by using a large variety of objects, especially tubes. Chapter 10 is another attempt to answer the same question using different kinds of objects.

Planning the Activity

From my previous observations I knew that four-year-olds are generally interested in blowing bubbles with plastic tubes and sucking water into them. I also knew that they have some unusual expectations about the movement of water in the tubes. For example, they frequently expect water to come out of the higher side of the "J" pipe shown in Figure 9.1 when it is poured into the lower side.[1] With these observations in mind, and intending to conceptualize more specific objectives by playing with water myself, I began shopping for materials that would encourage children to experiment in a focused way with the movement of water in tubes.

After forays into my basement, the hardware store, a drug store, a grocery, and the supply store of a nearby university hospital, I emerged with the following materials most of which can be seen in Photograph 9.1:

> Bottles:
>   1 glass gallon jug with a cork stopper
>   2 plastic shampoo bottles (12-ounce and 28-ounce)
>   4 plastic baby bottles with plastic collars but no nipples (two 4-ounce and two 8-ounce)

[1]All illustrations are drawn from the child's perspective.

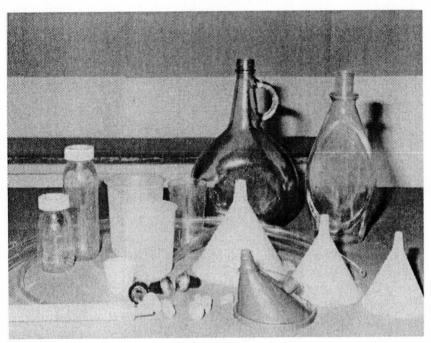

Photograph 9.1.

Cups:
    6 plastic beakers with lips for pouring (two 400-milliliter,[2] two 250-milliliter, and two 180-milliliter)
    8 plastic cups (four 50-milliliter and four 30-milliliter)
Funnels:
    6 plastic funnels (two 4-ounce, two 6-ounce, and two 12-ounce)
      2 asymmetrical plastic funnels with stopper caps (4-ounce)
Tubes:
    three to four feet of clear, flexible, plastic tubing in each of the following diameters:
      1 inch
      ¾ inch
      ⅝ inch
      ½ inch
      ⅜ inch
      ¼ inch
Drying tube:
    1 rigid plastic drying tube with two removable pointed end pieces with holes (8 by ¾ inches)

[2]One milliliter is equal to one cubic centimeter and approximately equal to 0.034 ounces.

Corks:
    18 assorted corks ranging from ¼ to ¾ inches in diameter
Sprinklers:
    2 laundry sprinkler heads
Scissors:
    1 pair of kindergarten scissors
Basins:
    4 plastic dishpans
Food coloring:
    1 bottle of red food coloring (2-ounce)
Cleanup equipment:
    4 sponges
    2 small terry cloth towels
    1 sponge mop with a shortened handle

Each one of the objects listed above was chosen with certain objectives in mind. I selected individual basins for each child rather than a single water table for two reasons. Individual basins permit each child to try out his own ideas without unintentional interference from others. At the same time, basins do not prevent children from cooperating when they want to play together. Basins also allow all materials to be displayed on the table top, between the pans, in full view and within easy reach.

Since an important objective of the activity is for children to put their actions and the movement of water into relationship, it is essential that they be able to see the level of water as it moves in a container. For this reason all the bottles, cups, funnels, and tubes I selected were either transparent or translucent.[3] To further enhance the visibility of the water both for the children and for the video camera, I planned to add food coloring to the water.

The objects listed above were chosen in hopes of encouraging a wide variety of actions and combinations of materials. For example, each size of tubing (with the exception of the largest and smallest) fit snugly into the next largest tube so that very long or circular tubes like those in Figure 9.2 could be created. The largest funnels fit both the 1-inch and the ¾-inch tubing. The middle-sized funnels fit the ⅝-inch tubing. The smallest funnels fit the ½-inch tubing. The pointed end of the drying tube fit into the ⅜-inch tubing, and with points removed, the drying tube fit into the largest tube. The sprinklers fit into the ¾-inch tubes. The baby bottles with plastic collars

---

[3]The asymmetrical funnels were the one exception. I was unable to locate them in transparent or transluscent plastic, but wanted to see if children would be interested in either the unusual shape or the stopper caps that came with these funnels. I discovered that these features were not interesting enough to warrant inclusion of the opaque funnels.

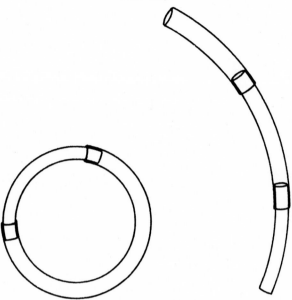

Figure 9.2.

intact fit onto the largest tubes, and the gallon jug fit the ¾-inch tubes. Corks were available to fit all of the tubes.

I cut the tubing into lengths varying from 4 inches to 30 inches and kept the scissors handy in case the children wanted to shorten the tubes. I included the sprinklers hoping the spray of water might increase the children's interest in getting water to flow through the tubes.

I expected the cups to be used as pouring vessels. I was interested in seeing what relationships, if any, the children would create between the width of a cup and the neck size of the bottle or tube into which they poured. Also, I wondered if the children would see that it is faster to use a large cup to fill a large bottle, that it is easier to pour into a wide tube than a narrow one, or that it is fastest and easiest to use a funnel when pouring into the narrow neck of a bottle or tube.

Although I expected most of the activity to center around tubes, I included the jug in case some children were interested primarily in filling containers. I thought that since this large container requires extended effort to fill, the children might come upon the idea of the usefulness of a funnel. Since the shampoo bottles had small necks, I expected them to be used either for pouring into the tubes or collecting water that flowed out of the tubes.

I wanted to provide an opportunity for children to think about the

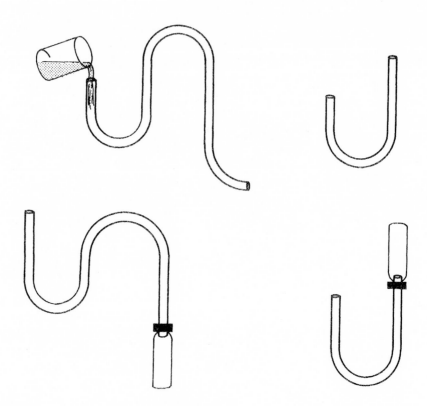

Figure 9.3.

relationship between the position of a tube and the movement of water within the tube. For example, I expected to ask such questions as "What happens when you pour the water into this tube?" and "Is there any way to get the water into the bottle?" in situations like those shown in Figure 9.3.

I decided to introduce the activity by asking, "What can you do with these things and the water?" (Alternative (2) of how to introduce an activity). Since the children were used to playing with water, I thought they would begin without hesitation. I planned to watch each child closely to figure out what he was thinking and then ask questions encouraging him to pursue his own ideas.

Part of my function would be to introduce new ideas. For example, I didn't think the children would realize that the various sizes of tubing could be fitted into one another. I planned to watch for opportune moments to show such combinations unobtrusively.

Spills, of course, are inevitable. Since I wanted to encourage the children to be responsible for as much of the cleanup as possible, I placed the sponges, towels, and mop on a low stool within easy reach of the children.

I filled the four basins with warm water[4] and placed them with the other materials on a table in an area outside the classroom. Then I went into the classroom to ask for volunteers to play with some things in the water. The reaction was somewhat hesitant, probably because the children did not know me well. The following four nevertheless expressed interest:

Lauren (4 years, 5 months)
Bobby (4 years, 9 months)
Erin (4 years, 10 months)
Alice (5 years, 1 month)

I suggested that they bring plastic aprons and we trooped to the prepared area.

Each child spontaneously chose a basin and began looking around at the materials on the table. I held up the food coloring and said, "The first thing we have to do is make this water colorful." Bobby took the bottle of coloring from me and poured about a third of it into his basin. When Lauren reached out declaring "That's enough!", he handed her the bottle.

I was impressed that she spoke directly to him rather than appealing to me for help.

Lauren poured a little into her basin and passed the coloring to Erin who emptied the rest into her water. Alice grabbed the empty bottle and shook it over her basin.

The other children had already begun to investigate the materials on the table and were not aware of Alice's predicament.

Since I had no more food coloring, and since I thought this situation might provide the children with a meaningful problem, I asked, "How can we make Alice's water red?"

Bobby glanced up and immediately assessed the difficulty. "Ain't no more, ain't no more, teacher!" His loud statement attracted Erin's attention. She dribbled a little of her colored water into Alice's basin.

I asked, "Will that help?"

Both girls watched Alice's water intently. Since Erin had added very little colored water, there was not much to see. Then Bobby chose the smallest

---

[4]Warm water was more pleasant on a cold March day and, in addition, the flexible tubing gets rigid and hard to manage when cold.

cup, filled it in his basin and emptied the contents into Alice's water. Alice
snapped with disgust, "Get a big cup!" Bobby obliged by choosing the
largest cup on the table and pouring from his basin into Alice's. He watched
as the colored water began to mix. "Her got some!" He poured another
cupful of red water from his basin into Alice's. She seemed satisfied with the
results and announced, "Now I've got some."

At this point all of the children began to try out various materials in the
water without encouragement from me. During the thirty minutes that followed, each child approached the objects and the water in a different way.
Lauren made a circular tube and a fountain by blowing into a tube with a
sprinkler attached. Bobby's interest centered around blowing bubbles, sucking water into the tubes and filling the jug. Erin spent most of the time
pouring from one container to another. Of all the children, she was the least
animated during the activity. Alice pretended to make Kool-Aid, juice, and
syrup. She was interested almost exclusively in symbolic play with the water.

Throughout the activity, I focused on one child at a time in order to
understand each child's actions from his point of view. I will describe in
detail the most interesting segments of each child's activity, along with my
observations and comments, beginning with Lauren, who came up with
more ideas and played more as I had expected than the other three. Bobby's
play represents the case of a child who had trouble finding something interesting to do. The activities of Erin, the least active, and Alice will be
described in less detail.

Lauren

Lauren chose a piece of 1-inch tubing which I had attached to a baby
bottle. She placed the bottle and the end of the tube in the water as shown in
Figure 9.4, and watched the middle of the tube intently. As though she were

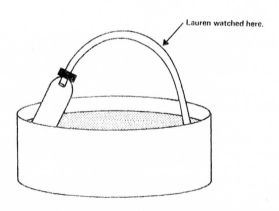

Figure 9.4.

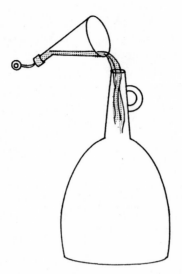

Figure 9.5.

trying very hard to make water flow into the bottle, she tilted the arched tubing almost flat on the surface of the water, closely watching various parts of the tube all the while.

Having no success, Lauren gave up this effort and turned her attention to the gallon jug, asking, "Teacher, what's that bottle for?"

Thinking that Lauren might become interested in figuring out how to use the funnel and/or a tube to fill the bottle, I responded with the suggestion, "Can you fill that bottle up?"

Lauren put the jug into her basin and started filling it with a beaker. The jug was floating unsteadily and she soon set it back on the table where it was stable. Suddenly, she grabbed an asymmetrical funnel with the cap on, dipped it in the water, and used it as a cup to pour into the jug as shown in Figure 9.5. Since the neck of the jug was quite narrow, most of the water spilled onto the table.

I thought she did not see the possibility of removing the cap from the funnel. When she put it down for a moment, I uncapped it and asked Lauren if that would make it easier to fill the jug.

"No. It won't help!" she muttered. Then, looking somewhat confused and discouraged, Lauren turned to leave for the bathroom.

Although my intervention was intended to introduce a new possibility to Lauren and to make it easier for her to fill the jug, her negative reaction and the fact that she stopped playing indicate that my suggestion was not helpful. Perhaps she knew that removing the cap made the funnel no longer useful as a cup. Since that is what she was interested in doing, and since she apparently did not see the value of the funnel for widening the neck of the jug, my action thwarted her initiative. No wonder Lauren seemed confused and discouraged! First she could not get the tube filled, and then I made a suggestion that served no purpose from her point of view.

As Lauren started to leave, she saw Bobby take her jug. "I was using that!" she asserted.

I hoped that the children could settle this problem for themselves, but since Bobby was ignoring Lauren, I intervened, saying, "Bobby, wait a minute, Lauren said something to you."

Lauren whispered to me, "I think I can get it." She approached Bobby, reached for the jug, pulled on it a little, and said, "Bobby, can I please have that?" Bobby abandoned the jug without comment. Lauren apparently forgot about her trip to the bathroom, and began filling the jug again—this time with a 250-ml beaker. She stopped to lift the asymmetrical funnel out of her basin, looking closely into it as the water ran out the bottom. "Hey, this looks like dark!" she exclaimed.

Photograph 9.2.

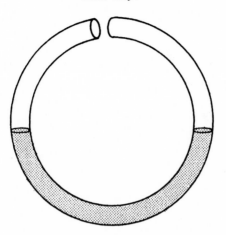

Figure 9.6.

I did not understand what she meant by "dark" but saw no point in intervening to find out.

A moment later, when the funnel was empty, Lauren looked through it, studying the hole intently. She dipped the funnel and lifted it up again.

Hoping she would see the possibility of using the funnel to fill the jug, I asked, "What happens when you hold it up?"

Watching the water run through the funnel, she only replied, "It goes out." Lauren then lifted the jug back into her basin and again found that it would not sit on the bottom, but floated. She put the funnel into the mouth of the jug and tried to pour, but could not steady it.

At this point I held the jug for her as I thought helping her to pursue the use of the funnel was more important than dealing with a floating bottle.

Lauren continued pouring until the jug was almost full, and then emptied it.

. . .

Coming back to Lauren later, I chose a 30-inch length of ¾-inch tubing, submerged it in her basin, and held it upright in a U.

Lauren was intrigued. "Wow, let me see. It looks silly!" she said as she took the tube from me and continued to hold it as shown in Photograph 9.2. She put the ends of the tube together, clearly trying to make a circle, as shown in Figure 9.6.

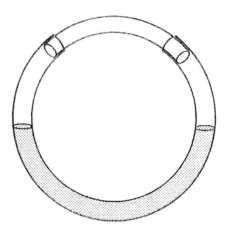

Figure 9.7.

Picking up on her idea, I asked, "Do you want to fasten it together? There's a way to do that." When Lauren nodded, I handed her a 6-inch piece of ⅝-inch tubing and helped her insert the smaller tube into both ends of her tube as shown in Figure 9.7.

Lauren held the circle of tubing in both hands and turned it slowly in one direction, then in the other (see Figure 9.8). She watched the water level in the tube and seemed puzzled. She looked only at one side of the column of water at a time.

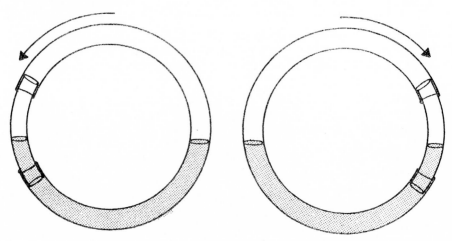

Figure 9.8.

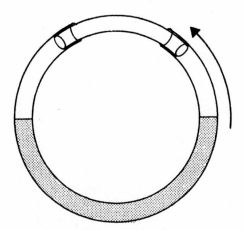

Figure 9.9.

My speculation is that she expected the water to move with the tube—to go "over the top" as shown in Figure 9.9.

Lauren then took her circle of tubing apart and blew into one end of the tube. This created a spurt of water from the opposite end as shown in Figure 9.10. Lauren looked quite surprised and blew again.

Noticing that her tube was empty, Lauren said, "It doesn't have anything in it." She dipped one end of the tube into her basin as shown in Figure 9.11. Not having achieved the expected result, Lauren tried the same approach, this time with the other end of the tube. Then she grasped one

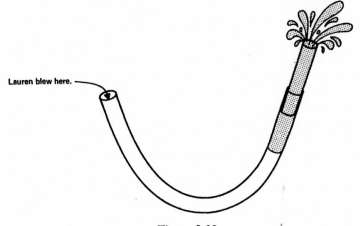

Lauren blew here.

Figure 9.10.

Figure 9.11.

end of the tube in each hand and stuck both ends into the basin as shown in Figure 9.12. When no water entered the tube, she immersed the whole thing in the basin. Lifting it out by the ends, she saw that it was about three-quarters full. She searched the table until her gaze fell on a sprinkler.

After asking her if that was what she wanted, I placed the sprinkler on one end of Lauren's tube.

She immediately brought the other end of the tube to her mouth and blew. This produced a fountain spraying in many directions. Lauren looked delighted and blew several more times (Photograph 9.3).

Lauren spent quite a lot of time blowing into the tube with the sprinkler on the end. After she blew all the water out of the tube, she submerged the sprinkler end and blew, making bubbles in her basin. Shortly thereafter, she removed the sprinkler and submerged the entire tube in the water. She lifted the full tube carefully by the ends and replaced the sprinkler.

Lauren apparently thought it was necessary to remove the sprinkler in order to fill her tube. Since she had only observed the water coming

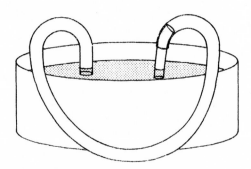

Figure 9.12.

Photograph 9.3.

out of the sprinkler, perhaps it did not occur to her that water could go in as well.

After more sprinkling, Lauren curved her tube into a circle, placing the sprinkler and the open end of the tube together as shown in Figure 9.13. She apparently saw that no connection could be made. She pulled the sprinkler off the tube and replaced it on the other end, as if this would make a difference (see Figure 9.14).

Bobby had gone looking for dry slacks. Lauren placed her sprinkler in the jug Bobby had filled. It fit loosely. Before she could develop her idea any

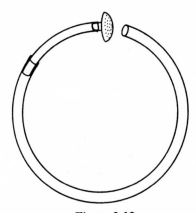

Figure 9.13.

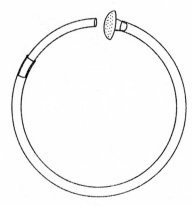

Figure 9.14.

further, Bobby returned on the run and screamed "NO!" Lauren took her sprinkler and returned to her own basin.

> I suggested that Lauren see if there were any other bottles that she could use with her sprinkler.

She tried the sprinkler on a baby bottle with a collar, but the mouth was too large. Then she removed the collar from the baby bottle and tried the sprinkler directly on the bottle.

> By this action Lauren showed either that she could not anticipate the size relationship without putting the objects in actual contact, or that she did not realize that by removing the collar, she could only make the neck of the bottle wider.

Bobby

After pouring some coloring into his water, Bobby held the edge of the basin, jiggling it gently and reaching out tentatively with one hand to touch and stir the water. He seemed fascinated by the swirling patterns produced as the coloring mixed with his water. He reached for a funnel and then for a sprinkler, asking, "What's this?"

> Hoping to encourage some action with the materials, I asked him what he could do with those things.

He went on to examine many other objects. He placed a funnel upside down on the jug. He looked the sprinkler over, dipped it in the water, and shook the water off. He turned his attention to a piece of 1-inch tubing attached to a baby bottle. He studied this apparatus carefully, turning it around in his hands and said, "Look, teacher."

Bobby's attention seemed more intently focused on this material than on any other object he had touched so far. Thinking that he might need a little help from me to find something constructive to pursue, I decided to attend exclusively to Bobby for a few minutes. I asked, "Can you make the water go into that tube?"

Bobby immediately put the bottle into his basin where it floated. Then he blew into the end of the tube. When nothing happened, he looked puzzled.

Clearly, he thought he could produce some effect by blowing. My guess was that he expected bubbles. I asked, "It didn't blow?"

Bobby shook his head and blew again into the tube. Again he looked confused. Picking up the bottle, he asked, "What's this?" and pulled halfheartedly at the tube as if he were thinking of taking it off the bottle.

I answered, "That's a tube with a bottle on the end." In retrospect, I think Bobby's real question was "What can you do with this?" Since his idea of what to do did not produce the expected results, he was probably asking me to show him a way to use the material. Realizing that Bobby was interested in blowing and that this action would not produce any observable results with the empty bottle on the tube, I helped him get the bottle off.

Bobby quickly dipped the bottle in his basin, partially filling it, and then tried to reinsert the tube.

I wondered if Bobby knew that with water in the bottle he would be able to make bubbles by blowing.

When he could not get the tightly fitting tube back into the bottle, he discarded it. He dipped more water into the bottle and shook it, covering the top tightly with the palm of one hand, and watching the water inside.

Bobby seemed to have lost a focus for his activity. I suspect his interest waned because none of his ideas about using the materials led to interesting results. My attention had turned to another child when he tried to reinsert the tube. In retrospect I think I should have helped him insert the tube at this point.

Bobby submerged an empty baby bottle in his basin and noticed the bubbles that rose to the surface. "Teacher, look at these bubbles!"

"How did you make those, Bobby, what did you do?" I asked.

By this time the submerged bottle was full and thus produced no more bubbles. Bobby jiggled the bottle under the water.

I think he was trying to produce more bubbles, but of course he got only waves. Again his spontaneous action did not produce the result he expected.

Bobby removed the full bottle from the basin, looking at it quizzically.

At this point Bobby surprised me. I thought he had been unaware of the other children at the table. But he apparently heard Alice saying "I can't get this off," as she struggled to disengage two large beakers that had been stacked together.

Bobby dashed around the table to the rescue, announcing, "I'll take it off." He carried the cups to me and indicated that I should hold one while he pulled on the other. In this way they were separated and Bobby handed one to Alice and one to Erin with a loud "Here!"

. . .

I offered Bobby a 12-inch length of ¾-inch tubing, asking, "Did you ever figure out a way to get the water to go up in this tube?"

Bobby immediately inserted the tube into an empty baby bottle, this time with no difficulty. As before, he blew into the tube as the empty bottle floated on the water. This time, since the tube did not fit tightly, the bottle flew off the end of the tube. He smiled and looked at me.

Bobby obviously expected a response. I said "Whoops!" and chuckled. He may have been interested in the bottle popping off, in trying to fill the tube, or in trying to make bubbles. As I was not sure what aspect of the event interested him, I decided not to suggest anything at this point.

Bobby replaced the tube on the half-full bottle. This time he sucked on it, and saw the water rise a few inches in the tube. "Teacher, watch this!" he exclaimed as he removed and discarded the bottle. He put the end of the tube directly into the basin apparently realizing that the bottle was unnecessary for making water rise in the tube.

Next, Bobby chose a 30-inch length of ¾-inch tubing, saying, "Teacher, this is a tall one." He put one end of the tube in the water and blew bubbles for a moment. Then he sucked water halfway up the tube, blew again, and sucked again, drawing the water almost to his mouth. He looked a little surprised and confused.

I was not sure Bobby realized what he had done, so I asked, "Did you see that water in the tube?"

Bobby took the tube out of his mouth momentarily and looked at it. He then sucked again, making the water come up to his lips. He watched the water rise, then lifted his head and said, "Look, y'all." He sucked the water up, blew it out and sucked it halfway up again. He sucked and blew, slowly and deliberately several more times watching the tube carefully all the while. At one point when he sucked the water up, he got some in his mouth. He seemed surprised and spat it out, laughing and coughing a little. He resumed sucking and blowing, pointing to the tube as the water rose. Then, when he had water in the tube, he lifted the end out of the water and saw some of the water flow back into the basin. After repeating this action twice, he called for my attention, but I was busy helping Lauren make a circular tube. Bobby continued to suck and lift, then added blowing to the following sequence which became very regular: suck/lift/blow/replace in the water.

. . .

Observing Lauren's circular tube, Bobby asked, "How you do that, teacher?" He held his tube in a U shape and moved the ends up and down so that the small amount of water in the tube swished back and forth. He watched the water, humming a little tune to himself in rhythm with his movements. When some of the water splashed out, Bobby slowed down and put the ends of the tube together. He glanced at Lauren, who was making spurts of water by blowing into her filled tube while pointing its end up. Bobby blew through his tube, imitating Lauren's spectacle.

At one point when he needed to fill his tube, Bobby tried to pour into it from the heavy jug. Unsuccessful, he thought of something else to do. He tried submerging the jug in his basin, but it was too small. When this did not work, he picked up a long piece of ¾-inch tubing and inserted it about 6 inches into the jug where it fit snugly, with about two feet extending from the opening. Choosing the smallest cup, he filled it and tried to pour the water into the tube, as shown in Figure 9.15.

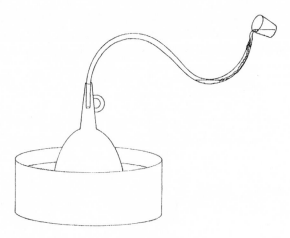

Figure 9.15.

Here, Bobby seemed to be thinking that in order to pour into the relatively small tube, he needed a small cup.

Because of the position of the tube, the water did not move into the jug. Bobby lifted the end of the tube straight up, but then it was difficult for him to reach high enough to pour. Happily, the bottle fell onto its side, and the tube then slanted downward toward the bottle as shown in Photograph 9.4. Bobby then poured the water slowly into the tube, and the water flowed into the bottle. Bobby blew into the tube, but nothing happened because the end of the tube did not reach the water in the bottle.

I handed him a funnel and asked, "Could you use this to help you fill it up?" Since he seemed to like using the tube in combination with the jug, I expected Bobby to put the funnel on the tube. In this way I thought he might get enough water in the bottle to make it possible to blow bubbles with the tube. I think it would have been more helpful to Bobby if I had simply pushed the tube further into the jug, and then suggested that he try blowing again. My indirect approach did not facilitate any interesting results.

Bobby removed the tube and put the funnel I had given him directly on the jug. He poured into the funnel with the small cup.

He seemed to appreciate the usefulness of the funnel, but did not think of using a larger cup for pouring.

Grabbing the 12-ounce shampoo bottle, Bobby began filling it using the same small cup, without the funnel, saying "I'm going to full this up, really."

Although he had just used the funnel, Bobby did not see its usefulness in this case, even when some of the water missed the bottle and spilled on the table.

When the shampoo bottle was three-quarters full, he poured its contents into the funnel on the jug. After filling the shampoo bottle again, he slowly poured it into the jug, watching the water level in the funnel go down. Finally, the jug was full to the brim, and Bobby appeared very pleased. He then mopped the floor a bit and left, saying that he intended to change his wet slacks.

Lauren lost no time in trying her sprinkler in the mouth of Bobby's full jug. When he returned a few minutes later, he saw this and shouted, "NO!" pushing her away. Unhappily, seeing that Lauren had spilled some of the water from his jug, Bobby took the largest beaker and poured an entire cupful over the top. Since only a tiny bit of water was required, most of the water ran down the sides of the bottle.

Deciding to try Lauren's idea for himself, Bobby found the other

Photograph 9.4.

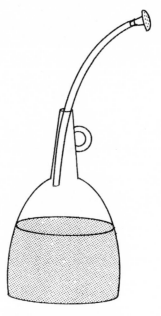

Figure 9.16.

sprinkler, put it on the mouth of the jug where it fit loosely, and turned the jug upside down. I don't know what he expected, but the sprinkler fell out of the bottle as the water flowed into his basin. Bobby picked up the sprinkler and blew through it, then fitted it on the end of a tube which he inserted into the jug (see Figure 9.16). He blew into the sprinkler, but nothing happened. Then he pulled the sprinkler out with his mouth and blew several times directly into the tube—harder and harder.

> Bobby obviously thought something would happen. From his subsequent behavior, it seems that what he expected was bubbles. However, since the end of the tube was not submerged, he got no results.

Lauren commented, "He's trying to drink it, I think." Bobby responded by sucking on the tube with all his might. By this time, the end of the tube had somehow become submerged, and the water rose slowly in the large tube. After a great deal of effort, the water finally almost reached Bobby's mouth. He took the end of the tube from his mouth and pointed it toward the basin (see Figure 9.17). Then he submerged the end of the tube in the basin, as shown in Figure 9.18. He kept watching the tube, apparently expecting to see water flowing. Getting no result, he twisted the tube several ways, but could not produce the desired effect. He sucked on the tube once more and called out for me to help him.

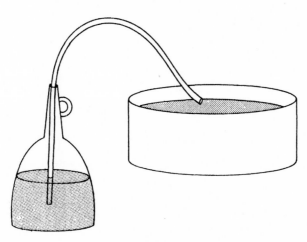

Figure 9.17.

I was occupied with Alice and did not respond. In retrospect I think this was one more example of a child's ideas and actions resulting in frustration rather than leading to interesting results.

Erin

As stated earlier, Erin was the least animated of the four children. She spent most of the time pouring from one container to another. What she did in between will be presented in summary form, except for one segment at the end, in which she made a circular tube and became involved in pursuits more in accord with physical knowledge objectives.

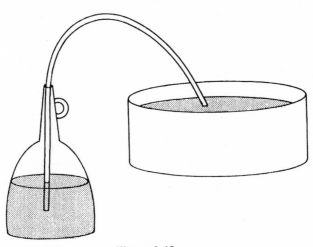

Figure 9.18.

Erin interrupted her pouring with several halfhearted comments to the other children. Occasionally she imitated their actions, but she never became involved in conversation or play with the others. She often stared at the video camera. When she heard Alice say, "It looks like Kool-Aid," Erin muttered, "That's what mine is, Kool-Aid." At one point, while pouring, she suddenly announced, "I'm a witch." Perhaps she was pretending to mix potions. For some time she was interested in collecting small corks in a baby bottle. She watched Bobby blow bubbles and imitated him. She watched Lauren fill her tube and make a "U" shape. Erin imitated Lauren for a moment, then stretched out the tube and blew bubbles in her basin for some time.

She began to alternate sucking and blowing, repeating this sequence about ten times. Then she sucked too hard, swallowed some water, coughed loudly, and began to cry.

> I lifted Erin onto my lap and tried to comfort her. When she had calmed down, I tried to get her interested in the activity again by offering a funnel and suggesting "Maybe you would like to do something with this instead of the tubes."

She reached down for a tube in her basin and threw it across the table declaring, "I don't like the tubes!"

. . .

Erin selected a long piece of ½-inch tubing. "Here's a snake, I want to cut it." I gave her the scissors. She thrust the tube at me, saying, "Hold this." I complied and she cut it twice. She chose two of the short pieces and dipped them in her basin. She held them under the water for quite a while. Then she pulled one out and twisted it, trying to make a circle. But the tube was so short that it would not curve easily.

> "Are you trying to make a round one?" I asked. When Erin nodded, I selected a longer piece of ⅝-inch tubing and showed her how to make a circle using her short piece as the connector.

> Her circle had only a few drops of water in it. Nevertheless, Erin seemed pleased with it. She held it up and turned it to the left and right.

> She watched the tube intently, but as far as I could see, there was nothing very interesting for her to observe. "How could we get more water in there?" I asked.

Erin unfastened the circle. She held one end up and with the other hand pulled the drying tube from the bottom of her basin. Erin positioned the full drying tube so that water would run out the pointed end and into her tube as

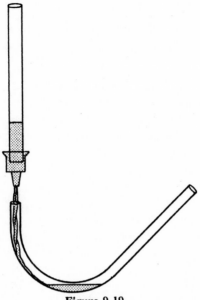

Figure 9.19.

shown in Figure 9.19. However, by the time she got the drying tube in this position, it was nearly empty. She stuck the point of the drying tube into the end of her tube. It remained upright and in place when she released it. She then grabbed a small cup and, dipping from her basin, poured into the drying tube as shown in Figure 9.20.

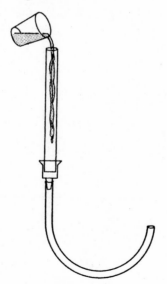

Figure 9.20.

After three pours, she disengaged the drying tube and reformed her circle. "Look what I did." She rotated the circle back and forth, studying it for a few seconds, and then, just as I thought she was about to experiment further, she announced, "I want to mop."

Alice

About five minutes into the activity, Alice held up the biggest beaker full of water. "This looks like Kool-Aid!" She sang, "Kool-Aid, Kool-Aid tastes great, Kool-Aid, Kook-Aid, I'm gonna have some. I'm pretending that this is Kool-Aid." Her song seemed to be more an accompaniment for her actions than a communication.

Many of Alice's comments were spoken too quietly for me to hear, but I did overhear three more of her playful statements. After pouring several times from the large beaker into the jug, she exclaimed, "Wow, it looks like wine." Sometime later, she said, "O.K., I'm a baby, goo, goo," as she pretended to drink from a baby bottle. She refilled the baby bottle mumbling "More milk, please." This seemed to be part of a conversation between two characters represented by the containers.

. . .

Photograph 9.5.

Photograph 9.6.

Holding a long tube with a funnel on each end, I inquired, "Alice, do you want to work with this?"

When she replied, "Yeah," I held the funnels up (the one in my left hand slightly higher as shown in Photograph 9.5). Alice poured into the one in my right hand. When it was full, no water entered the left one.

I asked, "If you pour more water in the funnel, do you think it will come out the other one?"

She shook her head.

Since I could not tell what she was thinking, and since the crucial factor is the relative height of the funnels, I handed the funnels to her. In this way I gave her control over where the water went in the tube and funnels.

Alice held the funnels at approximately the same height as shown in Photograph 9.6. The difference between the water levels varied between one and four inches and this relationship shifted back and forth as she moved the funnels up and down. Alice seemed unaware of the slight up and down movement of her hands. As she stared intently at the changing water levels, she seemed to be able to attend to both funnels at once, but I don't know what relationship she was putting the objects into.

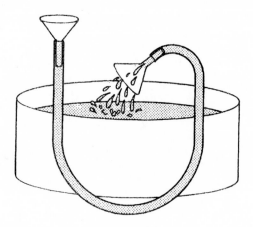

Figure 9.21.

I asked her if it made any difference if she moved the funnels.

She responded by jiggling both funnels horizontally a bit. She did not think of moving them up and down.

At one point she became excited and announced, "They're both full!" Both funnels were about half full. Suddenly she tilted her right hand down emptying that funnel into the basin as shown in Figure 9.21.

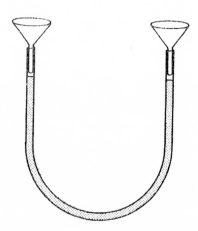

Figure 9.22.

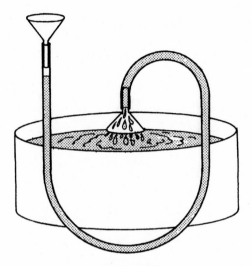

Figure 9.23.

I pointed out that the water in the left funnel was going down. Alice was amazed.

She held the funnels up again. A column of water rose in each side, almost to the bottoms of the funnels (see Figure 9.22). Alice lifted first one and then the other. When the left one was slightly higher, she again emptied the right one, as shown in Figure 9.23.

She started to tug on the left funnel, apparently trying to remove it, complaining, "I can't get this out. The water is stuck in there."

She seemed to think that she had to remove the funnel in order to empty the tube. I asked, "How can we get that water out?"

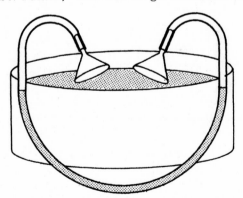

Figure 9.24.

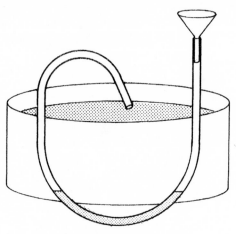

Figure 9.25.

She quickly turned both wrists so that the funnels pointed down as shown in Figure 9.24. A little water flowed out, but most of it remained in the tube which hung in a U between the funnels. She indicated that she wanted me to remove one of the funnels. I complied. She turned her left wrist so that the now open end of the tube pointed toward the basin (see Figure 9.25). No water flowed. Alice then quickly lifted the funnel high with her right hand (Photograph 9.7), and the water flowed right out. She beamed and giggled and began trying to remove the second funnel from the tube. "Oh, I can't get this doo-doo out."

I helped her by holding the funnel while she pulled the tube.

Joey and Danny

After the above activity, I felt exhausted and disappointed by my inability to keep track of the children's ideas. I therefore decided to try the activity again but with only two children. The volunteers this time were Joey (6 years, 2 months) and Danny (5 years, 9 months).

The two boys eagerly ran ahead of me toward the materials.

I began by saying, "There are a lot of things here to work with." Having noticed that the other children had not seen many ways to combine materials, but, once shown, were most interested in using two or more objects together, I suggested to Danny, "You know, there's one tube that fits right in the top of that baby bottle." When he responded with

Photograph 9.7.

interest, I helped him find the correct size and insert it into the full bottle. It became immediately apparent that these two children were more cooperative in their approach to the water than the first group.

Danny no sooner made the bottle-tube apparatus than he turned to Joey and asked, "Want me to get one that will fit in yours, Joey?" He picked a tube and handed it to Joey saying, "Try this." Joey inserted it into his bottle, but it did not fit snuggly because the bottle had no collar. He watched as Danny lifted his bottle as high as he could, letting the water flow down the tube into the basin. Joey giggled, "It's going pee!"

I wondered aloud, "How will you get the water back in the bottle now?"

This idea seemed to intrigue both boys. Joey responded, "Oh, that would be easy. Take it over and pour it through, and it goes rrrrrrr," pointing at the bottle and waving his arms.

I was baffled, but I soon understood what Joey meant.

Danny submerged about 6 inches of the free end of the tube and then lifted

Figure 9.26.

it high out of the basin. A little water flowed into the bottle. He repeated this action while Joey nodded with apparent satisfaction.

I remarked, "You have to do that a lot of times?"

Danny caught my suggestion and said, "Oh, here's a much faster way," as he grabbed a beaker, scooped water in it and poured down the tube. He then refilled the beaker, but this time inserted the end of the tube into the full beaker and upended it as shown in Figure 9.26. The result was that some water went into the tube, but most of it spilled back into the basin.

I was surprised that Danny did not seem in the least perturbed by the fact that most of his water was not reaching the bottle.

He repeated this procedure five times, watching the tube, apparently to see if any water was going down. Finally, he lifted the bottle and seemed pleased that it was full. He extended the tube to Joey, asking, "Here, want some?" Together, the boys placed the open end of the tube in Joey's basin. Danny lifted the bottle up so that some water flowed from the bottle as shown in Photograph 9.8. Joey laughed and said, "Oh, that's an easy way instead of taking it. . . . "

He seemed to be saying that transferring water from one basin to another by using a tube instead of dipping and pouring was pretty nifty.

Danny interrupted Joey by pointing to the tube as large bubbles moved upward. He commented, "I think I got more."

I'm not sure exactly what he meant, but perhaps he thought water was flowing up the tube since the movement of the air pockets was upward toward the bottle. As he was looking only at the tube, he did not notice that the bottle was emptying.

The boys continued to transfer the water from one basin to another. They exclaimed frequently, "Ooo, did you see that?" "Oh, wow! Neat! Wasn't that neat? I just got half a gallon!"

. . .

With various pieces of tubing on the table, Danny began making circles like the ones shown in Figure 9.7. "Let's make a whole bunch of these," he shouted. He placed each one in Joey's basin. At one point Danny asked, "Do you know how to make a inner tube?"

"No, how do you do it?"

Photograph 9.8.

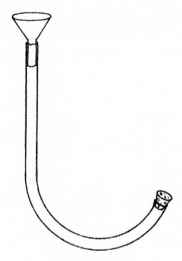

Figure 9.27.

"You make a lot of these and then you put lots of patches over it."

After reflecting over this puzzling remark, I wondered if Danny had observed inner tubes being tested in water for leaks, and patches being applied.

. . .

As I handed Joey a piece of tubing with a funnel on one end and a cork on the other (Figure 9.27), I said, "I wonder if you can do anything interesting with that." When he accepted the apparatus, I added, "Look, it has a cork in the end. Do you want it that way, or do you want to take it out?"

Joey answered, "I'll just have it that way." As I held it, he began to fill the funnel, using another funnel to pour as shown in Figure 9.28. He seemed not the least bit concerned with the fact that most of the water ran out before he could get it into the funnel and tube. As I continued to hold the tube in a U shape, Joey poured twice more in this way. Since there was a cork in the end of the tube, the water went only about halfway down as shown in Figure 9.29.

Joey did not seem to notice this so I called his attention to it saying, "The water is not going down. Look at it!"

Joey thought he had the solution. "It's because you've got it like that." He gestured to indicate the U shape. "If you turn it like this, it will go down."

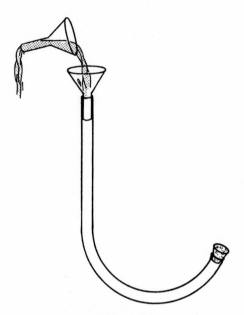

Figure 9.28.

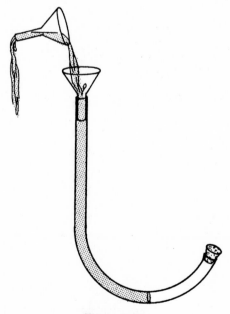

Figure 9.29.

Figure 9.30.

He took the tube and held it vertically. Some water flowed to the bottom but most remained above the air pocket as shown in Figure 9.30.

> I asked, "But what about this water?" pointing to the funnel. I doubted that Joey could understand this event, but thought that perhaps the observation of a little "magic" could inspire further investigation. At the same time I began to wonder if the corks were more confusing than useful. The children were already puzzled enough about the way water moves in tubes, and the introduction of an air pocket further contradicted their anticipations.

Joey was amazed. He lowered the funnel to his eye level and tilted it to look in. He pointed to the middle of the tube and said, "There's something in there, I think." He studied the tube carefully, bringing it close to his face, then looked at the cork, pulled it out, and watched the water flow into his basin.

. . .

Joey had a baby bottle attached to a long tube. He picked up a very large beaker and exclaimed, "Oh, wow! Look at this one! Look at this one, Danny. I'm going to put water in it and in there (indicating the bottle)."

I fully expected Joey to pour water from the beaker into the tube.

He surprised me by scooping the beaker full of water and inserting the end of the tube into it, as shown in Photograph 9.9. He stared at the empty tube.

He apparently expected the water to flow from the beaker through the arched tube and into the bottle. I was surprised.

After several seconds of expectant watching, Joey tilted the beaker with the tube still inserted, as if to start the water through the tube.

Apparently, Joey thought that the water needed a little help to get started into the tube.

Whatever he was thinking, the results of tipping the cup were unsatisfactory to him as the water merely poured from the cup into the basin as shown in Figure 9.31. In a perplexed voice, he said, "I can't believe it. It's going out there."

I shared his concern by saying, "It's going out the wrong way. I wonder how we could do it—how we could get the water to go in."

Joey began twisting the tube and talking to himself, "How can we do that?" He discarded the beaker and twisted the tube first into a circle, then into an arch. He left the bottle floating in the basin and stretched the tube straight

Photograph 9.9.

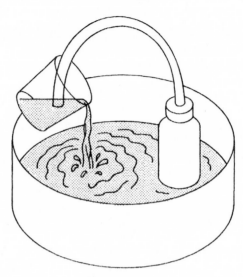

Figure 9.31.

out, almost horizontally, toward himself. When none of these approaches worked, Joey lifted the bottle out of the basin and attached a funnel to the free end of the tube. He dipped a large beaker of water, and poured it into the funnel. Since at this moment, the bottle happened to be dangling straight down toward the floor, the water ran easily into the bottle.

I asked, "Is it working?"

"Sure is, it's going pee." Joey continued to pour into the funnel.

"Where does the water go after it fills the bottle?" I asked, trying to get Joey to anticipate the fact that the water would fill the funnel after filling the tube.

"Up, up, up the tube," he answered.

"What will happen when it gets up here?" I asked, indicating the funnel.

"I'll have to pour it out." As the column of water reached the base of the funnel, Joey stopped pouring. "Wowee! It won't even go any farther. It's all over. It's got a lot of pee in it. Guess I'm going to empty it." Joey lifted the full bottle high in the air and held the funnel near the water in his basin as the water gushed out.

. . .

Joey found a funnel already attached to a tube about three feet long. "Wow! Look at this!"

I assumed that he would pour through the funnel into the tube and offered to hold it for him.

Joey had a different idea. He took another funnel and attached it to the other end of the tube (funnel *b* in Figure 9.32). Then he surprised me again by sticking another piece of tubing into the large end of funnel *b*. To this tube he affixed a third funnel, *c*. This apparatus, being longer than Joey himself, was quite unwieldy. Joey was thrilled with it. He kept muttering, "Wow!" He handed funnel *a* to me, instructing, "Now you pour the water."

"Show me what you want me to do."

"Put water in here (*a*). Wait, wait . . . not yet." He held funnel *b* in one hand, and extended funnel *c* with the other directly over Danny's basin. "Now pour it," he said. Just as I started to pour, funnel *c* and its tube became detached. Joey shoved these aside and impatiently told me to "pour the water." As I poured, he held funnel *b* slightly higher than I was holding funnel *a*, as shown in Figure 9.33. When he saw the water move into the tube, but stop short of entering his funnel, Joey raised it slightly and turned it upside down over his basin as shown in Figure 9.34. He told me to pour more. Again he seemed to expect the water to flow from my funnel through the tube, into his funnel, and out into the basin. This did not happen.

"Are you trying to make the water go out the side that you're holding?" I asked.

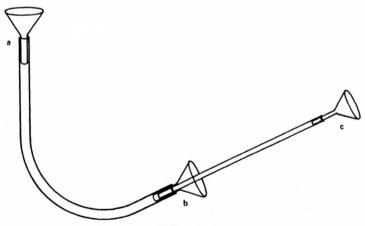

Figure 9.32.

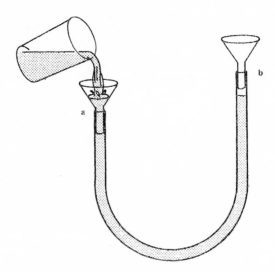

Figure 9.33.

Joey confirmed my suspicions with a somewhat dejected "Yeah, how can we . . ." He then turned his funnel upright but held it lower than mine as shown in Figure 9.35.

Knowing that in this position, the water would flow into his funnel, I quickly started pouring, saying, "Let's try it again." I could see that

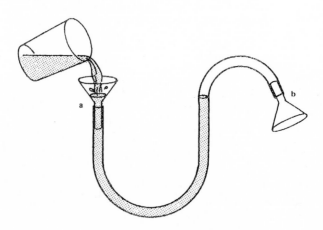

Figure 9.34.

Joey was very puzzled by the failure of the water to move in the way he expected. He seemed to have exhausted all his ideas, and I hoped that a little success might encourage him to try something new such as changing the relative heights of the funnels. As I poured, some water did rise in Joey's funnel, and I asked, "Is the water coming into your funnel?"

To my surprise, Joey said, "No."

Perhaps Joey was looking for something more spectacular (like a spurt of water from his funnel). His disappointment made me feel that my intervention had been inappropriate because I did not fully understand what Joey had in mind. I decided to let him try it his way and to support him in his frustration merely by staying close by and interested in his ideas. I said, "What should we do? There must be something to make this work."

Joey dejectedly tried emptying his funnel, holding funnel *b* tilted toward the basin. With the other hand, he held the middle of the tube in an arch extending higher than my funnel (*a*) as shown in Figure 9.36. He hesitated.

I asked, "Should I pour again?"

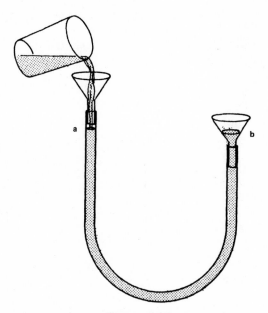

Figure 9.35.

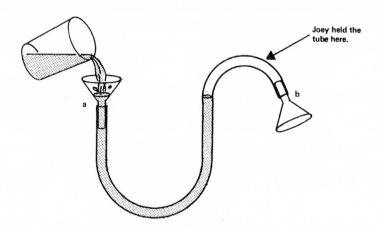

Figure 9.36.

He stared thoughtfully at the arched tube and at my funnel. As I poured into the apparatus, he noticed that the water did not go over the arch in the tubing. "But then it's got to go over . . .," he said as he pointed to the highest point of the arch. Joey's whiney tone indicated that he saw no possible solution to this problem. He made no move to lower the arch nor to raise my funnel. Suddenly he got an idea. He took my funnel so that he had a funnel in each hand. Announcing, "I'm gonna stretch it," he extended the funnels horizontally to the left and right as far as he could reach. Some water spilled from one funnel onto the table. Joey pulled hard on the tube, and seemed not to know what to do next.

I think he expected the water to come out of both funnels at once.

. . .

Afterwards, Joey constructed the very long funnel, tube, and bottle combination shown in Figure 9.37 and handed me the funnel saying, "Pour water in it."

I took the funnel and asked, "Where should I hold it?"

Joey was not concerned with the position of the tube, and impatiently told me, "Just pour it!"

I held the funnel chest high and poured as directed. Most of the water

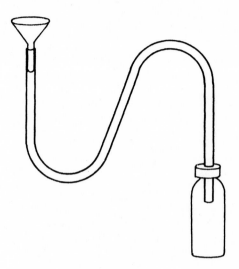

Figure 9.37.

went all the way into the bottle, but some collected in a curve in the tubing.

Joey immediately straightened out the curve, saying, "Now let's make it shoot down here."

In response to his suggestion "Higher!" I lifted the funnel as far as I could reach.

He looked up at the funnel extended way above my head. "Wowee!"

I noticed that in this particular situation, Joey knew how to change the position of the tube to produce the desired flow of water.

. . .

Danny picked up a tube and dipped it into Joey's basin just as Joey asked me to "Please pour some water into this"—the funnel, tube, and sprinkler combination of Figure 9.38.

I responded, "Maybe Danny can help you. Danny, do you have a minute to help Joey with this?" Danny's eager response indicated that I had made the right suggestion at the right time.

The words were no sooner out of my mouth than Danny was dipping a small cup into the basin and lifting it to pour some water into Joey's funnel. Then he dashed to the end of the table for a large beaker. "Here, I'll help you with a lot of water. Oh, wow!" From this point until the end of the activity, Danny and Joey played in close cooperation. At times they were working the same piece of equipment. At other times they were working alone, but on similar ideas.

As Danny began to pour from the beaker into Joey's sprinkler apparatus, Joey held the tubing so that the sprinkler was pointed away from the basins.

Concerned about a flood, I asked, "Where will that water go? Will it squirt out and make a fountain up in the air?"

Both Danny and Joey looked at the sprinkler. When some water did spurt out, Joey said, "Wait a minute," and tried quickly to move the sprinkler toward the basin. Unfortunately, the suddenness of his movement dislodged the tube from the funnel and even more water was spilled. We all said, "Oh, no!" Joey mopped the floor, and I wiped up the table.

In the meantime, Danny set about making a sprinkler apparatus of his own. He unfastened one of his circles and put the other sprinkler on this tube. He filled a cup and poured directly into the tube, making a shower in his basin.

Joey repaired his apparatus, then held the sprinkler over his basin with one hand and the funnel with the other. "I wish I had a million arms," he said as he struggled to hold the funnel, aim the sprinkler, and pour all at once.

I suggested, "Maybe if you made the tube shorter, you wouldn't have to reach so far. Do you think that would work?"

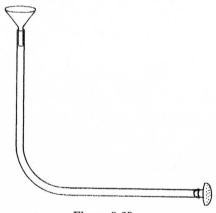

Figure 9.38.

But Joey had his own idea. "I need a chair to stand on."

I offered him my stool.

At one point, both boys had showers flowing at the same time. Danny admired Joey's impressive height on the stool, and asked to try it too. After a while, they did exchange equipment.

When I could see that the boys' interest was waning, I said, "It's almost time to go back. Is there anything else that you want to try with the water today?"

They looked around the table and decided that they were finished. They helped clean up everything and we walked back to their classroom together.

Evaluation

The children experimented actively with the movement of water in tubes. They all tried a variety of actions and strategies including sucking and blowing, pouring with cups and funnels, dipping the ends of tubes and submerging the tubes. Lauren, Alice, and Joey each struggled with the position of the tube in their attempts to get the water out. Bobby and Lauren blew water out in spurts. Joey and Danny figured out how to transfer a bottle of water from one basin to another with tubes. Though it is not clear what they were thinking, five of the six children became quite interested in watching the movement of water in circular tubes.

There was, however, at least one major problem with this activity. The children's investigations with water in tubes were short-lived and frustrating. The objectives of focusing children on the *movement of water in tubes* and helping them extend their investigations, were not met to my satisfaction. I think there are several reasons for this failure.

a.   The movement of water in tubes is quite complex, involving air and water pressure as well as the position of the tube. The children could not understand, nor adequately control, the ways in which water moved. A consistent problem was that they had no awareness of air pressure as a determinent of water level. For examples of this, see Figures 9.8, 9.9, 9.23–9.25, 9.29, 9.30, 9.33–9.35 and Photographs 9.2, 9.5 and 9.6. Also, they fully expected water to move through a tube, regardless of its position, as though it were a garden hose. When they could not get the water to flow in the way they expected, the children turned to other pursuits. My support and suggestions seemed helpful, but often not sufficient to combat frustration.

b.   The large variety of materials probably confused the children and pre-
     vented them from experimenting with a clear focus. For most of the
     children, simply filling and emptying the tubes would have been a
     realistic first objective.

c.   Some of the materials were more distracting than productive. Corks,
     for example, accentuate air pockets, which children cannot begin to
     understand. The jug, although attractive, did not contribute much to
     investigations of the movement of water in tubes. For Bobby, the
     sprinklers led nowhere; for Joey, however, they were useful in slowing
     the flow of water from his tube so that he could observe how much
     water was left and predict how this water would move in the tube. The
     scissors and the asymmetrical funnels contributed little or nothing to
     the children's activity.

Follow-Up

In setting up water play activities for a classroom, I would plan for the
children to have fewer materials, a lot of time, and as much teacher support
as possible. Since the movement of water in tubes is so complicated, I would
try to limit the variety of possible ideas, perhaps beginning with tubes only.
If water play were available daily, children would have the opportunity.to
extend their investigations of materials. I would observe and gradually, over
the course of the year, add more equipment as the children dictate by their
interest and requests.

The next chapter describes a water play activity involving materials
with much less variety.

Chapter 10

Water Play II

COLLEEN BLOBAUM

During one of our weekly seminars, we discussed the physical-knowledge aspects of water play and thought about the aimless and short-lived play which we had often observed. We speculated that part of the reason for this might be that the usual hodgepodge assortment of materials made available to children prevents them from noticing or producing intriguing phenomena. Chapter 9 was an attempt to be more selective about the materials so that the movement of water was clearly observable. As stated in the evaluation, however, the large number and the wide variety of materials led to short-lived sequences of activity. Therefore, we decided to use a smaller number and a narrower range of materials in the hope that this would enable children to focus on a specific phenomenon with less frustration and more concentration.

The materials selected were containers with holes which would allow children to focus on the movement of water. The use of these materials was inspired by Dr. Kamii's description of a water-play activity invented by three of her students at the University of Geneva [C. L. Capt, L. Glayre, and A. Hegyi (1976), who are teachers in the Geneva Public Schools]. These teachers punched holes in the bottom and sides of large, cylindrical cans and gave them to children to use in their water play. Among the phenomena that particularly interested the children were the following two:

1. When a can is filled and held over the dishpan, water runs out of the holes.
2. When an empty can is pushed *down* into the water, "fountains" spout *up* from the bottom holes and *in* from the side holes.

I decided to try this activity with my group of three-year-olds. I was not sure it would be successful—I did not know if they would be at all interested in

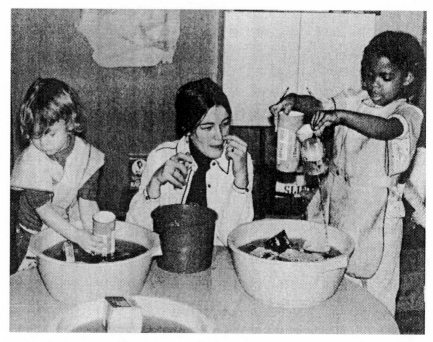

Photograph 10.1. Marita spontaneously compares what happens to the water in two juice cans—one with a hole and one without.

the water coming out of the holes, or indeed, even *notice* it. But I did think it was worth a try, and was interested in finding out just how much the children would observe.

Planning the Activity

I bought four plastic dishpans, the deepest I could find, so that each child would have his or her own space in which to work. I expected separate pans placed on the same table to clearly define each child's area, but at the same time not eliminate the possibility of imitation and cooperation.

In selecting containers in which to make holes, I looked for ones that could be punctured easily with a sharp instrument (without producing dangerously sharp edges), were fairly sturdy (styrofoam cups crumble when punctured), and were fairly narrow and deep.[1] With these criteria in mind, I selected the following materials:

---

[1]After doing this activity, we found a similar activity in *Activities for Lower Primary: Water*, by the African Primary Science Program (Education Development Center, 1973, pp. 4–6) and *Open Learning in Early Childhood*, by Barbara Day (1975, p. 159). In both these sources it is suggested that tin cans with holes punched

Orange-juice cans made out of heavy cardboard (6 oz., 12 oz., and 16 oz.)
Milk cartons (quart and half-gallon)
Yogurt containers made of plastic (8 oz.)
Cottage-cheese cartons made of plastic (16 oz.)
Juice cups made of plastic (4 oz.)

Before trying the activity with the children, I played with the materials myself at home. Since I had never used these objects before, I wanted to find out how well they worked in water. I also figured this would help *me* think of questions that would help the children focus on what was happening.

From my own experience with the materials, I was able to develop objectives for this activity. In terms of general goals of autonomy and initiative, I expected each child to decide how and where to pour the water, which containers to use, and where additional holes should be made. In terms of the goal of the child's observing the movement of water and putting things into relationships, I expected this to begin with the realization that when the container has a hole, the water runs out, but when the container does not have a hole, the water stays in. I also expected the child to put into relationship the various positions of the container and where the water goes. For example, when the container is held over the dishpan (or another container), the water goes there. When it is held over the table or floor, on the other hand, a messy spill results! Then, I hoped the child would form relationships between the water level in the container and which hole(s) the water comes out or goes in. That is, as the can drains, the water stops running out of the *upper* holes first, but when the empty can is submerged, the *lower* "fountains" stop first.

To achieve these objectives, I decided to punch a hole in about half of the containers listed above. All the holes were made in the bottoms of the containers, because I thought these would be the easiest for the children to observe. I planned to introduce side holes later in the activity, as explained below.

Another part of my planning was trying to think of questions that were open-ended and would stimulate the children's thinking about what they were doing. I came up with the following:

What's happening to the water?
Where is the water going?
How did you do that?
Where do you have to hold it so.it doesn't spill on the floor?

Later in the activity, if it fit in with their interests, I planned to introduce the idea of making additional holes in the containers, especially on the side at

---

in the bottoms and sides be used for sand and water play. However, since holes punched in tin leave dangerously sharp edges, we recommend using plastic or coated-cardboard containers instead. The cans used by the teachers in Geneva were ideal because they were made of a metal which resembled aluminum foil.

various heights. I thought I might suggest to one of the children, "What do you think would happen if we made a hole here (pointing to the side of a container)?"

I noticed that the white lining of many containers made the water difficult to observe. Having found that the addition of green food coloring made the water more visible, I decided to use colored water for the activity.

Trying the Activity[2]

To set up the activity, I placed the dishpans of water on a table in one corner of the room.[3] I provided large hollow blocks for each child to stand on, so the child's elbows would be higher than the top of the dishpan. All the containers were put in the middle of the table,[4] and two mops, with the handles cut to child size, and a small bucket and sponge were placed nearby to take care of floor and table spills.[5] Plastic aprons were available as usual. While I concentrated on this activity, the other teacher supervised the rest of the classroom.

The children who played with these materials on the two days were:

Lima (4 years, 3 months)
Ann (3 years, 5 months)
Marlena (3 years, 10 months)
Brenda (3 years, 10 months)
Andy (3 years, 7 months)
Judy (3 years, 11 months)
Marita (3 years, 11 months)

Lima noticed me filling the dishpans with water and adding the food coloring. She helped finish the job, then decided to play with the water. She put several containers into a dishpan, then held up two yogurt containers, one in each hand. Each had a hole in the bottom.

"What's happening to the water?" I asked.

[2]On two separate occasions, Drs. Kamii and DeVries came into my classroom with videotape equipment to record what was happening. The descriptions in this chapter are taken from those videotaped sessions. Because of equipment problems, however, no complete activity was captured on tape. The descriptions of events in this chapter thus consist of segments from those two sessions.

[3]I used only three of the dishpans at the beginning in order to limit the size of the group.

[4]I found that it was difficult for the children to reach the containers when they were placed in the middle of the table. A better way to begin is to place the containers between the dishpans or on a low shelf nearby.

[5]Another way to set up this activity is to place the dishpans in an *empty* water table. This eliminates table spills.

"It's coming out," she said, as she inserted one container inside the other, with an intrigued expression.

Marlena was attracted to what we were doing and scooped up water with a juice can. Water streamed from the bottom. She looked at it curiously.

"What's happening?" I asked.

Looking inside the can, she exclaimed, "Hey! I can't find the water." (It had drained almost empty.)

"You can't find the water? What happened to it?" I asked.

Marlena looked at the trickle of water still coming out the bottom. "It's running," she said.

"It's running?" I repeated, wondering if she would elaborate.

With a quizzical expression on her face, Marlena peered inside the can again, then shook the little bit of water that was left. (If the container is held at an angle, water collects in the bottom rather than running out the hole. The container has to be tilted or shaken in various ways to empty it completely.) Then she was distracted briefly by a heated discussion with Ann about who was big.

. . .

Ann exclaimed, "Look, Colleen, look!" as she held a juice can over a plastic cup, both producing streams of water out of the holes in the bottom (see Photograph 10.2 of a similar event).

"What? What's happening?" I asked, bending down to look.

"Got a hole!" said Ann, with a grin.

Laughing, I said, "You got a hole? What's happening to the water?"

Still grinning, she replied, "I don't know." Fascinated by the water running out of the can, she peered into it and turned it all around. Finally, she turned it upside down to look at the bottom—apparently not even noticing that she thereby dumped the water out onto the table as shown in Figure 10.1!

[Note: I could have pointed out to Ann at this point that she had spilled the water. However, the spill was not doing any damage, and she was

Photograph 10.2. A typical scene from the first day. Marlena has just observed the water running out of the container. Like many other children, she quickly reacted by moving another container underneath to catch the spill. If the second container also has a hole, the child finds out that this solution does not work.

so thoroughly absorbed in studying the container that I felt pointing it out to her would interrupt the very constructive process I had hoped to foster. I decided to wait for a better opportunity, or for another child to point this out to her. I also thought that perhaps she would notice it herself as she continued to experiment with the materials.]

Ann then focused on the water draining out of the cup in her other hand. She turned it upside down to look at the hole in the bottom—and spilled more water on the table. She then set both the cup and the juice can down on the table and picked out of her basin a milk carton (which had no holes), scooping up a bit of water into it. Expectantly, she moved a yogurt container underneath. Nothing came out. She tilted the milk carton just enough to see the bottom, then shook it lightly, as if trying to make the water come out. Then she turned the carton all the way over on its side to see the bottom again— and this time spilled the water on the floor. This event caught her attention, and she paused a moment to look down at the puddle.

[Note: Ann obviously expected the water to drain through a hole in the bottom of the milk carton just as it had through the juice can and the cup.]

Lima placed two nested yogurt containers, each with a bottom hole, in a juice can. She watched with a serious expression as water ran out the bottom. Then, with a grin, she held her hand underneath to feel the stream. Next, she added a milk carton under the juice can (it also had a hole in the bottom) and said she was "putting lots of stuff in it. They got holes in them."

Lima then tried to fit her milk carton into another one of the same size. Since the two cartons did not have tapered sides like the yogurt containers, this didn't work. So she discarded the second carton and picked up a cup, which also had a hole in the bottom. This she filled with water and set inside the top yogurt container, humming as she did so.

"Well, where is the water going now?" I asked.

"Out here," she replied, raising the whole construction and pointing to the hole in the bottom of the milk carton. After picking up one of the largest juice cans, Lima positioned it under the milk carton, saying, "I'm going to catch it with this." (See Figure 10.2.) As the water continued to run out the bottom can, Lima asked, "What should I do now?"

I replied, "I don't know. What should you do now?"

Lima then concluded, "I don't want no holes."

I looked for a container without holes, found a small juice cup, and gave that to her. Then I went to a nearby shelf to get some cans without holes.

Figure 10.1.

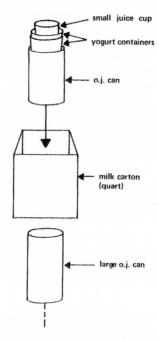

small juice cup

yogurt containers

o.j. can

milk carton
(quart)

large o.j. can

Figure 10.2. Each of these containers has a hole in the bottom.

Lima replaced the large juice can with the cup, using it to catch the water as it ran out of the milk carton. This took two hands, one to hold the milk carton (with the other containers inside it), and one to hold the cup. In order to free one hand, she dropped the cup. Then she put the large juice can in the top yogurt container and set the whole stack down on the bottom of the dishpan (see Figure 10.3). When she noticed me setting the juice cans without holes on the table, she told me, "I don't want none." She put the juice cup on the very bottom of the stack, under the milk carton. As she steadied the stack with both hands so it wouldn't topple into the water, she said, "It isn't going out."

"It isn't going out at all?" I wondered, not really sure what she meant.

At this point the bottom half of the stack was completely under water. Lima raised the whole thing so both of us could see it. Then, as the cup filled, she exclaimed, "It's all filled up!" She used the bottom cup to pour a cupful into the top juice can, and then put it back under the stack to catch the water as it came out.

I was amazed to see that Lima had worked out a whole recycling system! Lima repeated the same recycling procedure several times. Each time, she watched the water level in the top can closely, but no matter how much water she poured in, the level always went down. "It's going down," she commented.

Wondering if she was aware of where the water was actually going, I asked, "It's going down? How come it's going down?"
Lima ran her finger from the top to the bottom of the stack, and struggled with putting it into words. " 'Cause . . . 'Cause it got . . . 'Cause something . . . Probably the water likes to get out."

In this instance, I wanted to find out what Lima was thinking. By asking why the water level was going down, I found out that she did, indeed, seem to know what was happening to the water. She ran her finger from the top to the bottom of the stack of containers, and seemed to be visualizing in her mind the water going through all the containers and out the bottom, but she didn't quite know how to put that into words. Her answer is an example of animism—attributing to inanimate objects the qualities and feelings of a living organism (Piaget, 1926).

. . .

Meanwhile, Marlena scooped water into a juice can that had a hole in the bottom. Having placed a yogurt container in a milk carton (each had a hole in the bottom), she poured the contents of the can into the yogurt container and moved the can underneath to catch the water streaming out. "I'm making yogurt," she announced. "Me, too," said Ann. Then Ann giggled excitedly, "Hey, look!" She was holding a juice can with a hole in the bottom above a yogurt container that she was holding upright in the water.

"What's happening, Ann?" I responded.
"Mine's going like Lena's!" she said.
"It's like Lena's?" I asked.

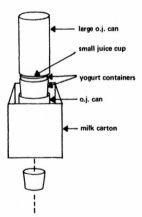

large o.j. can

small juice cup

yogurt containers

o.j. can

milk carton

Figure 10.3. This stack of containers is sitting in the dishpan of water. Lima is using the small cup on the bottom to pour water into the top can.

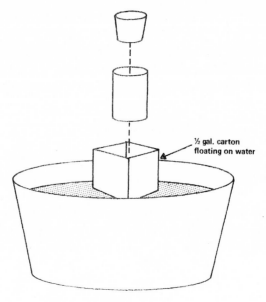

Figure 10.4.

"Yeah," answered Ann.

"What's happening to Lena's?" I wondered.

"Lena's went through there just like mine," she answered.

Marlena picked up her yogurt container, and water streamed out the hole in the bottom. "Hey, my yogurt coming out!" she exclaimed excitedly. She held her hand underneath, continuing to say, "Hey, my yogurt, my yogurt!" She grabbed a juice can and held it underneath the "yogurt," then held both of them over a milk carton that was floating on the water (see Figure 10.4). "My yogurt coming out!" she said again.

"Where's your yogurt going?" I asked.

Marlena peered over the top of the yogurt carton to look inside. "Down . . . Down in . . . (she rested the yogurt carton in the juice can to free one of her hands) . . . Down there," she said, pointing into the milk carton.

"Down there? All the way down there, huh?" I asked.

Marlena nodded.

"Where does it go after it gets down there?" I asked.

"I catch it in the cup," she replied, meaning the yogurt container. With this, she picked up the milk carton, now full of water, and began pouring the water back into the yogurt container. She did not examine the milk carton to see if it had any holes, but used it as an ordinary cup.

Ann next picked up a yogurt container without any holes. She turned it over, looked at it critically, and seemed dissatisfied with it.

Seeing that Ann seemed to be looking for a hole, I thought this might be a good opportunity to introduce the idea of making new holes. I therefore asked, "Do you want a hole in that one, Ann?"

She nodded.

"O.K., show me where you want the hole."

Instead of answering me, Ann began looking at several other containers, apparently searching for a particular kind.

Meanwhile Brenda, who had taken the basin vacated by Lima, picked up a yogurt container that had no hole and said, "I want a hole."

"You want a hole? Where do you want the hole?"

She turned the container over, and pointed to the bottom in the center.

I made the hole for her.

Ann had finally decided where she wanted her hole. "I need a hole," she said.

"Where do you need a hole? Can you show me?" I asked.
She pointed to the bottom center of the yogurt container.

As I punched the hole, I asked, "What's going to happen to the water after I make this hole?"

Before Ann could respond, Marlena held out a yogurt container, demanding, "I want a hole in this one."

I made the hole, noting that everybody was now clamoring for new holes.

Suddenly, Brenda exclaimed, "My yogurt's coming out!" She peered inside the container, then tilted it to look at the hole in the bottom. When the water stopped, she dropped the empty container in the water. Then she picked up a milk carton which had no hole, looked closely inside, and filled it with water. She waited a moment, but nothing came out. She then quickly dumped out the water and said to me, "I need a hole in here."

"You need a hole in there," I echoed.

[*Note: Perhaps Brenda was not sure what would happen without a hole, or perhaps she could not be sure whether there was a hole or not. In any case, she felt it necessary to fill the milk carton to see what happened.*]

Brenda replied, "Yeah—to make it go in here." She held the milk carton above the yogurt container to show me how she wanted to make the water drain.

"To make it go in there? So where should I make the hole?" I asked her, and punctured the bottom where she indicated.[6]

While Brenda continued to observe the water flowing from the milk carton into the yogurt container below it, Marlena and Ann each held two yogurt containers, one above the other. Each of the containers had a hole in the bottom. "My's going in this one," said Marlena. "My, too. . . . This, too," said Ann. "We got two things, right? 'Cause we got two," Marlena agreed. Ann picked up another yogurt container, one without a hole, and said, "I want a hole, too." She showed me where she wanted it on the bottom.

After making the hole, I asked, "Annie, what do you think would happen if I put a hole over here (pointing to a spot midway up the side of her yogurt container)?"

"Leak," she murmured, almost inaudibly.

"Do you want to try it?" I asked.

Ann nodded quickly, and Marlena requested, "Me, too."

I punched the hole for Ann and turned to Marlena, asking, "Where should I make the hole?"

---

[6]Since milk cartons are made from plastic-coated paper, the holes tend to clog up. Periodically, usually when a child asked for it, I would punch the hole again.

Figure 10.5.

When she pointed to a spot about one-third of the way up from the bottom, I punctured the container there. Ann dunked the container in the water, then lifted it up sideways, so that water streamed directly into the pan as it had previously from the bottom hole (see Figure 10.5).

> [*Note: I had not anticipated this idea, but, upon reflection, could see why this seemed "logical" to Ann. Previously, she had observed water coming out of a hole on the bottom. So it seemed obvious to Annie that, to get the water to come out of the side hole, she would have to turn the container on its side, thus making the side the "bottom".*]

Annie's actions caught the interest of Marlena, who stopped what she was doing to watch with an intrigued expression.

I asked Annie, "What happened?"

"It leaks," she responded. She picked up another yogurt container and examined it.

I asked, "Does that one leak?"

Ann nodded and showed me a crack near the top. Then she said, "Put a hole there," pointing to a spot midway up one side of the container. Marlena then asked for a hole on one side of her yogurt container, and Ann asked for another. Brenda joined in, "I need a orange-juice can, and a hole."

> She got no response from the other two, so I suggested, "Could you tell Lena or Annie what you want? . . . Maybe they'll let you use one of theirs."

Immediately Marlena, who had a juice can, said, "No!" Brenda began to whimper, "I want a orange-juice can."

"Are you using this now?" I asked Annie, indicating one of her cans.

Annie replied that she was using both of them and picked them up.

"Well," I said, "Brenda doesn't have any orange-juice cans, and she wants to use one."

Marlena reached over to take one of Annie's cans and give it to Brenda. "No!" objected Ann, hanging on to it. "She want a orange-juice—that one," explained Marlena. Seeing that Ann was not about to give up one of her cans, Marlena took a yogurt container from her own dishpan and gave it to Brenda. "She gave me one!" said Brenda, with a delighted smile.

[*Note: I felt that it was important that the children themselves arrived at the solution to this problem, so that it would be something they felt comfortable with rather than something I imposed on them. In a situation like this, I feel that my role is to ask questions, make suggestions, clarify the problem, and reflect children's feelings—but not to solve the problem.[7] I thus encourage the children to decenter, and to develop a sense of responsibility both for themselves and for others. Leaving the resolution of the problem up to the children contributes to the development of autonomy. Here, Marlena's offer of a substitute container was more acceptable than it would have been coming from me.*]

Andy was waiting for a turn to play with the water and asked what the mop was for. I told him that it was to wipe up water that spilled on the floor and asked if he wanted to be the "wiper-upper" until someone was finished with the water. Just then, Brenda announced, "This person is finished." Andy took Brenda's place at the dishpan, and Brenda stated that she was going to be the "cleaner-up."

This took care of the immediate problem of water on the floor. However, I still wanted the children to become aware of the water they were spilling.

---

[7]If Marlena had not offered this solution, I might have said to all three children, "What do you think we can do about this?" Sometimes it may take as long as ten minutes of discussion to resolve the problem. What I do depends partly on the personalities of the children involved, such as how much frustration a particular child can handle. It also depends on the context in which the problem arises. For example, during free play, I can spend more time helping children resolve problems than I can during group time.

Andy picked up one of the milk cartons and water came streaming out the bottom and one side. However, the side hole faced away from him.

Knowing that he couldn't see this, but thinking that he would be interested, I pointed this out to Andy and helped him turn the milk carton around so he could see it better.

Andy was delighted! "That looks like a sink coming . . . that looks like water coming out of the sink," he explained to me.

. . .

Ann picked up a cup, half full of water, and poured its contents into a yogurt container. Then she put the cup inside the yogurt container. In the process, she splashed some water on the table.

This had occurred several times, without her seeming to notice, and when she did notice, she didn't do anything about it. She didn't seem to realize that the water spilled on the floor or the table as a result of *her* actions. So I decided to call her attention to it. "Did you see what just happened?" I asked, pointing to the water on the table. "The water splashed out."

She took a sponge and gave a brief, cursory swipe to the table, then returned to her dishpan of water.

Ann obviously felt this was an interruption to her play. Although my objective in pointing out the spilled water was to help her realize the results of her actions, she interpreted it as an arbitrary request to clean up the water. It is not easy to decide whether or not to insist that a child clean up. At times it is necessary to impose adult authority. For example, if it seems that children may slip and fall on the floor, I insist that it be cleaned up.

. . .

Judy looked down at the dishpan. "Green water!" she exclaimed. "Ain't that *green* water?"

"It sure is green water," I agreed.

"How did we get green water?" she asked.

I replied, "I put some food coloring in it."

[Note: *This is an example of a question to which Judy could not find the answer from the materials themselves. By this time the other children*

*who watched me adding the food coloring could not provide the infor-
mation because they had moved on to other activities. Since I was the
only source for the information she wanted, I simply answered the
question.]*

Judy submerged both hands in the water. "I have green hands," she said.

"You have green hands?" I asked in surprise.

"Green arms and green hands," she elaborated, looking down at them.

"Green arms and green hands," I agreed, nodding.

"And green fingernails," she added.

"Green fingernails!" I said in mock surprise. "You're all green!"

"Now do you want to see? Now they're not," she said, as she pulled them out
of the water.

"Would my hands turn green if I put them in there?" I asked.

She nodded yes, with a broad grin on her face.

"You think so?" I said. I put my hand in the water. "Did it turn green?"
I asked, with my hand still in the water.

"Your hand turned green," she said, taking my hand and moving it in and out
of the water, "but your ring didn't. It turned purple!" (My ring was set with a
red stone, and it did, indeed, turn purple in the green water!)

[*Note: This is an example of how children can learn about colors in
ordinary, day-to-day situations. It was Judy's own interest that
prompted this discussion of color, rather than a teacher's arbitrary
demand that she learn the names of colors.*]

. . .

Judy picked up a large juice can and swished water around in it. Then
she held it upright and pushed it down into the water. Since the can had a
hole in the bottom, water spurted up like a fountain inside the can when she
did this. She put her hand into the can to feel the water. I was busy helping
Ann take off her apron and Brenda wipe up some water. So she said to Dr.
DeVries, who was taking pictures, "I'm putting it under water, and it's going
up."

"It's going up when you put it under water?" responded Dr. DeVries. At this point I came back to the table and asked Judy, "What's happening?" I looked in the juice can and exclaimed, "Hey! How did you do that?"

"I'll show you," said Judy. She pushed the can down into the water, explaining with satisfaction, "I put it down . . . and water runs out."

I picked up a milk carton, with holes on the bottom and side, and asked, "Do you think that would happen with this?"

She tried it, and watched water come up from the bottom and in from the side. She looked for something else that also had a side hole, and found a yogurt container. She filled the milk carton and held it over the yogurt container to catch the water coming out of one of the holes.

. . .

Judy picked up a juice can and stopped the flow of water from the bottom by plugging the hole with a finger.

"How come you're putting your hand on the bottom?" I wondered.

Photograph 10.3.

"I'm going to do something," she asserted. She then noticed water coming out of a side hole, and plugged that leak, too, with the other hand. Satisfied that no drips remained, she quickly moved the can from her dishpan to the bucket next to it (see Photograph 10.3).

Judy was able to anticipate the spill that would result if she moved the can from her dishpan to the bucket without covering the holes. For her it was a wonderful idea to move the container without dripping! "Oh, *that's* why. I see," I said.

Judy removed her hand from the bottom hole, let some water flow out, then covered the hole again and moved the can back to her own dishpan. She did this back and forth several times, covering the holes when the can was not over a container. Then she put her arms in the water to watch them change color. She held up some water in the palm of her hand and looked at it. Then she poured water from a yogurt container onto her hand. "It looks like plain water when I go like this," she observed.

"It looks like plain water?" I asked, not quite sure what she meant. "You mean the water is not green?"

"Yeah," she said. She put her hands and arms back in the water. "Now my hands are green."

. . .

Marita started playing in the dishpan next to Judy's. She looked at all of the containers already in the dishpan, and went through all of them, asking me, "Did you drink milk (or yogurt, or orange juice) out of this one?" Then she held out two juice cans of different sizes. "These aren't the same," she said. She found two of the same size, and said, holding them up, "These are the same."

[Note: As with Judy's interest in color, this was a spontaneous interest in comparing sizes of containers. I feel that this kind of spontaneous comparison is more valuable than giving a lesson on size.]

Then she asked, "Teacher, you want a drink of water? . . . I'll get you a drink of orange juice." She picked up a juice can full of water, and poured some into a yogurt container. As she handed it to me, water streamed out of holes on the bottom and side.

"Well, look at what's happening to it," I said, pointing to the water coming out of the holes.

She screeched in astonishment.

Judy was holding her juice can over the bucket. Marita watched, then took her own juice can, filled it, and moved it over to the bucket (see Photograph 10.4). However, she did not hold her hand over the hole in the bottom, and water ran onto the table as she moved it back and forth.

"What happened to it when you did that?" I asked.

"Where's the sponge?" she asked. She took the sponge out of the bucket, squeezed it, and wiped the water off the table. She picked up the juice can again, and held it first over her dishpan, then over the bucket. Again water ran out as she moved it.

"What happened when you did that?" I asked again.

"It spilled," she answered.

"Can you figure out how you could do it without spilling?" I asked.

Photograph 10.4.

Before Marita could answer, Judy solved the problem by moving both dish-pans right next to the bucket.

Evaluation

a.   The children did notice the holes, particularly those in the bottom of the containers. They were thrilled at the phenomenon of water streaming out of the containers. As a teacher, I found it exciting to watch the expressions of delight and amazement on the children's faces when they first observed water flowing out of the holes.

b.   All the objectives listed under "Planning the Activity" were met except the last two—the one concerning water on the floor, and the one dealing with the order in which the water stops running when there are many holes on the side.

c.   I started with the hypothesis that choosing a simple phenomenon, and limiting the number and variety of objects, would enable the children to focus their interest on the movement of water and to follow this interest in a variety of ways. This hypothesis was supported. All the children remained interested in the movement of water out of holes in containers. Within this focus, they each elaborated different combinations, ranging from "recycling" water through a series of containers to transferring it from one basin to another.

The Surprises

a.   I had not anticipated that children would turn the containers sideways to make the water come out of the side holes. As noted above, this does seem very "logical" from the child's point of view.

b.   Judy kept coming back to the color of the water. Since we played with colored water before, I did not expect such preoccupation with it at this time.

Follow-Up

a.   The second or third time that any child played with these materials, he or she had to recreate some of the relationships that had been constructed before. For example, on two separate occasions, I asked Ann what would happen if we made a hole in the side of the container. Each time it seemed a very new idea to her. So follow-up to this activity would include more of the same, at least for children this young.

b.   Other relationships that might be established in the future are those between water in a container and water on the floor or table. It was

Photograph 10.5. Children can participate in this water play activity without the constant supervision of a teacher. Here, Marlena is holding a milk carton, not realizing that it has a hole on the side away from her.

    much easier for children to notice the movement of water in relation to a container than in relation to either the floor or the table.

c.   These materials could be tried with sand instead of water. Perhaps the holes would have to be a bit bigger for the sand to flow through easily. Children might notice that it is possible only with water to make "fountains" that gush *in*.

PART III

How to Go
Beyond This Book

Chapter 11

How to Develop
Physical-Knowledge
Activities

When we discussed how we planned each of the activities in Chapters 4–10, we usually started from a point at which certain decisions had already been made. In the chapter on Target Ball, for example, we began by saying that we decided to develop an aiming game with balls and the action of throwing. In the present chapter, we would like to discuss the thinking that led to this kind of decision, to help the teacher become able to develop physical-knowledge activities of his or her own by using the same sources and line of reasoning.

Ideas for developing physical-knowledge activities come from a variety of sources which often converge. We begin with the most important consideration, the child's actions on objects, in light of the four criteria of good activities discussed in Chapter 1 (the *producibility*, *variability*, *observability*, and *immediacy* of the object's' reaction). We will then discuss other sources to which the teacher can turn for specific ideas, such as early-education texts, sports, party games, toys that can be bought or made, and ideas suggested by children.

Actions the Child Can Perform on Objects

As stated in Chapter 1 and illustrated with the activity on crystals, one of the fundamental differences between "science education" and physical-knowledge activities is that the former emphasizes teacher-directed observation and the social transmission of knowledge, while the latter puts the accent on the child's own actions on objects and his observation of how the objects react. In Chapter 2, we also pointed out that there is not much the child can find out about a ball by observing it and listening to adult explanations. It is only by dropping the ball on the floor, rolling it, throwing it in the air, throwing it against the floor, throwing it against a carpeted surface, throwing it against the grass, throwing it against a wall, varying the force applied, trying to catch it, chasing it down a stairway, kicking it, and so forth, that the child can come to know the ball. These actions do not refer to the same thing as what is called "manipulation" in educational parlance. "Manipulation" refers to actual physical contact with objects as opposed to dealing with them in representational forms such as words and pictures. Manipulations can thus include random, mindless fingering. In contrast, the term *action* as used by Piaget refers to the two interrelated actions discussed in Chapter 2—physical and mental action. The two are interrelated because what the child does physically is guided by his mental activity. When the children described in Chapter 5, for example, put an object on one end of a lever in order to make it fly in the air, this choice of action was guided by an inner organization of knowledge and intention. It is by acting on the object in a particular way that the child can see how the object reacts, and the intelligence which produced that particular action is the same intelligence that interprets the significance of the object's reaction.

One of the ways we invent physical-knowledge activities is by focusing on a particular action children can perform on objects. We then wrack our brains to think of objects suitable to that action. For example, when we focus on the action of throwing, we can think of objects such as balls, bean bags, rings (for ring toss), darts, and paper airplanes. Our next task is to find out by trying the effects those that children might want to produce. For example, hitting a target is an effect that makes throwing interesting. Good targets for balls or bean bags might be constructions such as those described in Target Ball, or perhaps buckets, baskets, or a board with holes. For ring toss, the leg of an upturned chair can be used. Paper airplanes, on the other hand, do not need a target as children spontaneously try to produce long, smooth flights.

It is thus by focusing on an action that the teacher can often invent activities. To provide further examples of this process, we list a variety of actions children can perform with objects and indicate briefly some kinds of activities that can be developed around each. This list of actions contains many overlaps. However, to focus on actions seems a natural way for the teacher to approach the invention of activities. We begin with the movement of objects and then go on to the changes in objects.

Actions Producing the Movement of Objects

The movements of objects are produced basically by two actions: pushing and pulling.

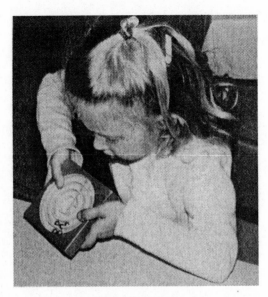

Photograph 11.1.

Pushing.   Objects often move when pushed, and the way they move depends on the relationship among a variety of factors such as shape, size, weight, friction, and force. The same action on different materials can thus result in activities that are very different. For example, in shuffleboard the objects do not move in the same way as in pool. Pushing a child on a board on rollers, as we saw in Chapter 4, is another kind of possibility that involves the action of pushing.

Rolling.   The child can roll a ball by pushing it across a flat surface, but on an incline he has only to let go. Like throwing, rolling can be used for the purpose of hitting a target. The child can roll an object by pushing it underhanded across a floor (as in bowling), hitting it with a stick (as in croquet and pool), or by flicking it with a finger (as in marbles). Games like these can be modified into appropriate activities for four-year-olds. A target activity involving rolling on an incline was described in Chapter 7. In addition to spherical and cylindrical objects, pear-, egg-, and football-shaped objects as well as tires and tapered papercups should also be used occasionally so that children can compare the differences these shapes make.

Rolling can also lead to activities such as roller skating or riding on boards on top of wooden rollers. A good resource for activities involving the making of wheeled objects is *Wheels*, developed by the African Primary Science Program of Education Development Center (1973). (The making of soapbox racers is a sophisticated elaboration of this activity that can be interesting even for adolescents and adults.)

Photograph 11.2. By tilting the board, this child succeeded in getting the styrofoam piece around all holes but the last one.

Sliding.   The child can make certain objects slide by pushing them or putting them on an incline. We often see children spontaneously trying a variety of objects (such as a pair of scissors and a lunch pail) on an indoor slide to see what happens to them. Sliding can lead to variations of shuffleboard (though young children are more interested in the effect of making a puck *hit* or *fall into* something than in simply reaching a point in space). When children go down a slide, they themselves are the objects observed. Skiing, sledding, and ice-skating are other forms of this action.

Tilting.   By tilting, children can make temporary inclines in order to direct the movement of objects. Toys such as Labyrinth (made by Creative Playthings and shown in Photograph 11.1) and the board with holes and hairpins shown in Photograph 11.2 can be bought or made.

Throwing.   We have already described how bean bags, balls, rings, darts, and airplanes lend themselves well to the action of throwing, and lead to variations of games like basketball, ring toss, and other target activities.

Dropping.   The relationship between throwing and dropping is similar to that between rolling a ball on a horizontal plane and letting go of it on an incline. In dropping an object and letting go of a ball on an incline, the

Photograph 11.3.

child can make the object descend simply by letting go of it. An example of an activity using the action of dropping is Drop the Clothespin. In this activity, children stand at a certain distance above a container and try to drop clothespins into it. Beans and seeds of various sizes (from lentil to lima beans and avocado seeds) can also be used to aim at containers of different sizes.

Another activity involving the same action is that of dropping parachutes made with paper napkins or plastic wrap (Photograph 12.7). This activity should be varied according to the children's developmental level. At age four, dropping the parachute and choosing a good weight for it may be all they can be expected to do. Later, however, making the parachutes also becomes a significant part of this activity.[1]

Blowing.   Blowing is like pushing and rolling, but instead of pushing the object directly the child "pushes" the air that pushes the object. Examples of blowing activities were cited in Chapter 1 (blowing things across the floor) and Chapter 3 (blowing floating objects across the water).[2] The action

---

[1]This activity is discussed later under the heading of "Toys That Can Be Made by Children."

[2]Characteristically, when the children could not make things move across the water because they sank, they came up with what the adults had not anticipated. They found out that they could blow through the straw in the water behind the sunken objects and make bubbles that pushed them across to the other side!

Photograph 11.4.

of blowing can thus be elaborated into making things move with an instrument such as a straw or a cardboard fan, a machine—perhaps an electric fan— or the wind. Children can be helped to make pinwheels or they can make "kites" from paper bags with holes punched in them (Photographs 11.3 and 11.4). To make it fly, they can either run to create a wind effect or make use of the natural wind on a windy day. (They usually do both!) Other activities involving the action of blowing are making soap bubbles[3] and blowing a ping-pong ball within a curving path taped on the floor (Photograph 11.5).

Sucking. By sucking through a straw children can transport a small piece of paper. The teacher can put out pieces of paper, tin foil and

---

[3]When Ms. Ellis was teaching a kindergarten class, she made circular, triangular, and square bubble blowers, and asked, "What would happen if you used these?" The children said that the circular one would make round bubbles, the triangular one would make triangular bubbles, and the square one would make square bubbles!

cardboard of various sizes, paper clips, and rubber bands, for example, and ask, "Which ones can you carry with the straw from that box to this box?" Children thus have the opportunity to find out that certain objects "stick" to the straw while others do not. In water play with a tube, to cite another example, children are intrigued by their ability to "pull" the water up. One child experimented with a long tube and was amazed that she could back far away from the table and still pull the water. Children's use of the term *pulling* to refer to this action is one more confirmation of the fact that the actions listed in this section are variations of two actions—pushing and pulling.

A machine that can serve as a toy in this connection is a vacuum cleaner. For example, at the end of an activity involving dropping beans and other seeds, the teacher can suggest cleaning up the mess with a small vacuum cleaner. Children can then use sieves to separate the different-sized objects sucked up, and the materials will then be ready for use on another day.

Pulling.   The action of pulling an object with a string is too easy for four-year-olds, since toddlers already play with pull toys. A more appropriate kind of pulling activity for four-year-olds is shown in Figure 1.3 where a child can make an object go *up* by pulling a rope *down*. When children drop parachutes from high on the jungle gym, for example (see Photograph 12.7), one child usually loves to be in charge of sending the parachutes up to the top in a bucket. They are fascinated by the fact that, by pulling a rope, they can make the bucket go even higher than their heads. Other activities involving the action of pulling which seem more appropriate at age five than

Photograph 11.5.

Photograph 11.6. This activity with pulleys developed into a race. Players sent their buckets as fast as possible to the teacher, who quickly dropped an object in each one. The buckets were then pulled back, emptied, and sent again to the teacher. At the end of the game, they counted to see who had the most objects.

at four are play with pulleys, as shown in Photograph 11.6, and spinning a top by jerking the string wound around it. Aiming an arrow with a bow is a good physical-knowledge activity of this type that is appropriate for older children.

An activity we originally thought was too dangerous is aiming with a slingshot. Mr. Gleeson developed the toy shown in Photographs 11.7 and

11.8. In this toy, he inserted two clothespins into holes in a board, making them stand up. He then put a rubber band around these clothespins and taped down its front half so that the back half could be used as a sling. After finding out that this taping did not work satisfactorily, he decided to make two slits in the board as shown in Photograph 11.8 so that a rubber band inserted through them would be half under the board. But this sling still presented problems because the children's natural tendency was to put the ball under the rubber band (and the rubber band then served only to hold the ball on the board)! The third and final version he devised is shown in Figure 11.1. It is a board with two big nails, a rubber band around them, and a small washer. The child pulls both halves of the rubber band as he places a ball on the washer (which keeps it from rolling away). When the initial plan for this toy was to make an aiming game with a target, it became clear during the course of the activity that their interest was primarily in shooting the ball as far as possible. A target in this situation would have been too hard and frustrating. The children were soon using only ping-pong balls when they concluded that they went much farther than balls made of styrofoam.

Swinging.   The pendulum (Chapter 8) is an example of an activity that involves the phenomenon of swinging. The result of releasing a pendulum is similar to the result of releasing a ball on an incline or dropping clothespins. These movements are determined more by gravity and the spatial relation-

Photograph 11.7.

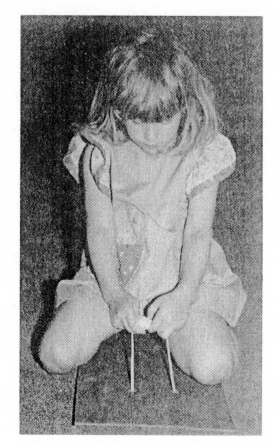

Photograph 11.8.

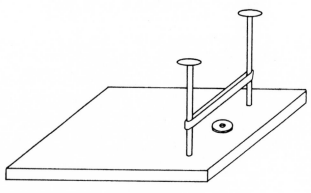

Figure 11.1.

ships among the objects (the point of release, the length of the string, and the position of the target) than by the child's action. In light of this analysis, it becomes easier to understand why three-year-olds tend to push or throw the bob rather than simply to let go of it. Their experience with the movement of objects leads them to expect that it is necessary to push or throw the object. They are unable to understand that their own action of throwing is unimportant in this situation, and it does not occur to them that what is important is *where* they release the bob.

Twirling. An example of twirling an object on a string was given in Figure 3.3. A similar example is the cowboy's lasso. Still another example is the use of a Hula hoop which most four-year-olds can learn to make go around and around their waists with amazing skill. It is by repeating such actions of twirling that children build a foundation for understanding centrifugal force.

Balancing. Balancing here refers to arranging objects in such a way that there is equilibrium and an absence of movement. The most obvious example of an activity involving balancing is play with a balance. Other examples are

building a tower with blocks
making a tall construction with cans, cylinders, and milk-carton blocks as we saw in Target Ball (Chapter 6)
walking with various objects stacked on one's head
making mobiles (see pamphlet by the Education Development Center, 1969)
making constructions with cards or plaques
balancing objects on a cardboard disc on a ball resting in a cup, as shown in Photograph 11.9.

Kicking. Kicking shares many similarities with pushing, rolling, and hitting. All activities suggested under these headings can therefore be considered for modification into kicking activities. Kicking may be particularly good for outdoor target games and games such as Dodge Ball.

Jumping. A good activity involving the action of jumping is that of making a lever with a roller and a board as described in Chapter 5 and shown in the film, "Playing with Rollers" (Kamii, DeVries, Ellis, and Zaritsky, 1975). By jumping on the high end, the child can make all the objects fly up in the air. This is an example of an activity we did not invent. It was a four-year-old who invented it, and an observant teacher who picked up on it.

Photograph 11.9.

Actions Producing Changes in Objects

We now turn to the second category of physical-knowledge activities, changes in objects, where the role of observation is primary and that of the child's action is secondary. Taking cooking as an example, we list below common actions and some of the different ways different objects react to the same action.

Putting in water.   If the child puts sugar in water, the solid dissolves. Flour does not completely dissolve, and clouds up the water. A radish cut in a certain way does not dissolve at all but reacts in the opposite way—it opens up like the petals of a flower and becomes even stiffer than before. Rice and beans left overnight in a pan of water expand and become softer.

Heating in water.   The rice and beans mentioned above expand even more when cooked in water. The vegetables in vegetable soup become soft when they are cooked. Eggs, in contrast, become firmer when they are cooked.

Heating in oil. Popcorn makes a popping noise and expands enormously and changes color. Pancakes do not pop but only change from a sort of liquid to a solid.[4]

Heating in the oven. Cakes and breads expand and change in color and consistency. Cookies and pizzas expand less than cakes and come out crusty.

Cooling in the refrigerator. Jello and melted butter come out firmer than when they went in, but fruit, vegetables, and milk come out only colder. Ice cream, popsicles, water, and everything else harden in the freezer. Some come out feeling like rocks.

Making pottery, candles, and playdough are very similar to cooking. Mixing paints is also similar in the sense that mixing certain colors leads to a predictable outcome based on the properties of the objects that were mixed together.

Actions Producing the Third Category of Phenomena

The third category of physical-knowledge activities, those we described as being between the other two categories in Chapter 1, involves making objects interact and producing results that depend on the unusual properties of objects. Some of the actions the child can perform on objects in this kind of activity are the following:

Putting in water. Some objects which do not dissolve react by floating, others by sinking.

Pouring, sifting, making flow, spilling, sponging, and draining. Up to a point, sand, salt, cornmeal, and rice have in common with water the quality of flowing. This quality can be used to develop activities that are similar to water play in some ways but different in others.

[4]Ms. Laura Gross, a teacher colleague who works with three-year-olds, introduced the making of pancakes after the children had made popcorn many times. As she was about to put the pancake batter onto the frying pan, she asked the children, "What do you think will happen when I put the batter in?" Some predicted, "It'll pop." By thus making empirical generalizations and modifying them, children develop their knowledge about the properties of objects.

Sifting. This is a kind of "unmixing" of different-sized objects which we mentioned in connection with sucking.

Running to step on other people's shadows. (See Education Development Center, 1963.)

Deflecting (in play with mirrors).

Yelling (in producing echoes). This is not a classroom activity, but we could not resist including it.

Holding a magnifying glass above various objects.

Touching things with a magnet

Our suggestions for actions and activities are intended to serve only as a starting point. The teacher can elaborate these in three ways—which are not mutually exclusive:

1. By combining actions
2. By developing actions into group games
3. By integrating physical knowledge with other aspects of knowledge.

Photograph 11.10.

When a creative teacher begins inventing activities and picking up on children's ideas, he or she may even combine all three categories of activities and many actions which do not appear on the above list. For example, Mr. Aborn, a former teacher at Circle Children's Center, invented the following activity after noticing that objects can be made to move on water when the water is gently stirred back and forth with a spoon. He decided to make a maze with blocks in the water table as shown in Photograph 11.10, so that children would have to figure out how to direct their "boats." For "boats," he chose a variety of small objects such as round, rectangular, and triangular wooden blocks, paper boats, and checkers. He also provided a straw and a spoon for each child so that he or she would be able to compare the effects of moving the air that moves the "boat" with the effects of moving the water that moves the "boat." This activity thus cut across the movement of objects (category 1), the changes in objects (category 2)—since the paper boats absorbed water and unfolded as they became soggy—and sinking and floating (category 3). Once the activity started, one child became interested in rearranging the blocks on her side to make different "harbors" to navigate her boat in and out of. Another wanted to have "high water" on her side of the water table and added a bucketful of water (Photograph 11.11). When she noticed that the added water did not make it higher on her side but made the blocks float and destroyed the maze, she stopped.

Another example of a creative elaboration of a common activity is given below in the words of the teacher:

> Last time when making Jello, I asked the children to save a little. Then at group time I asked all the children if they could think of a way to change the Jello back to the red water it was at first.
>
> There were many ideas such as put salt in it, put baking powder in it, put water in it, and let it stand all night. The next day the cooks from the day before tried all of the suggestions. The Jello changed, but it still was not like before. No one thought of heating it; so finally I suggested it. To my surprise, all the children thought that was a dumb idea and didn't even want to try. I persuaded them and they did try it and were surprised at the result. (Reported by Ms. Maureen Ellis)

Another way in which actions can be elaborated is to extend the activities into group games. The group game format can greatly enhance interest in the physical-knowledge activity as can be seen in the following examples reported by two kindergarten teachers.

Marbles

The first time I played with a small circle taped on the rug, I asked three or four kids if we could make up a game. First, they made up impossible tasks—line marbles up around the circle and shoot one so it

Photograph 11.11.

hits and causes others to hit, or try to make one marble go around the circle following the line of the tape!

After some exploration, I introduced the game of take four, keep one for a shooter, and put three in the middle. The ones you knock out of the circle you keep, and whoever has the most wins. The children changed the rule to "the ones you hit you keep."

The game was very successful and has been played again and again. Recently, a new game has developed in which everyone starts with seven marbles, and when you don't hit any, you have to give your marble to the person next to you. (Reported by Ms. Maureen Ellis)

Balancing

This game has already been mentioned in this chapter under "balancing." A disc like the one shown in Photograph 11.9 is placed on a rubber ball which is in a cup. When the teacher feels that the activity is becoming boring but might regain the children's interest in the form of a group game, he or she introduces a die, and players take turns placing an object of their choice on the number they throw. The object of the game is to avoid making the disc topple. (Reported by Ms. Geri Mann[5] as a modification of a commercial game which could not be identified)

The third way in which the teacher can elaborate a physical-knowledge activity is by trying to integrate other aspects of knowledge. For example, "Marbles" can encourage numerical reasoning in a natural and meaningful way. "Balancing," when played with two dice, integrates the addition of two numbers (logico-mathematical knowledge) with the reading of written numbers (social knowledge). Group games have the further advantage of integrating moral development by encouraging social organization, legislation, and the enforcement of rules among children.

The Games and Sports of Older Children and Adults

At the beginning of this chapter, we said that ideas for physical-knowledge activities can come from a variety of sources which often converge. We will now discuss how the beginning teacher can develop physical-knowledge activities by thinking about adult sports and asking him or herself whether the child can perform the action involved in light of the four criteria discussed in Chapter 1, and also whether the child will be motivated to produce a desired effect and whether the activity promotes logico-mathematical and spatiotemporal reasoning. Some sports such as tennis, ping-pong, baseball, and volleyball are obviously too hard for young children. Others, however, can be modified in appropriate ways. For example, the following games provide good starting points from which the teacher can begin to develop physical-knowledge activities.

Golf, miniature golf, pool, and croquet. These activities have in common the fact that the player uses an instrument to hit a small ball to make it roll to(ward) a target. They illustrate the variety of targets that can be used, such as a hole into which the ball must drop or another ball that must

[5]Formerly a kindergarten teacher at Washington School in Evanston, Illinois.

be hit. They also illustrate the different paths that the ball can be made to take, such as passing between two points and ricocheting against the side of the table (or a bumper as in bumper pool).

The teacher can vary the kinds and number of balls to use in each one of these activities. The ones that are easily available are golf balls, tennis balls, ping-pong balls, styrofoam balls, marbles, ball bearings, wooden balls, Nerf balls, baseballs, and all kinds of rubber balls.

Bowling.   Bowling is different from the above activities in that (1) the ball is rolled directly with the hand, and (2) many objects are used as the target, thus making the number knocked down dependent on the spatial arrangement of the "pins." The teacher can vary the size and weight of the balls to be used, as well as the number and nature of the targets. Commercially available, lightweight, plastic pins often fall over too easily, and it is frustrating to spend a lot of time setting them up before each aim. Cardboard blocks or empty juice cans are easier to set up and enable children quickly to get on with the game.

Basketball.   This activity involves throwing a ball into a container. The size, height, and distance of the container can be changed to make the activity appropriate. As mentioned earlier, bean bags and buckets or a board with holes are versions of the same activity.

Tetherball.   Four- and five-year-olds can obviously not play this game according to the standard rules.[6] They can, however, invent ways to play with this equipment when they are encouraged to use it in any way they like. The teacher can also suggest that two players cooperate in trying to wrap the cord around the pole (see Photograph 11.12).

Ice-skating and hockey.   On ice, everything slides much more easily than on the floor. Ice-skating and hockey are obviously impractical ideas, but we list them to illustrate what older children can learn as they play outside the classroom.

Roller skating.   Although roller skating may be too difficult for four-year-olds, it is a natural extension of the action of rolling, and we include it here because it offers good possibilities for older children.

Skiing and sledding.   While sledding is a more practical idea than skiing, both involve the action of sliding on an incline. As in the case of

---

[6]That is, players facing opposite one another try to wind the rope around the pole in opposite directions.

Photograph 11.12.

skating, children can find out how fast they can slide when friction is reduced.

Jumping on a trampoline.   For some day care centers such as ours at a university, this activity is available in physical education facilities and is excellent, as each child can invent his own way to jump and land.

In presenting these ideas, we have only scratched the surface of many possibilities. Most importantly, the teacher should keep in mind that these activities are used not merely for recreation or for the child's physical and perceptual-motor development, but also for his intellectual, social, and moral development.

Early-Education Texts

A third way of developing physical-knowledge activities is to search for them in early-education texts such as Hildebrand (1971); Leeper, Dales, Skipper, and Witherspoon (1974); Pitcher, Lasher, Feinburg, and Braun (1974); Read

(1976); Stant (1972); Taylor (1964); and Todd and Heffernan (1970). This may seem like a surprising suggestion in light of our criticism of "science education." Although we find that such texts pay little attention to the importance of actions on objects in the context of science, we do find good ideas in chapters on art, music, and outdoor play. We shall, therefore, discuss some of these activities and try to show how Piaget's theory can be used to recognize physical-knowledge possibilities.

Chapters on Art

For children who do not yet use materials representationally, "art" activities have primary value not as art but as physical-knowledge activities. (At age four, these activities are sometimes physical-knowledge and sometimes representational activities—and sometimes both.) Let us consider some examples which offer possibilities for children to act on various materials, find out what happens, and then try to produce particular effects.

Painting.   Painting involves changes in objects, the second category of physical-knowledge activities. In the following examples, children can vary the results they get by varying their tool (hands, brush, straw, roller, and so on), the way in which they use it, and the material (finger paint made with wallpaper paste or soap flakes, tempera mixed with sand or sawdust, and so forth). Such possibilities for variation facilitate comparison of similarities and differences.

Finger painting: By using commercial fingerpaint and by participating in making paint with cornstarch, soap flakes, wheat paste, and flour, children find that it can be made from combinations of different materials. They also find that different actions with their hands produce different results (using all fingers, side of hand, palm, or fingernails).

Roll-on painting: A cardboard roller or rolling pin creates a unique effect. When paint is dripped on the paper and then rolled, the effect is different than when the roller is dipped in paint. Thin paint reacts differently from thick paint.

String painting: The resulting design depends on how the paint-soaked string is arranged on the paper, and children can vary this action by pulling the string between folded paper.

Spatter painting: Children can vary the spatter effect by using fine and grossly meshed screen. They can plan different silhouettes by anticipating the effect that will be produced by spattering over a leaf or key.

Blow painting: Children must vary how hard they blow on paint and the direction they blow in order to create particular effects. They have the opportunity to think about how to drip the paint and how to combine colors to get particular effects.

Squeeze-bottle painting: Different effects can be achieved by squeezing paint from plastic mustard bottles, food-coloring bottles, and detergent bottles.

Printing: Children can compare differences in prints made with sponge, cork, potato, their hands, a fork, and the top of a can. Group printing to make a mural is a particularly good activity because it is one in which cooperation is possible but not necessary.

Dry-powder painting: Children can paint with dry powder by dipping a brush into water and then picking up dry tempera with the wet brush. They can also sprinkle powder on wet paper, or they can dip a wad of cotton into dry powder paint and apply it to damp paper.

Sand/sawdust painting: Children can make a design on colored construction paper with paste and then shake sand or sawdust mixed with tempera on it (from a shaker with large holes).

Cutting, tearing, pasting, and gluing. In making collages and building "sculptures" children have occasion to observe the properties of glue and other materials, as well as to engage in balancing and spatial reasoning. We list some examples.

Collages: The variety of objects to compare in making collages is endless—tissue paper (which can be cut or torn), cloth (which has to be cut), beans, egg shells, egg cartons, glitter, leaves, magazine pictures, straws, popsicle sticks, shells, nutshells, wire and pipe cleaners. The effectiveness of paste and glue in holding various objects can be compared. Spatial reasoning comes into play when children put the glue on the side of the picture they want to show and are then surprised that they have to turn it over to affix it!

The making of paper bag masks can involve pasting, and the reader can undoubtedly think of many other examples such as the making of paper lanterns for Halloween and the making of Easter baskets.

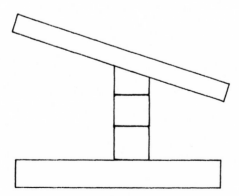

Figure 11.2.

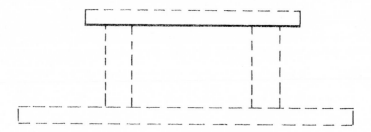

Figure 11.3.

Wood "sculptures": These are especially good physical-knowledge activities because they involve the action of making things balance. One typical four-year-old, for example, put glue all over the entire surface of the heavy board shown in Figure 11.2 to make it stay balanced on top. When it nevertheless fell off, his solution was to add gobs of glue all over the surface of the board! The teacher knew that this solution would not work, but encouraged the child to try out his idea to see what would happen. Figures 11.3, 11.4, and 11.5 show other examples of spatial reasoning and the action of trying to make things balance (reported by Ms. Liliane Glayre, a teacher in the Geneva Public Schools). In Figure 11.3, to glue the top piece onto the two vertical pieces, the child put glue on the entire surface shown with a solid line. In Figure 11.4, to glue the flat piece (a) onto the one already glued and standing up (b), the child put glue on the sides of "a" indicated by the solid lines and was later surprised that the glue was not where he wanted it to hold the two pieces (a and b) together. When another child found out that the plaque (a) shown in Figure 11.5 was too thin to stand up with glue alone, he came up with the solution to support it with the two sticks (b and c) glued on either side. Woodworking, too, is an excellent opportunity for the child to act on objects and find out how they react under various conditions. Attempts to balance objects can be classified under the movement of objects, whereas the painting of a finished product can be considered as belonging to the second category, the changes in objects.

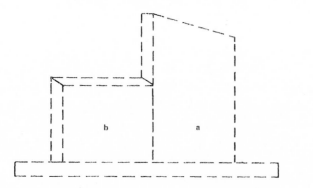

Figure 11.4.

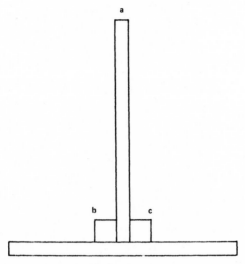

Figure 11.5.

Making mobiles. This activity has already been mentioned in connection with the action of balancing. One of the favorite objects to hang from a mobile is fish that are either simple paper cut-outs or two cut-outs glued together and stuffed with paper. Figuring out where to make a hole to hang the fish horizontally is in itself a physical-knowledge problem.

Modeling. The making of playdough, baker's clay, and sawdust dough are similar in value to cooking. Like painting, activities with playdough begin by being physical-knowledge activities. Children's interest first centers around the material and what happens when they pull it apart, roll it, pound on it, press down on it, and so forth. It is when the physical aspect of the material is well known that the child begins to use it deliberately as a medium of representation—perhaps a "snake," or a "pancake."

In the above discussion, we did not mean to imply that all art activities can be reduced to physical knowledge. What we tried to point out is that when a material is first presented to the young child, he approaches it as something he wants to know by acting on it in a variety of ways. The teacher who is aware of how the child approaches the material as a physical object will intervene differently from the one who thinks that the child is merely "manipulating" it or that he is merely practicing his motor skills or is in his "scribbling stage." The child does manipulate, does practice motor skills, and does scribble, but the significance of these behaviors is that they are part of his construction of knowledge about objects in his environment.

The context of Chapters 2 and 3 makes it clear that the different techniques mentioned, such as string painting, should be presented to children not as artistic skills to be learned but as interesting ideas someone came up with to make pretty things that might be fun to try. The emphasis would then be for each child to produce the different effects *he* wants and not for him to produce exactly the same thing the teacher modeled.[7] We emphasize again that the importance of children's coming up with their own ideas is based not on the arbitrary adult value of "creativity" drawn from some "bag of virtues," but on Piaget's constructivism; this scientific theory shows that knowledge can be built only by construction, or creation, from within.

Chapters on Music

Like art and science, the two traditional subjects discussed so far in this book, music is also presented in early-education texts as an area of knowledge which is defined and given. The objectives of music education can be found in the following typical passage:

> . . . Basically, children get a great deal of pleasure through singing and responding to music. This then becomes one of the objectives—sheer enjoyment. Music does "have charms to sooth" and, therefore, another objective might be the releasing of tension, or the quieting influence of special music.
>
> Another goal might be to have children learn something from the song or music. It might be the sequence of the song that the teacher feels is important for children to be exposed to. They listen to the tune so they can respond in accordance with this sequence. It may be that concepts are a part of the song—a shape, a distance, an animal. There is also the possibility that some songs or rhythms might be used to stress change in tempo, making the body respond fast on some sounds and slowly on others. (Stant, 1972, p. 65)

This atheoretical approach is not unlike the honey-and-vinegar approach to medicine. Honey may be soothing and good for some people, but the fact that practitioners found this value by trial and error hardly helped develop the science of medicine—nor will it help education to advance beyond its current state.

Music in preschool can be viewed in two ways: (1) as the culmination of centuries of evolution like science, art, or any language; or (2) as something early man invented by acting in various ways on certain objects to produce interesting sounds. The first conception, the social-knowledge approach, is the one universally adopted by all the early-education texts we

---

[7]If a child is spontaneously intrigued with reproducing a clever idea the teacher has shown, this should of course, not be prevented. What should be avoided is making children feel that they are expected to do so. (Even when children make something that does not look at all like the teacher's, they often have *tried* to make it identical.)

have seen. Just as various languages evolved in different cultures over the centuries, each culture developed its own music, and many educators believe that they should transmit this heritage to the next generation.

Although the learning of a common repertoire of songs is in itself highly desirable for the development of group spirit and a sense of belonging, it is also important to encourage children to invent their own music. The music of primitive civilizations actually involved a good deal of physical knowledge—both in the choice of certain objects to hit, rub, pluck, blow through, and shake and in the modification of these instruments to produce desired sound effects.

Stant (1972, pp. 69–70) gives good examples of home-made instruments, but she recommends that the teacher make these instruments. For the development of both physical knowledge and intelligence, it is better to have children make their own instruments, no matter how crude they may be. One note of caution, however: Teachers of young children need to keep in mind that musical instruments that do not sound good are no fun and too hard for young children to modify. Teachers of older children will find *Musical Instruments Recipe Book* (Elementary Science Study, 1971) a rich resource.

Chapters on Outdoor Play

On the playground, children spontaneously gravitate to a variety of equipment recommended in all early-education texts, including swings, seesaws, slides, merry-go-rounds, rope ladders, and single climbing rope. Children act on all these pieces of equipment and observe the reactions of the objects. For example, they find a correspondence between how high the swing goes forward and how high it goes backward. On a seesaw, they find out that when they move forward toward the fulcrum, they go up and the child on the other end of the seesaw goes down. They also find out that a steeper, longer, and/or bumpier slide is scarier and more fun than the tame kind that three-year-olds like. Wagons and balls, too, are objects children can act on in various ways and observe their reactions. Thus, the playground is an environment that is not limited merely to opportunities for physical and perceptual-motor development. On the playground, preschool children learn an enormous amount of elementary physics at the level of practical intelligence.

Chapters on Science

Ideas that can be developed into physical-knowledge activities are rarely found in chapters on science. The reason for this, as has been pointed out many times, is that "science education" is oriented toward the teaching of content. The following are examples of the kinds of topics often found in traditional texts:

Air
Electricity
Magnetism
Temperature
Volume
Length and Distance
Size, Shape, and Weight
Balance
Speed
Machines and Tools
Sounds   (from Hildebrand, 1971, pp. 157–161)

Obviously, "instructing" children in these contents is antithetical to Piaget's constructivism. Occasionally, however, there are certain overlaps between what we advocate and what authors of early-education texts recommend. To illustrate what we mean, let us take as an example the first item on the above list and consider each statement from the point of view of physical knowledge.

> *Air.*   Provide opportunities to show that air is all around. Make or buy pinwheels to watch in the breeze. Build and fly a kite. Fill balloons with air. Have the child hold his nose and mouth to see how long he can go without breathing. Place a glass over a lighted candle to demonstrate that fire needs air to burn. Have the children learn words like air, wind, breeze, oxygen, and movement. (Hildebrand, 1971, p. 157)

Piaget's theory leads to the view that one should not try to show to young children that "air is all around." Since air is invisible, this is a statement the children cannot understand. On the other hand, we would agree that it is good to encourage children to play with pinwheels, kites, and balloons. Our rationale, however, would be not to "demonstrate" that air is all around us but to have children themselves act on the objects. The next statement in the above quote, "Have the child hold his nose and mouth to see how long he can go without breathing," is presumably an activity intended to show that each child has to have air. Perhaps the child will thereby become more conscious of the fact that he has to breathe, but what he learns about air is again questionable. "Place a glass over a lighted candle to demonstrate that fire needs air to burn," violates the fourth criterion of good physical-knowledge activities—that the reaction of the object must be direct and immediate in order to be understandable to a young child. Why things burn or stop burning is a content that is completely beyond the comprehension of young children. Finally, the list of words recommended at the end of the quote, "air," "wind," "breeze," "oxygen," and "movement," likewise belongs to the verbalistic instruction of "science education."

Most chapters on science also include activities centering around the raising of animals and plants. This reflects the fact that the physical and biological sciences are grouped under one heading in the traditional classification of academic disciplines. Biological phenomena, however, do not belong to "physical knowledge" as we reserve this term for elementary physics and chemistry. Plants grow not as a direct consequence of the child's action on them. Animals move on their own without having to be pushed or pulled by the child. Certainly there are many reasons why it is good for children to raise animals and plants and learn eventually about the germination of seeds, the reproduction of animals, and the similarities and differences between animals and humans. However, biological objects are different from inanimate objects and, therefore, do not contribute to physical knowledge in our use of the term.

Toys That Can Be Bought or Made

Many toys that can be bought or made are good for physical-knowledge activities. These have, by and large, been invented not by educators but by adults who have retained a certain playful attitude. Recognizing those toys that may be appropriate for physical-knowledge activities demands familiarity with the criteria discussed in Chapter 1. To provide a basis for selecting good toys, we list examples from three sources which are not mutually exclusive—toys that can be found in stores, those that can be found in catalogs such as teachers regularly receive in the mail, and toys that can be made in the classroom or at home. Our list is by no means exhaustive—in fact, we were tempted to add construction toys such as those that involve nuts and bolts. However, we decided to restrict our examples to a few toys which either meet the four criteria of good physical-knowledge activities well, or seem good at first but fall short in practice. We hope the contrast between the two types will help to further clarify our criteria. Although the most valuable toys are those the children themselves make, we begin with those that can be bought, because they make life easier for the beginning teacher who has to equip the room with a variety of good materials that children can choose from.

Toys That Can Be Found in Stores

Many commercially available toys have already been mentioned, such as Hula hoops and bowling, croquet, dart, ring toss, and basketball sets. Others worth discussing include one which we have found clearly appropriate for four-year-olds (Water Wheels), one which is better when played with other materials (Pick-Up Sticks), one whose value we are uncertain about (Jumbo Tiddledy Winks), one which looked excellent but turned out to have serious drawbacks (Don't Break the Ice), and one often seen in pre-school classrooms which has little value (Shape-Sorting Box).

Water Wheels   (manufacturer unknown). The plastic toy with three wheels shown in Photograph 11.13 was found in a variety store in Chicago about the summer of 1972 and we have never seen a similar one since. We nevertheless describe it as an example of a good toy for water play because it meets all the criteria of a good physical-knowledge activity described in Chapter 1, and similar toys may possibly be found elsewhere. When the child pours water at the top, he can see that the water comes down and makes the first wheel turn. This wheel makes the second wheel turn, and the second, the third. The child thus produces the movement of objects, movement that is immediately and clearly observable. He can also dispense with the water for a while and make each one of the wheels turn by using his finger, watching what happens to the other two wheels when he moves one clockwise or counterclockwise.

This is a plastic toy, but it is unusually sturdy. The only piece that breaks off easily seems to be the top funnel, and this breakage is a blessing! We have observed that when children can pour water into the funnel, they tend to concentrate on pouring water and do not pay much attention to what happens to the wheels. When the funnel is gone, on the other hand, as can be seen in Photograph 11.14, the children pour water on the top wheel in

Photograph 11.13.

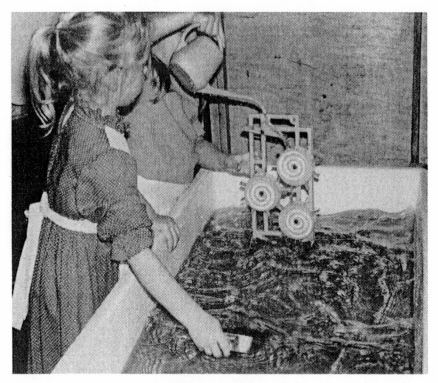

Photograph 11.14.

various ways and find that if they pour it to the left, the wheel turns counterclockwise, and if they pour it to the right, it turns clockwise. The spiral-like pattern painted on each wheel adds to children's fascination with the resultant optical illusion.

Don't Spill the Beans (Schaper Mfg. Co., 1967).   As can be seen in Photograph 11.15, this plastic toy consists of a stand having two arms on which a covered pot rests. Since the pot is thus held in equilibrium by resting on only two points, it tips when beans are concentrated more heavily on one side. The toy comes with a bag of about 200 beans and plastic dishes for four players.

The game begins by dividing all the beans equally among the players, who take turns placing one bean at a time on the pot, trying not to make it tip over. When a player makes the pot tip over, he has to take all the beans he spilled. The one who gets rid of all his beans first is the winner.

In addition to being a good physical-knowledge activity, this game is excellent for numerical reasoning for children who are five years of age or older. Before the game can begin, the 200 beans must be divided among the

Photograph 11.15.

players. Four- and five-year olds have a variety of ways to accomplish this "equally." Sometimes they give each player one at a time, and go around until all the beans are gone. (Whether or not someone gets skipped here and there, or someone gets a double dose, may or may not be of importance to anyone!) Sometimes a child may think of giving two at a time to each player, or five to each, to expedite the process.[8]

Some children figure out that the imaginary line across the pot connecting the two points of suspension is the safest place to deposit a bean (see Figure 11.6). However, the difference between placing a bean at "X" or at "Y" is much harder to figure out. According to Inhelder and Piaget (1955, Ch. 11), proportionality in distance from the fulcrum of a simple balance is a problem that cannot be solved before the formal-operational stage. Thus, when the beans spill, young children often seem to attribute this to an

---

[8]What happens in the execution of this procedure is often amusing. When one child counted and discovered that her opponent had five more beans than she did, she decided that the way to make the number equal was to put the five "extra" beans in the pot and not use them!

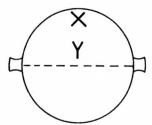

Figure 11.6.

unfortunate accident and they do not look for an explanation. Nevertheless, with practice, they gradually become conscious of the fact that some places are better than others to drop the beans, and that the side which is beginning to go down is the side to avoid. We have one suggestion for the manufacturer: the balancing mechanism on this toy should be made more sensitive, as the pot does not tip easily enough to provide clear feedback from the object.

Pick-Up Sticks. Commercial pick-up sticks are made of bamboo and are thin and sharply pointed. They are thus too dangerous and too hard for

Photograph 11.16.

Photograph 11.17.

four-year-olds to pick up. (The teachers with whom the senior author has worked in Geneva do not agree with this opinion.) We prefer to use Japanese chopsticks of all kinds—those made of bamboo and other wood, round ones, laquered ones, square plastic ones. (Chinese chopsticks are usually too long and too large.) The number can vary from 30 to 50 or more.

To play this game, one person bunches up all the sticks and holds them vertically in one hand in such a way that one end of each stick touches the floor (or table). He then removes his hand quickly so that the sticks fall in a scattered pile. Players take turns picking up one stick at a time so as to avoid moving any other stick. When a player makes another stick move, it is the next person's turn. The rules call for scoring based on the color of the sticks collected, but with younger children the one who collects the most sticks is the winner. As shown in Photograph 11.16, some five-year-olds don't feel the necessity to take turns when they first begin to play this game—and it doesn't seem to matter how many sticks move!

This game is a good physical-knowledge activity because players have to scan the chopsticks to figure out which one is on top of all the others, and whether the pointed end, the blunt end, or the middle is best to touch. For the person who begins the game by holding all the sticks vertically, this is an occasion to figure out how to release them to disperse them as much or as little as possible. Opportunities to engage in numerical comparisons are obvious.

Jumbo Tiddledy Winks (Milton Bradley, 1963). The basic materials are 16 plastic discs (Winks) ⅞ inch in diameter (four each of red, white, blue, and yellow), four larger plastic discs (Tiddledies) 1½ inches in diameter (one each corresponding to the colors of the smaller chips), a round glass cup about 1½ inches tall and 1½ inches in diameter, and four stiff green felt pads about 3½ × 2¾ inches. The object of the game is to snap the Winks from a pad into the cup with a Tiddledy as shown in Photograph 11.17. Players select a color and take turns trying to get a Wink into the cup. Each time they succeed, they get another turn. After the game starts, players must jump their Winks from where they landed on the previous turn. The first player getting all his Winks into the cup wins.

The game may be played with the cup alone or with the cup inserted in a cardboard scoring frame divided into four areas, two marked "5," and two marked "10." Using this frame, each player jumps his four Winks and counts his score according to where they fall. Any falling in the cup counts 25, and any falling on a line between a 5 and a 10 counts 15. A modification of the game, called Party Tiddledy Winks, is to snap Winks from the floor onto tables, up on chairs, over obstacles such as a low stool or a pile of pillows, through the rungs of a chair, and so forth. Scorekeeping may or may not be appropriate for four-year-olds.

In this game, the child has to establish correspondences between the force applied and the distance traveled, as well as between the point of application of the Tiddledy on the Wink and the direction of the Wink's jump. These correspondences can be established by a child (or adult) only up to a point, since the action of the Tiddledy on the Wink involves slippage which takes place too fast to observe. (Both of the authors were rarely successful in getting a Wink into the cup.) The Party version is, therefore, the best place to begin this game, since larger targets are easier to hit. The teacher might also use a larger container and make a larger scoring board. Even when the game is thus modified, the teacher must remember that, although there is an action-reaction sequence, the action of the Tiddledy on the Wink is to a large extent unobservable. We conclude, therefore, that this game is not one of the best to recommend for four-year-olds.

Don't Break the Ice (Schaper Manufacturing Company, 1969). Materials for this game, shown in Photograph 11.18, consist of a square plastic frame about 8½ × 8½ inches, 33 white plastic cubes measuring about 1⅛ inches on a side, and one block measuring about 2¼ × 2¼ inches, four legs for the frame, two plastic mallets, and a small plastic man in a seated position, which can be inserted into the large block. Players begin by fitting into the frame the large block and the 32 small cubes (one extra cube is included). The fit is tight and, when completed, the legs are added to the frame and the

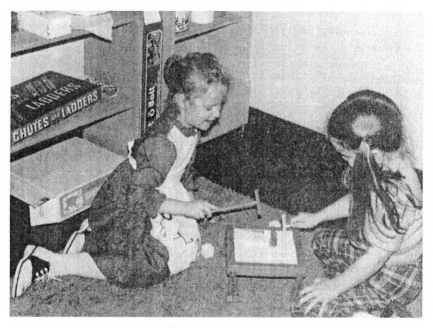

Photograph 11.18.

pieces form a sheet of "ice" on which the man sits. Players take turns using a mallet to tap out a block of "ice" of their choosing. The object of the game is to tap a block out without causing the man to fall through the ice.

The primary cognitive task in this game is to figure out the minimum support necessary for the large block (on which the man is sitting)—a problem which changes as the large block is placed in different positions within the frame. In deciding which block to tap out, players have to anticipate the effects on other blocks, since several are often dependent on a single block. Toward the end of the game, when players can anticipate the final sequence of turns, they can often figure out who will inevitably be the one to make the man fall.

This toy also challenges children to fit all the pieces of "ice" into the frame and to adjust four legs onto the frame, in preparation for playing the game. However, these tasks are much too hard for four-year-olds, and sometimes for five-year-olds as well. When a toy thus requires excessive teacher input, it should be taken out of the room and offered to older children who can play with it without continually calling for adult help.

Like many other plastic toys, this one breaks very easily and is, therefore, not worth its price for use in a classroom. We include it as an example of a toy which would make an excellent physical-knowledge activity if it were sturdy and easier to assemble. In other words, what we are endorsing here is only the educational soundness of the basic idea of the toy.[9]

Shape-Sorting Box.   One often sees in classrooms a hollow wooden or plastic box with holes cut in various shapes. Three-dimensional shapes can be poked through these holes. Although this toy does involve the dropping of objects into a container and may be thought to provide an opportunity for a physical-knowledge activity, the child's action is little more than unreasoning manipulation. We have seen children trying hard to force a shape through an impossible hole. The same child might then push a shape through a hole it does not match but which is big enough to let the object pass through.

Toys That Can Be Found in Catalogs

Teachers, supervisors, and administrators regularly receive catalogs from manufacturers of children's toys. These catalogs may be generally thought of as a more fruitful marketplace to locate toys that are suitable for physical-knowledge activities. Commercial establishments doing business with schools usually have some ideas about what might be educational and appreciate the importance of making toys that are sturdy. Toy catalogs are similar to early-education texts in that they do not include good physical-knowledge materials under the heading of "science," where we characteristically find the same content approach as in early-education texts. Science materials tend to be fancy, unusual objects, such as magnifiers, stethoscopes, magnets, and "Chick-U-Bators"—which hatch chicks. Good toys for physical-knowledge activities are found instead in other sections, such as those labelled "manipulatives."

We list here some examples selected from a few well-known companies. Obvious materials such as water tables, standard playground equipment, and musical instruments will be excluded from this discussion. Our selections come from the following catalogs, which are listed in alphabetical order:

Childcraft Education Corporation (1976)
Community Playthings (1976)
Creative Playthings (1976)
Ideal Toy Corporation (1975).
Mead School Products (1973/74)

[9]In a home situation this toy can be valuable if it is used carefully. When an adult is available to help with putting the game together and to play with the child, the advantages we discussed may be realized.

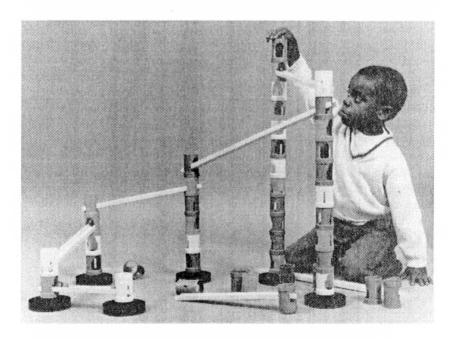

Photograph 11.19. Courtesy of Childcraft Education Corp.

Marble Railway (Childcraft Catalog No. 6M 509).   As shown in Photograph 11.19, this is an activity with inclines and towers. This toy is easier for four-year-olds to handle than the Multiway Rollway put out by Creative Playthings, which we also describe. It is, therefore, a better toy for young children whose motor coordination is not as well developed as that of kindergarten children.

Blockhead (Childcraft Catalog No. 6G 174).   As can be seen in Photograph 11.20, this is a balancing game in which children take turns trying to place a piece onto the structure without tumbling it. This is an excellent physical-knowledge activity in which we can see a great deal of sorting taking place. For example, children systematically look for a cylinder having the same height as another one, in order to make a "bridge" that will be stable.

Derrick (Community Playthings Catalog No. T50).   This toy (Photographs 11.21 and 11.22) can be found in many classrooms, but we have not yet had occasion to study it very closely. It invites the actions of pulling, turning (winding and unwinding), lifting, and lowering, and seems excellent for children who are advanced enough to put a whole variety of parts into relationships.

Multiway Rollway (Creative Playthings Catalog No. G0651). This toy, shown in Photograph 11.23, is one of the most popular physical-knowledge materials we have tried in kindergarten classrooms. Although some teachers wish the pieces were bigger for easier handling, even teachers of three-year-olds have expressed enthusiasm for the versatility and potential of this toy for putting objects into relationships. For example, children make horizontal "bridges" and expect the marble to roll, and then find out the necessity of making an incline! They also make arrangements such as the one shown in Photograph 11.24, and expect the marble to go around from one end of the path to the other!

Photograph 11.20. Courtesy of Childcraft Education Corp.

Photograph 11.21. Courtesy of Community Playthings.

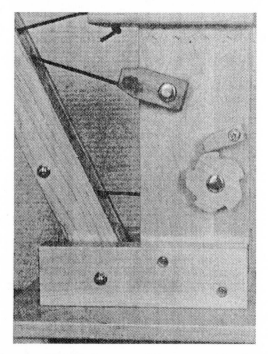

Photograph 11.22. Courtesy of Community Playthings.

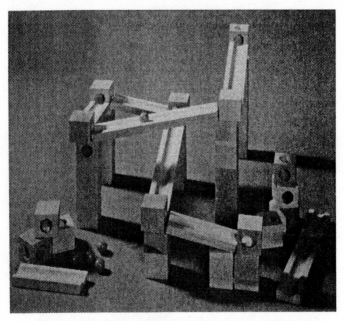

Photograph 11.23. Courtesy of Creative Playthings.

Labyrinth (Creative Playthings). This is a type of maze which the child tilts in all directions to make the balls all go to a particular spot (see Photograph 11.1). This toy is no longer marketed by Creative Playthings, but we list it anyway because similar toys using the same principle can often be found in stores.

Spindle Top (Creative Playthings Catalog No. C0606). This is a special kind of top that keeps spinning longer than an ordinary top because it uses a string which is wound around and then pulled to give it momentum (see Photograph 11.25). The interest in this toy is short lived because there is only one thing children can do with it. Winding the string is in itself hard, and four-year-olds tend simply to watch the five-year-olds play with this toy. It is thus not a priority item but nevertheless an excellent toy to put on the shelf from time to time.

Beat the 8 Ball (Ideal Catalog No. 2106-3). As can be surmised from Photograph 11.26, players take turns dropping the "8 ball" into the funnel. At what he thinks is just the right moment, each player presses a lever to start his own ball rolling down an incline. All the balls roll under the funnel and down the scoring chute. The object of the game is to beat the "8 ball" there, but just barely. The player whose ball reaches the bottom first because he released it too soon gets only one point. The one whose ball ends up *just* before the "8 ball" gets four points. If the "8 ball" beats a player's ball, he loses one, two, three, or four points, depending on how many other balls

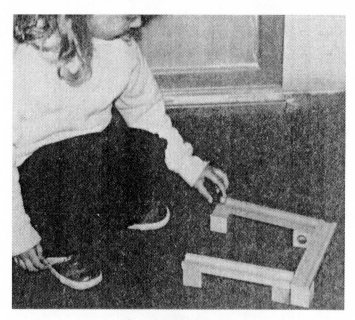

Photograph 11.24.

come down after the "8 ball." The winner is the one who first collects 10 points. All the rules about scoring must be either modified or dispensed with entirely when four-year-olds play this game. For example, the object of the game could be to be the first one that comes down *after* the "8 ball."

The cognitive value for the player who drops the "8 ball" lies in how unpredictably he makes the "8 ball" behave, thereby increasing his own chances of earning points. He can spin the "8 ball" around the funnel to make it take a long time before it reaches the scoring chute. He can also drop it straight down the middle. The other players have to judge the time it takes for their balls to roll down so as to arrive at just the right moment.

This is an excellent toy for learning about the movement of objects that four- and five-year-olds like very much. However, as with several other toys

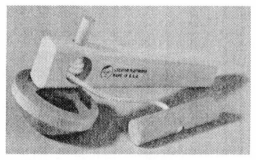

Photograph 11.25. Courtesy of Creative Playthings.

Photograph 11.26.

made by this company, the flimsy plastic construction makes it impossible to take the normal wear and tear of a preschool classroom.

Toss Across (Ideal Catalog No. 2117-0). As can be seen in Photograph 11.27, this is a giant tic-tac-toe game. The idea is to toss a bean bag at a square mounted on a frame and turn it so that an "X" or an "O" comes up. The first to turn up three of his symbols in a row is the winner.

This is theoretically a good aiming game as well as a game of strategy. Unlike the regular tic-tac-toe game, this one offers the possibility of undoing what the opponent (or oneself) did. For example, if an "X" is already up, it is possible to change it to an "O."

However, although the game is theoretically sound, we found out that in practice we cannot recommend it. In several trials, for example, the squares, which give the impression of rotating freely, sometimes rotate easily in one direction but fail to rotate in response to pressure from the other direction! Since each square rests on a plastic frame that is molded in a particular way, it rotates in a rather erratic way. We thus found out that an "X" sometimes turns up for no reason that *we* could understand, and sometimes does not turn up when we fully expect it to. For us, therefore, it was impossible to establish correspondences between our actions and the reactions of the objects.

Photograph 11.27.

Giant Tinkertoy (Mead School Products Catalog No. 123-5300).　Unlike Spindle Top, this is a versatile toy that can be used in a wide variety of ways. It is not a toy for the beginning of the school year, since it is potentially dangerous for children who cannot judge how far the other end of a long stick goes. Since construction with the large pieces can often not be accomplished by a single child, interindividual coordination is encouraged by this material. Being able to use the set outside is an advantage, especially when the classroom is small.

Toys That Can Be Made by Children

When a child uses a good ready-made toy, he can learn a great deal by acting on it in different ways and observing how the object reacts to the variations in what he does. However, when the child makes the toy, he can learn even more by varying the characteristics of the toy as well. For example, most of us remember folding paper in different ways trying to make airplanes that flew as far and smoothly as possible.

Sources of ideas for toys children can make include many books in the general category of "arts and crafts with junk for young children" or "how to entertain your child when he has nothing to do." Most of these books deal literally with arts and crafts, for example, how to make dolls or puppets. Occasionally, however, one gleans an idea for a toy that can be used for physical-knowledge activities. Even if one finds only a few good ideas, they are worth the price of the book. We list four such books, with the ideas found in each for making toys that involve the movement of objects.

Fletcher, Helen Jill, *The Big Book of Things to Do and Make*. New York: Random House, 1961.

Making tops (p. 23).   The materials can be cardboard, bottle caps, jar lids, empty spools (of thread or typewriter ribbon), acorns, or any other round object through which a hole can be punched. If there is already a hole in the object, the problem will be how to secure the pencil (skewer, or stick) to make the top work.

A Mexican balero game (p. 52).   This toy, shown in Photograph 11.28, requires only a milk carton, a 20-inch piece of string, and a washer.[10] After cutting off the top of the milk carton, the child makes two holes in it with scissors or a nail. He then ties the washer in the center of the piece of string, and ties each end to the box through the holes. To play with this toy, the child tries to flip the washer into the box, as can also be seen in Figure 11.7.

Parachutes (p. 22).   The materials recommended in this book are a paper napkin, four pieces of string (each 12 inches long), and a small cork. The child ties a piece of string to each corner of the paper napkin. The other ends of the strings are then tied together and onto the cork.

One of the teachers with whom we work at Circle Children's Center tried making more durable parachutes by using a variety of thin and thick cloth and paper napkins. She found that most of these materials were too heavy to drift in air and concluded that the cheapest kind of paper napkins tore easily but worked the best. Later, another teacher came up with an idea that worked even better—using plastic bags that come from the cleaner's (Photograph 12.7). During hours of experimentation with these toys, the teachers found many factors they could vary to make the parachutes work better. One important variable was the length of the string—it has to be long enough so that the cork can stabilize the whole thing. This example illus-

[10]A cork or any other softer material than a washer is less likely to hurt the child on the chin. A large carton such as the one shown in Photograph 11.28 makes it easier for young children to catch the washer. The length of the string can also be varied.

Photograph 11.28.

trates how essential it is that the teacher familiarize him or herself with how to make a toy before introducing it to the children. These preparations have often turned out to be an education in physical knowledge for the teachers and for us, and we have been struck by how little physics we know, even though, as adults, we have been observing physical phenomena a good number of years and have even had a few courses in physics.

The above toys are too hard for most four- and five-year-olds to make. We cite them nonetheless to show how physical-knowledge activities can be extended to the primary grades, as well as to show what teachers and volunteers *can* do with preschool children. The best way to use these ideas seems to be for the teacher to bring from home two or three of these toys already made, so that children can immediately get the idea of how to play with them. Once they have played with the finished product, they tend to be-

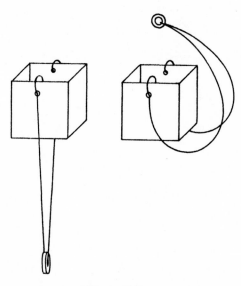

Figure 11.7.

come intrigued with the process of making it. If this task is too complex for preschoolers, they can observe how the toy is made and participate in certain decisions, such as where to cut the string and whether to use a big cork or a small one for a given parachute.

Caney, Steven. *Steven Caney's Toy Book.* New York: Workman Publishing, 1972.

Kazoo (p. 26). The materials used for this musical instrument are a paper tube (paper towel or toilet paper roll), wax paper, and rubber band. The child wraps a piece of wax paper around one open end of the tube as shown in Photograph 11.29, and puts a rubber band around to hold the wax paper tightly in place. About one inch from the same end, he punches a hole with a pencil.

To play this instrument, the child presses the open end of the kazoo against his face around his mouth, puckers his lips, and sings or hums any song.

Sand Combs (p. 79). Heavy cardboard (about 8 × 11 inches) is simply cut into various shapes such as those shown in Figure 11.8. (Thin wood is preferable, but requires a saw to cut it.) Children moisten sand as necessary to make patterns on it.

Photograph 11.29.

Ring and Pin (p. 100).   This toy resembles the Mexican balero discussed earlier, and is adapted for young children as shown in Photograph 11.30. It is made by tying one end of a string to a short stick, and the other

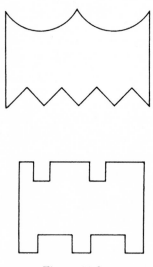

Figure 11.8.

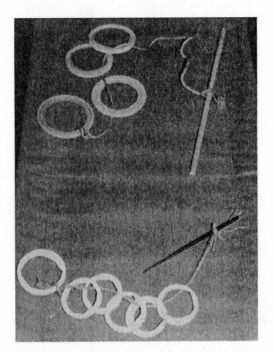

Photograph 11.30.

end to a ring, with a number of other rings placed in between (plastic lids with the center cut out). Photograph 11.31 shows the children trying to ring the pin.

Milk Carton Boat (p. 147).   Photograph 11.32 is self-explanatory, and children can see how the addition of the paper plate makes a difference in the way the boat moves.

Caney, Steven. *Steven Caney's Playbook*. New York: Workman Publishing, 1975.

Building with Cards (p. 25).   This activity involves making playing cards stand and lean against each other so as to retain their balance. Constructions with playing cards are too difficult for four- and five-year-olds, however, because cards are too thin. With thicker plaques, they can make elaborate constructions.

Pin Ball Machine (p. 28).   The materials required for this game are a piece of heavy cardboard, bobby pins, wax paper, and a button (or BB, bean, or coin). The child makes a kind of maze such as the one shown in Photograph 11.2, and the teacher cuts out holes that objects can fall through.

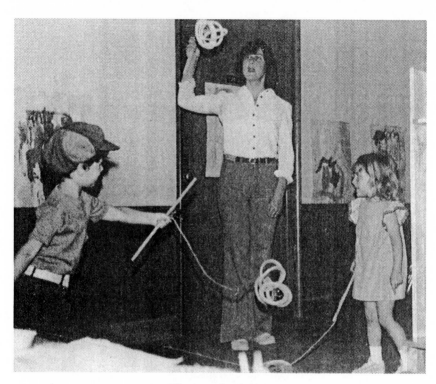

Photograph 11.31.

Photograph 11.32.

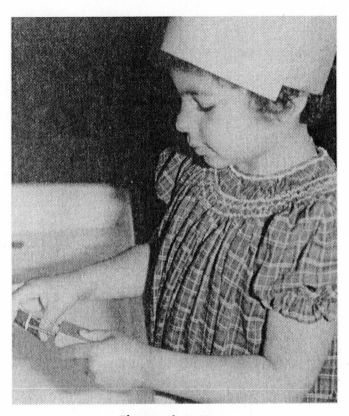

Photograph 11.33.

(Rubbing a piece of wax paper all over the surface of the cardboard makes it slippery.)

The object of the game is to tilt the board and make the button go from "Start" to "Finish" without falling off.

Paddle Block Boat (p. 113). The materials necessary for making this boat are a scrap block of wood, a thin, short strip of wood, two long nails, and a rubber band. The children (or teacher) make the boat, wind the paddle (Photograph 11.33), and then release it in the water (Photograph 11.34).

This is another example of a physics activity which served to educate both the teacher and the authors. We found that if the paddle is wound in one direction, it *pulls* the boat, thereby making it move slowly. If the paddle is wound in the opposite direction, it *pushes* the boat, thereby making it go much faster. The width and length of the paddle also make a difference, as do the width and length of the rubber band.

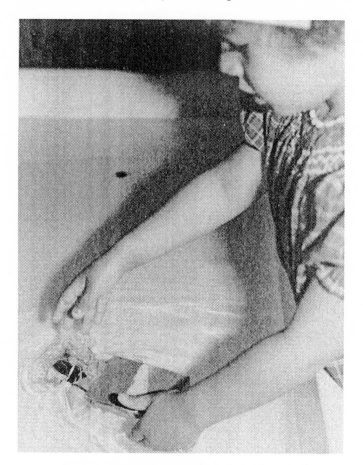

Photograph 11.34.

Children

Another important source of activities is children themselves. For example, the activity reported in Chapter 5 was developed by a teacher who picked up on a child's fortuitous discovery of a lever. In Chapter 1, we cited four projects suggested by children—putting a mixture of popcorn grease, water, and food coloring on the window sill to make "something"; demonstrating an experiment seen on television; putting a bar of soap into a cup of water; and cooking a mixture of beans, blue water, styrofoam packing materials, and Q-Tip.

Ideas like the above do not occur to children without cultivation by the teacher. They are generated and expressed only in an atmosphere created to

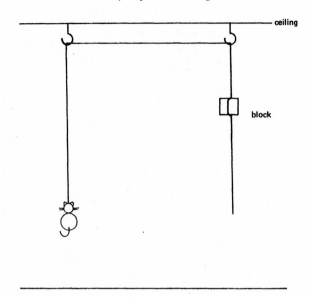

Figure 11.9.

open the way to experimentation. Then, as children begin to come up with ideas, the teacher encourages and elaborates them. To illustrate how the teacher can pick up on children's ideas, we present below an example from Capt, Glayre, and Hegyi (1976).[11]

In a class of four-year-olds, the teacher noticed one day that the children had great fun jumping up in order to touch the mobiles that were hanging down. Building on this action (one not listed at the beginning of this chapter), she made the arrangement shown in Figure 11.9. The cat could be held at various heights by pulling the other end of the string and holding it in place. (The block served as a counterweight as well as a stopper to maintain the string in position.) At first, the children jumped while the cat was swinging. Then they began to offer advice to each other such as:

"You jump too fast (= too soon)."

"Wait. It's moving!"

The children then began to vary the height of the cat in relation to their own height.

"Pull a little. I'm bigger," one said.

"It's too high," said another.

"Teacher, *you* don't even have to jump up," said a third.

[11]The memoire de licence of three teachers in the Geneva (Switzerland) Public Schools, written under the direction of the senior author of this book.

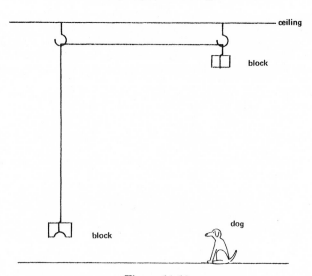

Figure 11.10.

After succeeding in touching the object, they usually asked to have it held higher and higher, until they could no longer reach it.

After some time, a child asked if he could have something else rather than the cat at the end of the string. The teacher tied a block to the string and introduced a toy dog as shown in Figure 11.10. The children first aimed the block at the target by pushing the string. They then moved the dog farther and farther away, continuing to push the string to hit the target, until, accidentally, one child let go of the string and saw that the block knocked the dog down. They then continued to release the pendulum, letting its own momentum take over.

Chapter 12

How to Integrate
Physical-Knowledge Activities
in an Ongoing Program

At the beginning of Part II, we explained that the activities described in Chapters 4–10 were carried out for three purposes: (1) to test and evaluate each activity to make sure that it is a good physical-knowledge activity; (2) to obtain the raw material for conceptualizing the principles of teaching that were presented in Chapter 3; and (3) to collect detailed materials for teacher training. Because we wanted to focus on how individual children played, we videotaped small numbers of children in each of these activities. In real life, however, the teacher has a much larger group of children and an ongoing program that includes a variety of other activities, such as pretend play, movement, stories, and so on. In this concluding chapter, therefore, we would like to discuss how the teacher can integrate physical-knowledge activities in an ongoing program.

The integration of physical-knowledge activities must be guided by the overall objectives of teaching that we discussed at the beginning of Chapter 3. The reader will recall that Piaget's constructivism implies first of all a socioemotional context which encourages the child's development of autonomy—his exchange of opinions with others, and his initiative, curiosity, and confidence. The teacher's first task is to create the kind of psychological environment which fosters these. Therefore, at the beginning of the year energy will be focused primarily on socializing children in classroom routines and getting them to pursue activities of their choice without continual conflicts. While children are still grabbing, hitting each other, and monopolizing toys, physical-knowledge activities which are easy to manage should be planned. Quiet activities like art (discussed shortly in connection with activity cards) are usually manageable during this period, but more boisterous ones like Rollers (Chapters 4 and 5) should be avoided until children can be trusted to play safely.

Piaget's framework / Child-development curriculum activities	Physical knowledge	Social knowledge	Logico-mathematical knowledge					Representation		
			Logico-arithmetical knowledge			Spatio-temporal knowledge				
			Classification	Seriation	Number	Spatial relationships	Temporal Relationships	Index	Symbol	Sign
Block building	X								X	
Painting	X								X	
Printing	X							X		
Pretend play		X							X	X
Listening to stories	X	X							X	X
Movement									X	
Cooking	X									
Playing with sand and water	X								X	
Playing with playground equipment	X									
Putting puzzles together									X	

Table 12-1. Activities other than "science" which are found in early education texts as well as in classrooms of teachers who use Piaget's theory.

The art of running a classroom which provides a good psychological environment has been mastered by many child-development teachers. In this and other ways, an educator who uses Piaget's theory to develop a preschool program can be said to be building on the child-development tradition in early education. In fact, a program derived from Piaget's theory includes most of the activities found in a child-development program (see Kamii and DeVries, 1977). Table 12.1 lists common aspects of both programs. the X's indicate what aspects of intellectual development are especially fostered by each activity when it is analyzed according to Piaget's theoretical framework.[1] While the types of activities that can be seen in our classrooms

[1]Since, in reality, all aspects of knowledge are present in all activities simultaneously, we could have put an "X" in almost every box of this matrix. However, it is useful to be aware of the predominant aspects of knowledge involved in each activity. In the logico-mathematical realm, we shaded the columns rather than putting in any "X" because a logico-mathematical framework is always involved in all activities.

are thus very similar to those that can be found in traditional nursery schools,[2] our reasons for including them are different. When the rationale for teaching is different, the "how" of teaching sometimes differs from the child-development approach. We saw one example of this at the beginning of Chapter 3, pp. 38–39.

One of the similarities between a child-development program and ours is that the day includes the following blocks of time: free play, snack, group time, and time for play outside. The question of how to integrate physical-knowledge activities will, therefore, be addressed in terms of how the teacher can plan these blocks of time. In addition, we will discuss the kinds of incidental situations which are golden opportunities for physical-knowledge activities because they arise naturally as part of life in and out of the classroom. Within this framework, we hope to give to the reader some "feel" for the continuity of activities over several days or several months.

During Free Play

Free play in our classrooms looks very much like that found in a child-development program. For this block of time, the teacher sets up the environment in such a way that children can freely choose from a variety of activities such as pretending in the "house" corner, building with blocks, painting, playing card and board games, putting puzzles together, and looking at books. Physical-knowledge activities can be integrated in this block of time in three ways which are not necessarily mutually exclusive: (1) by making materials available so that children can choose them just as they can choose any other activity; (2) by introducing an activity with a view to decreasing the teacher's involvement as children become more independent; and (3) by introducing an activity and staying involved with it for a relatively long period of time.

Making Materials Available for Children to Choose

The environment most conducive to the development of autonomy and initiative is one in which materials are easily accessible so that children can find interesting things to do with little or no help from the teacher. Autonomy and initiative are discouraged if children have to ask the teacher to hand them everything from a high shelf. Many alternatives from which children can choose should, therefore, be available on low shelves. Among the toys that the teacher can put out either on shelves or on tables are the following (which were described in Chapter 11): Multiway Rollway, Beat the

[2]One activity that we emphasize which is not found in child-development curricula is group games such as Tag.

8 Ball, Blockhead, and Don't Spill the Beans—all commercially available—plus such homemade toys as Pick-Up Sticks, the balance game, and Drop the Clothespins.

Every teacher knows that it takes more than good materials to achieve a smoothly running free-play time. However, the availability of fascinating materials contributes a great deal to the development of children's ability to choose and pursue activities on their own. Many readers, too, must have observed the dramatic change in a group of fretful, quarrelsome children when the teacher introduced something interesting for them to *do*! Arguments can come to a quick halt, and aimlessness can suddenly change to focused curiosity. The first goal for free play is to create the kind of physical and psychological climate in which children have so many delightful possibilities for action that "discipline" becomes only an occasional problem. This goal is not achieved overnight. It requires considerable investment of the teacher's energy at the beginning of the year to communicate expectations and possibilities to children, and to develop a relationship with each child. During free-play time, the teacher generally keeps an eye on what the entire group is doing, and goes from one activity to another unobtrusively to observe what might be going on in children's heads, raise a question if appropriate, and lend help when necessary.

Introducing an Activity with a View to Decreasing the Teacher's Involvement

Once the teacher has a smoothly running free-play period, he or she can begin to initiate some activities requiring concentrated involvement, especially when there is more than one adult in the room. Cooking and woodworking are examples of the type of activity requiring constant involvement at first which can be decreased as children become more independent. Although woodworking, especially, will always require supervision in terms of safety, it is realistic to expect children to become able to pursue these activities with very little help.

Cooking.[3]   Planning for independence in cooking (as part of the teacher's effort to foster the child's development of autonomy) means setting up the situation so that children can figure out what to do and how to do it.

---

[3]Although we mention cooking as an activity to introduce only after establishing a smoothly running free-play period, one teacher colleague expressed the view that there are sometimes advantages to introducing it earlier. She recounts her experience in a difficult kindergarten class, where she was having trouble establishing a cooperative socioemotional context partly because children did not believe her.

Teachers with whom we have worked find it indispensable to have available homemade recipe books which the children can follow. Figure 12.1 shows the pages from one of the easiest recipes—popsicles—which they use early in the year when children are learning the routine of cooking. The final page shows the end product, and the first page pictures all the necessary ingredients and utensils. Each page thereafter contains a single direction, with a clear picture of what to do. Figure 12.2 shows the pages from a more difficult recipe—one for cupcakes.

The untrained adult tends to focus on getting a cooking project completed successfully rather than on helping children to learn. When the purpose is viewed as getting the cupcakes made for snack time, too much help of the wrong kind is usually given to children. Cooking should be used as an occasion for children to *co-operate*, thereby developing autonomy. In this socioemotional context, the teacher can also consider the intellectual possibilities of cooking—temporal reasoning, quantification, and the "reading" of pictures and words in recipes.

The routine for cooking in one of our classrooms of four- and five-year-olds begins with the selection of the cook. On the wall is a list of all the children in the class, and everybody knows that the person whose name is at the top of this list is the next cook. This cook picks an assistant cook, and the two decide together which recipe to select for the next day. They check to make sure they have everything they will need, and the teacher makes a list of what is needed if something is missing. (Later in the year, the children can make the list themselves.) They "read" the recipe to make sure they know what to do. The next day, they have to decide who is going to break the egg, stir, put in the chocolate chips, and so forth. Finally, they serve their classmates.

Co-operation often begins with a disagreement over what recipe to select! We observed one cook spend a long time trying to persuade his assistant that popsicles really *will* taste better than pudding. When this argument did not work, he finally got his friend to agree to popsicles because he was cook; he promised to go along with his friend when the roles were later reversed. Such situations are invaluable for moral development, as the children are highly motivated to negotiate and compromise, both in order to have the fun of doing the project and to accomplish something.

In the beginning, it will be necessary for the teacher to help children

---

(Their experience in the institution had already convinced them that teachers were not to be trusted.) Cooking turned out to be the political magic this teacher needed. In order to demonstrate that they would get their turn to do something special as promised, she planned cooking every day. After a while, they became convinced that this teacher was one whom they could trust.

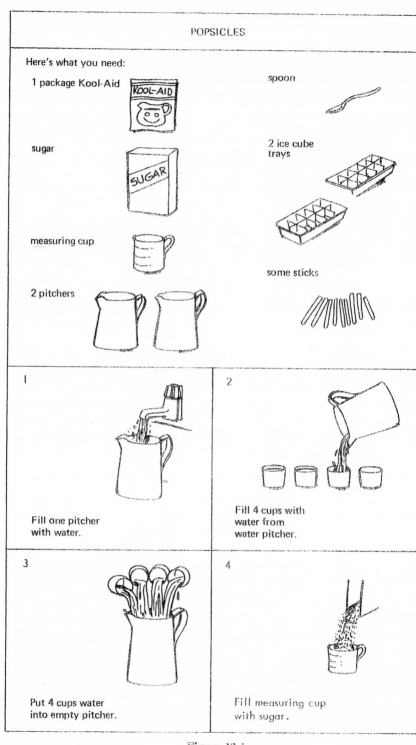

Figure 12-1.

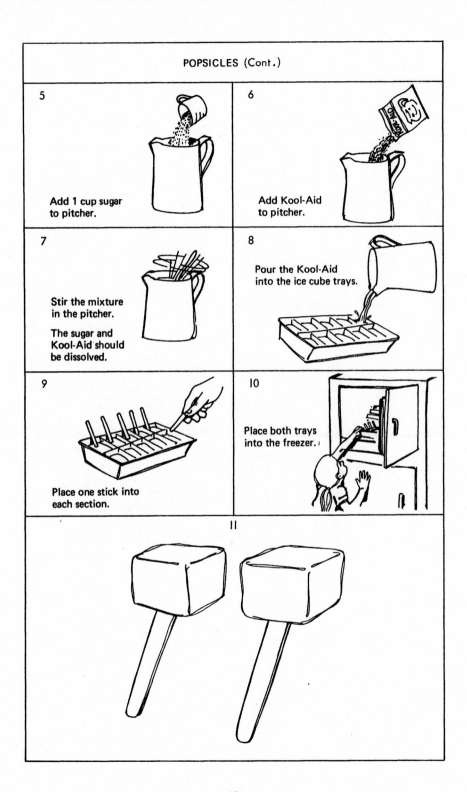

POPSICLES (Cont.)

5 Add 1 cup sugar to pitcher.

6 Add Kool-Aid to pitcher.

7 Stir the mixture in the pitcher.

The sugar and Kool-Aid should be dissolved.

8 Pour the Kool-Aid into the ice cube trays.

9 Place one stick into each section.

10 Place both trays into the freezer.

11

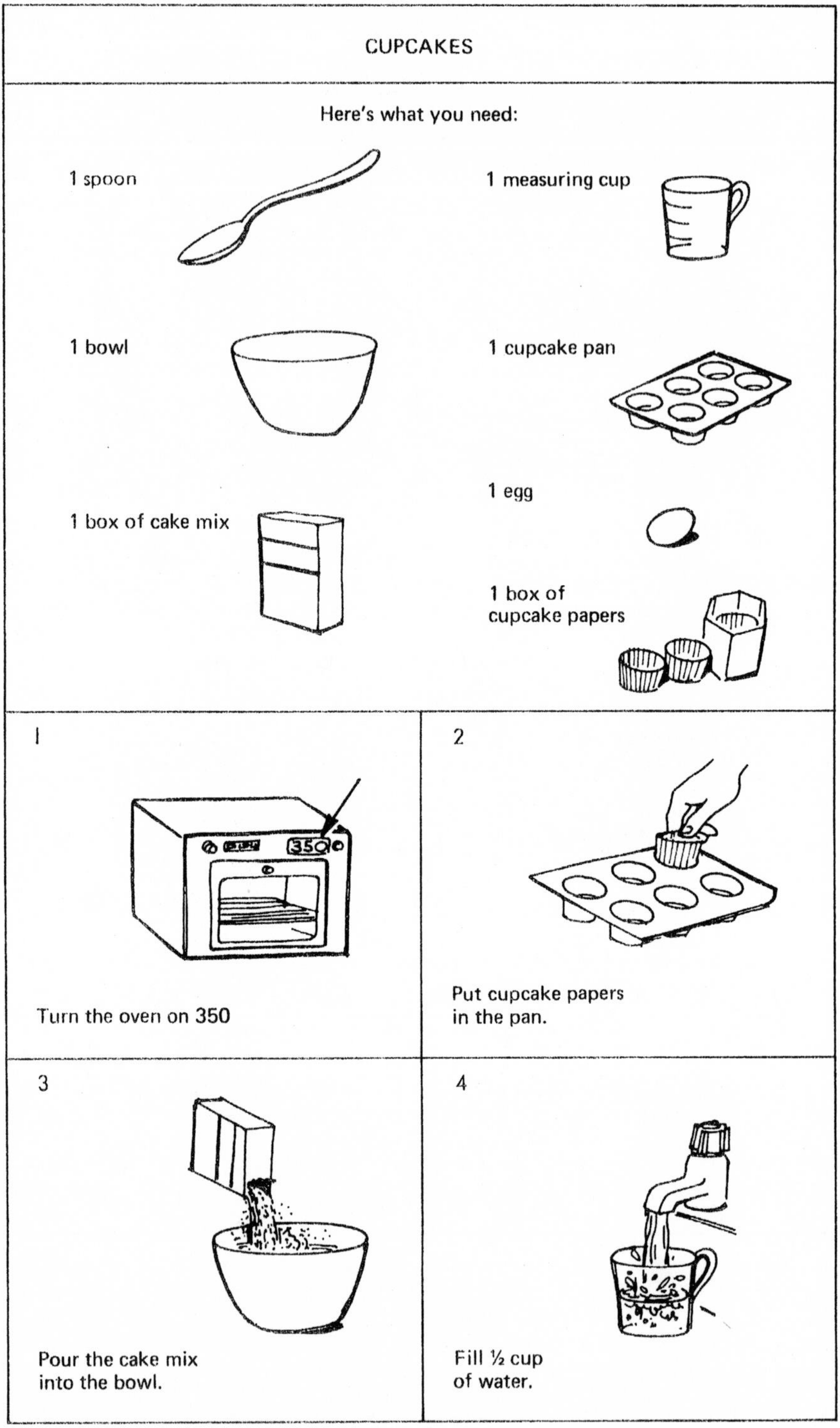

CUPCAKES

Here's what you need:

1 spoon

1 measuring cup

1 bowl

1 cupcake pan

1 box of cake mix

1 egg

1 box of
cupcake papers

I	2
Turn the oven on 350	Put cupcake papers in the pan.

3	4
Pour the cake mix into the bowl.	Fill ½ cup of water.

Figure 12-2.

5

Add the water
to the bowl.

6

Add one (1) egg
to the bowl.

7

Stir all the ingredients
until they are mixed
together.

8

Fill each cupcake
hole ½ full.

9

Put the pan
in the oven.

10

Bake for 20 minutes.

11

become conscious of the need to cooperate and anticipate events by asking questions such as:

> Whom would you like to ask to be your assistant cook?
> How can you agree on what to cook?
> Did you ask your assistant if that's O.K. with him?
> Have you checked together to make sure you have everything you will need?
> What does the recipe say to do first?
> How can you decide who gets to stir first? Maybe you'd better talk it over and come to an agreement. Can you figure out a fair way?

In this social context, cooking provides opportunities for children to use—and thereby develop—their intelligence. The advantages of being able to "read" the recipe motivates children to try to read the pictures and accompanying words. It is in such a highly meaningful and useful situation that beginning reading is best taught. Children who want to cook have their own reason for wanting to read, rather than somebody else's reason—such as the teacher's desire to conduct a scheduled reading time. Cooking also motivates children to think about time. They have to anticipate the ingredients and tools they will need, and decide what has to be done first, second, and third (sequence of events). After putting the cupcakes in the oven, or the Jello in the refrigerator, they have to wait for a certain interval. Cooking also promotes quantification. If they add too much or too little milk to the pudding, the "proof of the pudding" will let them find out that it is important to mix the right amounts. Preschool teachers should note, however, that children do not have the same conventional tastes as adults. Therefore, *anything* they make can taste super, and we must be careful not to impose our own, perhaps jaded, standards on them.

Interacting with children in a way that fosters their independence is truly a difficult art. The principle to keep in mind in cooking is to encourage children to figure out what to do next by relying on the recipe rather than on the teacher. There are, however, times when the teacher has to intervene directly rather than allowing children to make discoveries that are irreparable and traumatic. How to be out of the picture as much as possible and yet present when necessary can be learned only by trial and error and by knowing each child's personality. By spring of the school year, many pairs of four- and five-year-olds are able to carry out entire projects from beginning to end (including washing and cleaning up), and they surprise us with how much they can do when they are encouraged to become independent. By Mother's Day, for example, some four- and many five-year-olds can make ready-mix cupcakes with almost no help from the teacher.

Woodworking.   In woodworking, children find out and compare the properties of objects and figure out how to cut things and make them stay together. They thus engage in spatial reasoning as well as representation. For example, if they want an airplane or boat for their pretend play, the teacher can suggest that they make one out of wood.

If the project is putting nails in a board for a design with string, rubber bands, or yarn, the teacher can ask, "What design will that arrangement make?" or "What kind of design do you want to make?" At first children are interested mainly in the action of nailing. However, as they get experience with stringing, they begin to be more aware of the relationship between the placement of nails and the resulting design. The teacher can show these designs at group time and casually remark, "Jennifer made a wide design by spreading her nails far apart," or "Does the design look different when you wind the string around a lot?" These kinds of comments and questions have the effect over time of helping children anticipate and plan how they want their design to turn out.

Seeing a filmstrip on the making of musical instruments inspired one group of children to make guitars out of wood, nails, and rubber bands.[4] In this activity, the teacher helped the children think about what they were doing by judiciously asking questions such as the following:

How should we fix the rubber band?
What does the loose band sound like?
How can we change the sounds?
Are you going to make a lot of low sounds (in low voice) or a lot of high sounds (in high voice)?
Are there things in the room that will make musical sounds?
Can you invent your own instrument?

In this activity, one child made a drum out of wood. He worked for a long time and finally had a reasonable facsimile of a box. Everyone else had drums made out of oatmeal boxes, and he was extremely proud to have the only wooden one. However, when he played it with his hands, he was disappointed to find out that the oatmeal boxes sounded a lot better. It was at this point that the teacher suggested he try a stick.

Like cooking, woodworking is a physical-knowledge activity from which the teacher can withdraw when the children have had enough experience in how to produce desired effects and what precautions to take. Although the teacher's role *then* becomes primarily advisory, he or she still has to remain alert to problems preschoolers cannot always anticipate.

Introducing an Activity and Staying with It

Although children can have many good physical-knowledge experiences without the teacher, or with limited teacher supervision, it is important as soon as possible after the beginning of the school year to plan at least one activity per day in which the teacher stays involved in a concentrated

[4]They also made tambourines out of paper plates, bottle caps, and seeds, shakers out of toilet-paper rolls, cardboard, and popsicle sticks, various mouth instruments, and African thumb pianos. The teachers found the book *Musical Instruments Recipe Book* (Elementary Science Study, 1971) an excellent resource.

way. This may require a second adult in the room to oversee other activities and free the teacher from interruptions. Teachers whose children develop the most initiative and the richest ideas feel strongly that this would not occur if they did not regularly and intensively involve themselves in physical-knowledge activities. They state that the more the teacher introduces exciting activities and is available to intervene at appropriate moments, the more often children come up with ideas of their own.

The principles of teaching presented in Chapter 3 are intended especially for concentrated physical-knowledge activities. Most of the activities discussed in Chapters 4–11 could be selected as the "special" physical-knowledge activity of the day. We cite three additional examples for a variety of reasons. The first one, Shadow Play, was selected because it is limited in scope and relatively easy for the beginning teacher to do. The second example, Making Boats, was selected because it illustrates continuity and elaboration over about two weeks with a large group of kindergarten children. The third example, Printing, was chosen because it is an old and familiar activity which can be done differently by using Piaget's ideas.

Shadow play.   Setting a light source (a slide projector) so that a clear shadow can be produced against a wall, one teacher brought a variety of objects collected from around the room and began by asking children not to look, but to guess the object by looking at its shadow. Then the children collected things for one another to guess, and when one child made no effort to conceal his objects, the others said, "You're not supposed to let us see 'cause then we know what it is." The teacher suggested they try to guess people from their shadows, had the children hide their eyes, and tapped one at a time to stand in front of the light. When this got too easy, the teacher took a turn and put on a hat and scarf. All the children then began to try various disguises to fool the guessers. The activity concluded with the children making silhouette drawings of one another.

Making boats.   An activity on sinking and floating led to an interest in making boats. At group time at the end of one day, Ms. Ellis mentioned, "Tomorrow there will be some special things at the water table. If you want to, you can check to see if they sink or float when you put them in the water." Over the next three or four days, children tried the objects and added many of their own choice from around the room. At group time each day, the teacher asked what they were finding out. She made cards with a picture of each object, and the children discussed whether it should go on the "float" or "sink" side of a large cardboard on which she drew a line in the middle to separate the two categories. Differences of opinion arose over some of the objects. For example, some children found that the bottle cap floated, and some found that it sank. The teacher suggested that they show one another the next day how they got the cap to do both. This discussion led to the need for placing certain cards *right on the line* dividing the display into two distinct categories so that the card would straddle both.

This discussion on sinking and floating led the teacher into questions about boats. She asked what boats are made of and how such heavy things could float. The lively responses were of the type "Because boats always float," and "Oh, no, they sink sometimes." The teacher encouraged this exchange of opposing views, left the question open, and offered to meet the next day with anyone who wanted to find out more about boats in a book about them. To the five who responded the next day, she showed *The Big Book of Real Boats and Ships* (Zaffo, 1951), read a bit of it to them, and showed them pictures of a fireboat, an ocean liner, a tugboat, a hospital ship, and other boats. Ms. Ellis then asked if the children would like to make their own boats. When they said they would, she said she would bring things the next day for them to use.

As promised, the teacher brought soap, sponges, styrofoam, wood, nails, washers, bottle caps, lids, toilet paper rolls, and other similar materials. She asked, "Which things can you use to make a boat?" As the children began their projects, they found out that the sponge got soggy and, therefore, did not work, and that some cakes of soap did float while others did not. Most of them thus ended up making their boats out of wood. After selecting or cutting the wood, the teacher encouraged them to check to make sure it would float. The children then elaborated their boats. Inspired by the pictures they had seen, they often had ideas they could not carry out by themselves. The teacher helped them take nails out, put pieces together in ways *they* decided on, and figure out, for example, how to make a toilet paper roll stick on the wood. When Jim tried to use his boat before the glue was dry, the paper roll fell off, and the teacher asked, "Do you think it might work if you let the glue dry first?" When some children put so many nails in their boats that the wood sank, she asked, "What can we do to fix it so it will float again?" She encouraged the children to test their boats in the water each time they added something new.

When one child wanted to put a flag on his boat, Ms. Ellis brought in a book of flags, and everyone got interested in making cloth and paper flags for their boats. Two filmstrips on boats were shown, and, finally, the teacher suggested having a boat race. Some children were reluctant, and the teacher suspected they knew that their beautiful boats were actually unwieldy in the water. When she assured them that everybody could be a winner, however, they all responded enthusiastically. Preparations were elaborate—children even made tickets and planned who would make and sell Kool-Aid and popcorn. The teacher suggested that four children at a time race their boats, and she worked out groupings so that the matches would not be too one-sided. The children voted that everyone could have four tickets, and that they could each decide whether to buy two Kool-Aids and two popcorns, or one popcorn and three Kool-Aids, etc.

When it was time for the race, the teacher asked, "How can you make your boat go?" At first, the racers decided to move their boats by pushing them with their hands, and the teacher asked, "Don't you think it's too easy that way? Is there another way you can figure out to make them move?" Somebody suggested blowing them, so this technique was used for a while. Then the teacher set up a fan and asked, "Do you think the fan will move the boats?" Everyone received a ribbon and was pleased, even though they knew whose boats were first, second, third, and fourth.

This activity spanned a period of about two weeks, and is an example of how physical knowledge (about floating and sinking, construction, and movement across the water) can be integrated with social knowledge (about names of boats, flags, social and moral rules), ordering (who finishes the race first, second, third, and fourth), and number (four tickets being used in a combination of ways). The teacher's role was critical for the organization of this rather complicated activity as well as for the usual intervention to pose questions and extend children's thinking.

Printing. Over several weeks, the teacher introduced blow painting, string painting, and various kinds of printing. After making prints with sponges, raw potatoes, and carrots, the teacher asked children one day if they could find things in the room to make prints with. She showed them how a Lego block could be used to make an unusual print, and the children excitedly ran around the room to see what they could find. Some tried other Lego blocks, and others brought Tinker Toys, spoons, beads, forks, and small blocks. As they worked, the teacher tried various objects along with the children and encouraged them to place the objects on their sides or along an edge.

After several experiences with a variety of objects in the room, the teacher asked the children at group time if they thought they might be able to find things outside that would make interesting prints. When they went outdoors, the children collected many things, including a dandelion, cotton, a beer can, leaves, sticks, bottle tops, gum wrappers, and rocks. The children talked excitedly about what they were going to print. Everybody scoffed at the beer can, saying, "That's dumb! You can't print with that!" Jean told Kevin that his gum wrappers would get wet in the paint. He responded with conviction, "I'm gonna' make a gum wrapper print." Later, there were many surprises. Sara was surprised that the dandelion withered and she was unable to make a flower print. The blob she got with the dandelion was not at all what she expected. The cotton failed to make a fluffy shape! To everyone's amazement, including its discoverer's, the beer can turned out to be the most exciting of all, and the teacher encouraged the children to roll it, make circles, and use the rim to make surves.

After about two months of many kinds of painting and printing activities, the teacher decorated the bulletin board with pieces of the children's work she had saved. For about two weeks, no one seemed to notice the new array. Then, one day during lunch, Jeff sat facing the board as he munched on a sandwich. Suddenly, he pointed to a print and said to his friend, Jessie, "There's mine. I made that with a potato." Jessie responded, "Oh, yeah, I remember that. There's mine." The teacher picked up on this interest and asked, "How did you do your design, Jessie?" Jean ran to get a Lego and pointed to a print, saying, "This is that." The children excitedly talked with one another, saying, "Where's yours?" "That looks like a horse." "That looks like a firecracker." "How did you do that?"

Printing involves causal relationships between objects and the traces that can be made with them. In the above situation, the teacher encouraged children to find a variety of objects *they* wanted to make traces with. She also encouraged them to use the same object in different ways to create a variety of traces.

It is extremely interesting to note the physical knowledge of the children who thought that a dandelion and a piece of cotton were better materials than a beer can. They expected the dandelion and cotton to react to the action of printing in a way more similar to the materials they had tried than would a beer can. Young children have to act on the object in many different ways physically before they become able to manipulate it mentally and anticipate how different objects will react.

Holiday themes work well into these physical-knowledge activities in which the teacher remains involved in a concentrated way. At Halloween time, making costumes, roasting pumpkin seeds, and making paper lanterns are popular activities. Making candles for Mother's Day, dyeing Easter eggs, and making Christmas ornaments must already have come to the reader's mind.

Sometimes, an "ordinary" activity should be selected for concentrated involvement The water play in Chapters 9 and 10 illustrates how, by staying with children, the teacher can help them enrich their play in an everyday activity. Such enrichment of an "old" activity raises the level of play when children are again left to their own devices.

For days when a "special" activity seems appropriate, many teachers make the planning of physical-knowledge activities easier by developing activity cards filed and cross-referenced under such categories as "Holidays," "Wax and Crayon," "Painting," "Dyeing," "Construction," and "Musical Instruments." We give some examples from the card file of Ms. Ellis and Ms. Fineberg, whose observations are sometimes recorded as helpful reminders of what to expect and what mistakes to avoid. Although we are unable to trace the sources of these ideas, most undoubtedly came from books such as those referred to earlier on arts and crafts and how to make toys.

Under "Christmas Presents."

Snowstorms

"Snowstorms" makes use of the phenomenon of sinking in water. Each child takes a baby food jar and uses marine glue to stick a plastic snowman, Santa or deer to the inside of the cover. He then fills the jar with water (when the glue is completely dry), adds about one teaspoon of glitter or moth flakes, and screws the top on *tightly*. When he shakes the jar and puts it down (upside down), he gets the effect of a snowstorm just like those he may have seen in souvenir gift shops.

Under "Wax and Crayons."

Making Candles

For Mother's Day presents we made candles, which is really a simple process. Kids tie a 4-inch wick to the end of a pencil and, holding on only to the pencil, they dip the wick in and out of colored hot wax. After each dip in hot wax, they dip it in cold water. Eventually a small candle is formed. It was a good physical-knowledge activity and children even learned how to make layers of color.

Wax Paper and Crayons

Shave or finely chop old crayons of different colors. Place a piece of wax paper on a towel, then crayon shavings, then another piece of wax paper, then another towel. Iron, counting to 25, 30, or whatever. Crayon will melt to make pretty designs. Leaves, flowers, glitter, etc., can also be placed between the wax paper.

Wax paper can be cut into circles, squares, triangles, etc., to influence designs.

Under "Painting."

Marble Painting

At group time, I showed the children a design I had made and asked them to guess how I made it. After a number of guesses, I said, "Those are good guesses. I probably could have done it like that, but let me show you what I did." I showed them a shoebox and a marble and demonstrated dipping the marble in paint and rolling it in the box. I asked if anybody wanted to try marble painting the next day.

The next day, I had various sized boxes and construction paper. The children cut the paper to fit inside each box. During the activity, I asked questions such as:

Where do you need to tip the box to make the marble roll this way?
How can you get the marble to make a zig-zag design?
How can you get your marble to make a design over here?
What would happen if you used more than one marble?

Salt Snow Paint
(Dries very hard. Looks like snow.)

Mix the following together and paint:

1 part liquid starch
1 part water
2 parts salt
Few shakes white powder tempera paint

Can substitute sand (and different color tempera) to make sand paint for desert scenes.

Tempera Shake

Put dry powdered tempera in yogurt containers. Put water in other yogurt containers. Punch holes in top. Shake paint and water onto construction paper in either order. Provide pans to shake/roll excess off paper. Makes pretty designs.

Under "Dyeing."

Tye-Dye

We wrote notes home to parents asking for white T-shirts or cloth that we could use to tie-dye. We used Rit dye: blue, yellow, and red. We mixed dye in large bowls. (Dye crystals dissolved in hot water.) Kids put rubber bands around sections of material to be dyed. Dipped protruding portions of T-shirt into dye. T-shirts were dried and rubber bands removed.

Paper Towel Tie-Dye

Prepare various jars of food color water, fold thick paper towel into square, triangle, rectangle, etc., wads, and dip corners into different colors. Open paper towels and let dry.

Under "Constructions (Balancing)."

Straw Construction I

Cut straws into various lengths. Leave some whole. On corrugated cardboard bases, use small straight pins to build straws onto bases and off of other straws. Paint or decorate when finished (Photograph 12.1).

Photo 12-1.

Straw Construction II

By sucking string through straws and eventually connecting them many "fluid" constructions can be made. The straws bend and fold, making interesting shapes (Figure 12.3).

Spaghetti and Clay Construction

Materials: Cardboard or posterboard cut into various shapes, uncooked spaghetti, and clay.

Play with clay until soft. Use small pieces and stick spaghetti into them and build off one another. Clay bases will stick together (Photograph 12.2).

Figure 12-3. Straw construction II.

Photo 12-2.

Styrofoam Structures

Use small bits of styrofoam and toothpicks to build interesting structures.

Paper Strip Sculptures

I initiated this activity by putting out on the art table a model I had made (Photograph 12.3). When several children came over to look at it, I asked

Photo 12-3.

Photo 12-4.

them if they wanted to try to make one. I put out glue, cardboard for bases, and precut strips of construction paper. As the children set to work, I noticed that they were putting glue over the entire length of the paper strip. Several glued one strip flat on the base, and others were struggling in various ways to get a curved piece to stay on. Jim began by curving one long strip over the wide base. I then showed the children how to fold the ends of a strip slightly and put glue just on the edges. They easily learned to do this, and nearly everybody succeeded in making a row of loops on their bases (see Photograph 12.4).

When they began the second row, however, no one realized that each loop had to begin at the middle of a bottom loop. Everybody had the idea of putting loops directly above the bottom ones, and they were quite surprised when the weight of the top loop made the bottom one sink (see Photograph 12.5)! I sympathized and wondered aloud, "How can we fix it so it stays up?" I suggested looking at the model, and one child figured out what to do. He showed the others, and everyone went on putting on more loops.

At one point Ann arranged a wide loop on her base, looked closely at the model, and then decided she wanted a loop underneath. "I want one to go from here to here," she told me. I asked what she had to do, and to my surprise, Ann responded by taking off the first big loop in order to put the other one beneath! I asked, "Did you have to take the top one off in order to get the other one under?" and Ann nodded with certainty.

One child commented, "It's stretched funny." I asked, "Is it harder to put the loops on top?" and Kevin offered helpfully to a friend who

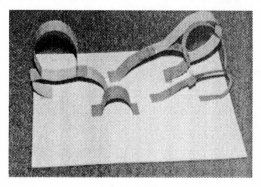

Photo 12-5.

Photo 12-6.

was having trouble getting his top loop to stick, "You have to count to ten. You only have to count to five on the flat cardboard." I joined in counting to ten as I worked on a sculpture of my own, occasionally asking children to suggest how I could get a piece to stay on or whether there was any way to get a piece to go from one point to another.

Roly Poly Dolls

I showed the children a doll I had made by cutting a ping-pong ball in half, stuffing it with modeling clay, and decorating a stick stuck in the clay as a doll (see Photograph 12.6). I demonstrated how the doll always popped up again when rolled on its side. The children were fascinated with this toy and eagerly set to work to make their own. When a child failed to get his stick in the middle, the doll would not stand up, and I helped by asking questions such as, "Is there another way you could fix the stick so the doll will stand up?" I was also available to help with problems encountered as the children worked to attach a body and head to the stick and to decorate it.

As they began to play with their finished products, I asked, "Do you think you can do anything so it won't pop back up?" Several children tried in various ways to see if they could make the doll lie down. One child tried holding the doll on its side awhile, then longer and longer. Others tried dropping the doll on the floor, and were amused each time the doll popped back up. One child thought that if she dropped it from a high enough point, it might stay down. She climbed on a chair to drop it, then on the desk, and then asked me to help her pile books on the desk! After four or five days of playing with the dolls, the children noticed that the clay had shrunk and that the ping-pong ball came off. They were surprised that the dolls still worked.

Under "Magnets."

Fishing

The children put one or more paper clips on the fish that they had cut out. After putting them in the "ocean" (on the floor), they took fishing poles with a magnet at the end of the string and fished from a platform. Aiming the magnet to make a contact with a paper clip is not easy and is, therefore, a physical-knowledge problem in itself. The integration of physical-knowledge activities into this kind of pretend play seems often to increase children's involvement.

Under "The Movement of Objects."

Hockey

Version 1:   The children make an enclosure with blocks and use a checker and two chopsticks. Each player tries to flick the checker with his stick through a corner gap between the blocks. Players keep score of the number of "goals" each gets.

Version 2:   The same enclosure with blocks is used, but the "goals" are arch blocks that stand like tunnels. The children use a marble (or ball bearing) and a stick to roll the marble through their "tunnels."

Version 3:   The players use straws to blow a ping-pong ball into their opponent's shoebox as shown in Figure 12.4.

Version 4:   The idea is exactly the same as Version 3 except that the ping-pong ball floats on water in the water table. The goal for each player is anywhere on the side where the opponent is standing.

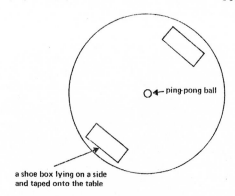

a shoe box lying on a side
and taped onto the table

Figure 12-4. Blow soccer.

In concluding this section on free-play time, we would like to emphasize once again the importance of the teacher's planning this block of time so as to allow him or herself to get involved intensively in at least one physical-knowledge activity every day. In classrooms where we have observed the children to be full of initiative and creative ideas, we find teachers who regularly involve themselves in a concentrated way in these activities. In one teacher's words, "The more excited and interested I am in children's ideas, the more contagious the spirit of experimentation is, and as the year goes by, I hear more and more children saying to one another, 'Hey, I have an idea . . .,' 'Let's try it this way . . .,' 'I know what we can do. . . .' "

During Group Time

Some activities that are well suited for group time include singing, finger plays, movement, listening to stories, acting out stories, and certain group games such as "Indian Chief."[5] While group time is thus not especially appropriate for physical-knowledge activities, it can be used to support them. The few minutes the teacher spends introducing or discussing an activity, for example, can make an enormous difference in how it later begins or becomes elaborated. (When we say "group time" here, we include snack and lunch time as periods the children spend together rather than being engaged in various activities of their own in different parts of the room.)

The only way group time can be used in connection with physical-knowledge activities is to focus children's thinking on them beforehand or afterwards. Before an activity, the teacher can introduce it, encourage children to compare predictions, and discuss different ways of producing a desired effect. After an activity, he or she can reflect with children on what they did and found out and what ideas they had. We give examples of each of these approaches.

Before an Activity

Introducing a new activity or a new toy. We saw in the activity on making boats that *after* reading a book about boats, the teacher asked if any children wanted to make their own boats. When they all responded positively, she promised to bring in materials the next day. Another example of introducing a physical-knowledge activity at the end of group time was seen

[5]In this game, "It" goes out of the room while the rest of the group sitting in a circle selects an Indian Chief. The Chief does a variety of actions for the other children to imitate, such as clapping, then shaking both hands, then hopping. By watching the group who imitate the Chief, "It" has to guess which child is the Indian Chief.

in the printing activity. After some experience with printing, the teacher asked the children if they might be able to find things ouside that would make interesting prints.

It is not always a good idea to introduce an activity the day before because, sometimes, children cannot wait to get started. However, the groundwork that is laid the day before often makes the difference between the success or failure of an activity. When children have chosen to make boats, for example, they come to school having thought about what to do and are committed to a certain idea.

Another example of using group time to introduce an activity is the introduction of the workbench. The teacher can explain what it is for and what safety precautions must be taken. She can also try to get an agreement about how the group will take turns using the workbench.

An effective way to introduce the making of certain toys is for the teacher to make two or three models and show them to the entire group. For example, at the end of group time, just before going out, he or she can show a couple of homemade "kites" and explain that they can be flown outside (see Photographs 11.3 and 11.4), and that later on those wanting to make their own may do so. If the teacher is careful not to pressure children into making a replica of the model, this is a good way to introduce a toy for children to make. Children need to have a clear idea of the finished product before they can be motivated to make a toy. It is interesting to note that, when they are encouraged to do the same thing in different ways, children will "copy" a model in many different ways. With the "kite," for example, some children attach two strings to the brown bag but do not even open the bag as they run around "flying" it. Others open the bag but make a much smaller hole in the bottom of the bag. *Generally, we find that creativity is stimulated when children have a limited range of possibilities within which they are encouraged to come up with their own ideas.*

Comparing predictions.   An example of comparing predictions was given when we discussed printing. As the reader will recall, all the children thought the beer can was a dumb idea. One child told another that his gum wrapper would get wet (and messed up) in the paint, but the latter insisted, "I'm gonna' make a gum wrapper print!" The comparison of predictions is a good way to get children to think about the outcome of an action. It is also a good way to get them committed to an idea and to see that other people have different ideas.

Another example of this approach was used by the teacher who picked up on one child's idea of cooking a cupfull of stuff (beans, blue water, styrofoam packing materials, and a Q-Tip). She asked him to tell about his experiment at group time, and everyone became involved in making predictions, which she wrote on the blackboard. The next day, after the child did his experiment and wrote down the results with the teacher's help, the group discussed what happened and which predictions were borne out. We feel that this is one of the best ways to introduce reading and writing. As the teacher writes down each child's prediction, and reads back what he or she wrote the previous day, the children get the idea that this is a neat way to remember what might otherwise be forgotten.

Discussing how to produce a desired effect.   In Chapter 11, we referred to Ms. Ellis' idea about how to make Jello turn back into a red liquid. She asked all the children to save a little bit of their Jello, and at group time wondered aloud if they could think of a way to turn it back into red water again. As we reported there, the children suggested putting various things in, such as salt, baking powder, and water, and letting it stand all night. When they could see that nothing they had suggested worked, Ms. Ellis proposed the idea of heating the Jello. All the children thought that was a dumb idea and did not even want to try it. She persuaded them to try it anyway, and the result was a big surprise to them.

This discussion approach was also helpful in solving another physical-knowledge problem: children's tendency to pick up long blocks with one end and hit someone or something because they are not aware of how the other end of the block is moving. When such problems arose during free play, the teacher asked at group time if the children could think of a way to carry the blocks so they didn't hit anything. One child suggested holding the block over their heads. The teacher asked him to demonstrate, and the children decided that it was still sticking out and might hit something—like the teacher. After a while, they decided that they should carry the long blocks down close to their bodies.

Group time can be used to discuss how to produce other desired effects that are inextricably related to children's moral development. Some examples are the problem of messy soap and paint in the bathroom sink, how to get the griddle clean, and how to repair broken things. By respecting every idea that is offered and caring about the feelings of each child, the teacher can stimulate a feeling of community in which children will construct *their own rules*, rooted in the need *they* feel for cleanliness and objects that are not broken.

After an Activity

Discussing what the children did and observed.   In the activity involving the sinking and floating of objects, we reported that at group time each day the teacher asked the children what they were finding out. We also noted that the teacher made cards with a picture of each object, and that the children discussed whether it should go on the "float" or "sink" side of the chart. Reflecting on what happened during an activity is important not only because children may now be able to create connections they could not previously establish, but also because it can enable them to find out that other people observed different phenomena.

The follow-up after the printing activity is another example of a discussion that stimulated children to think about what they did. As the reader will recall, the teacher put the children's artwork on the bulletin board. After quite some time had elapsed, one child spontaneously noticed, "There's mine. I made that with a potato." Another child ran to get a piece of Lego and said, "This is that." On these occasions, the teacher can ask questions such as, "Can you pick out all the other traces Paul made with his beer can?"

It is easy to overdo this aspect of discussion. It should always be kept in mind that children's interest in talking about activities is limited. Again, we invoke the word "sparingly" to describe the amount of teacher talk. To the extent that children seem interested, discussion may be good, but the teacher should be sensitive to responses which indicate that the discussion is more for the teacher's benefit than the children's.

Pointing out the "wonderful ideas" children had. As we mentioned in connection with woodworking, the teacher showed certain products at group time and casually made remarks such as, "Jennifer made a wide design by spreading her nails far apart." On another occasion the teacher observed one child's variation of a pendulum experiment. The pendulum consisted of a block (the bob), a pulley attached to a light fixture hanging from the ceiling, and a rope. One end of the rope was free so that the height of the bob could be adjusted by pulling it or releasing it. Usually, when pairs of children played together, one child held the rope at the proper height, while the other aimed at the target. One day, however, Randy could find no one to play with, and his problem was what to do with the rope. For a while he held the end of the rope as he aimed the bob with the other hand. Deciding that this was too awkward, he then thought of tying the end to a chair. Then, however, he had to adjust the location of the chair to make the bob stay at the right height. Since this was a solution the teacher thought would interest other children, she said at group time, "I saw some really interesting things today. One of them was Randy's idea of how to play with the pendulum all by himself. Would you like to show us what you did, Randy?"

For the child who is asked to show what he did, this is a moment of recognition, as well as an opportunity to practice public speaking. We feel that this is a much better way for children to take turns talking about something than the usual "show and tell," which tends to be a juxtaposition of unconnected accounts rather than an opportunity for children to compare the interesting things they did. If the teacher is careful not to praise the same children all the time, this kind of discussion can stimulate the interest of others. Also, without taking time for a discussion of details, the teacher can remark that "Jean figured out a new game with the rollers. If you ask her, maybe she will show it to you."

Group time is obviously an appropriate time for using certain objects children made, such as Halloween costumes, musical instruments, and tops. This time can also be used to make group decisions, including those that involve physical-knowledge activities. For example, the teacher can consult the group and ask them to vote on whether to put the pendulum away to make room for some other equipment that requires a big space, such as Giant Tinker Toys. Projects which extend over a period of days also lend themselves to group planning. For example, a wood-"sculpture" project elicits discussion about what materials are needed and how to go about gluing the pieces, and painting and shellacking the product.

During Playtime Outside

The size of many classrooms precludes activities such as Rollers indoors. However, teachers often have access to a large playground or gym and can schedule a large block of time to spend outside. The provision of the following materials can increase children's opportunities for physical-knowledge activities:

Rollers
Croquet set
Kites
Parachutes (Photograph 12.7)
Tetherball
Balls and beanbags for target games
Hula hoops.

The principles of integration in the above activities are the same as for free play. Sometimes, children naturally gravitate to objects (such as tetherball), and the teacher's involvement is neither necessary nor desirable. At other times, he or she introduces the activity with a view to withdrawing from it (Hula hoops and kites). In certain situations the teacher can introduce an activity and stay with it in a concentrated way (croquet and kites).

Other possibilities include sledding and making a snowman in the winter and shadow play (Education Development Center, 1963). Using a grassy slope as an incline was mentioned in Chapter 7. When children are playing with standard equipment such as swings, slide, seesaw, and climbing rope, the teacher can occasionally make comments such as the following:

Photo 12-7.

Swing: How can you make it go by yourself (rather than asking me to give
           you a push)?
           How can you make it go higher?
Slide: Can you come down in a different way?
Seesaw: How can you make me go up (with the teacher sitting on one end)?
           What do you think would be heavier than this hollow block (which
           the teacher places on one end)?

We conclude this section with an example from Capt, Glayre, and
Hegyi (1976) to show another aspect of integration—the integration of
physical-knowledge activities in kindergarten and first-grade programs. This
example illustrates the possibility of beginning arithmetic in a natural context. It also provides a glimpse into how this integration develops over a
year's time.

One day, while looking at the teacher's notebook of activities, a five-
year-old got the idea of making bowling pins with plastic bottles. At the
teacher's suggestion, many children brought mineral-water bottles from
home. (Mineral water is widely consumed in Switzerland and comes in
one-liter plastic bottles.) They painted the bottles and filled them up with

sand. Below are excerpts from the teacher's notes on what happened during the subsequent months.

June, 1975 (around age five).

The children arrange the bowling pins in a line, one against another, explaining that this way is "easier to knock them over."
At first they did not take turns. The one catching the ball was the one who threw it next. Later, they organized themselves into taking turns.
For each throw, they counted the number which fell down, without putting them into relationship with the number they knocked down on the previous throw.
They do not feel any need to stand at a specific spot to throw the ball. Some stand far away from the target, some very close to it, and some at the side.
Later, they varied the spatial arrangement by lining up the bottles in straight lines and in circles and ovals.

September, 1975

Another way of playing has appeared. The children arrange the pins spaced out in a line. Each time a pin falls over, they take it out of the game. When there is only one pin left, since aiming becomes difficult, they bring the pin closer and closer. The game has thus become more structured with the following rules:

Arrange the pins on a certain line.
Eliminate those that fall.
Bring closer the last one.

January–February, 1976

The children now feel the need to draw a line beyond which they cannot go when they roll the ball, but there is no competition among them.
They now write numbers on paper, and some add up their total score. For example, Laurent's column shows that $0 + 1 + 3 + 4 = 8$ (as can be seen in Figure 12.5). The other children's "columns" are not as well structured. It is not clear from this figure whether the three children had unequal numbers of turns, or whether some children practiced writing numbers in their "columns." In any event, the desirability of making a matrix with three columns has not occurred to these children.
Another way of playing the game is to try to make all the pins fall, and to count the number of throws necessary to achieve this result.

May, 1976 (around age six).

The children now organize themselves tightly before they begin the game. They decide how they will play and how they will keep score.
Figure 12.6 is an example of the record kept by four players. Although this score sheet is not in matrix form, its columns are much better structured than those in Figure 12.5. The children more or less designated the columns by their initials and apparently wrote down the number they knocked down each time. (The teacher was somewhere else throughout most of the game and did

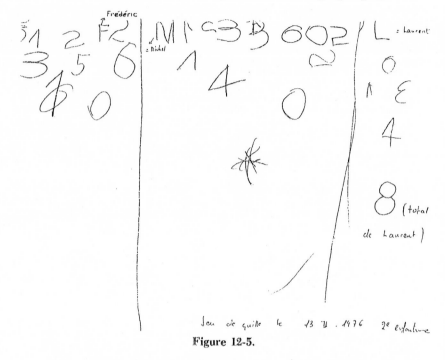

Figure 12-5.

not observe how score was kept.) There is no zero on this sheet (the one "O" is Olivier's initial) because the following line of reasoning reigned:

Jean-François came to record a zero after he failed to knock any of the pins over.
Marc intervened, "No, you know, you don't need to make the zeros."
The teacher asked, "You don't write the zeros down?"
Marc explained, "No, you see, we don't need to because zero means 'nothing.'"
Vincent agreed, "That's right. Zero is 'nothing at all.' So we don't write it."

It was thus in the context of a physical-knowledge game that the need to co-operate and debate record keeping as well as the notion of zero emerged.

Incidental Situations

Physical knowledge is involved in countless situations that spontaneously occur throughout the day. In this section, we discuss several examples with which all teachers are familiar—spills, dirty objects and breakage. The reader who is familiar with *The Moral Judgment of the Child* (Piaget, 1932) will recognize these situations as those that are involved in the child's moral development as well.

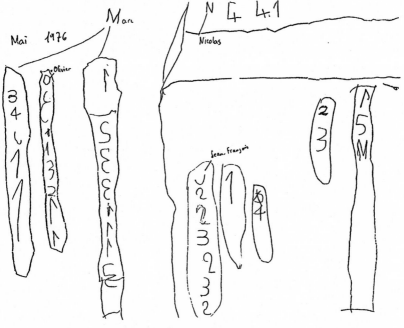

Figure 12-6.

Spills

Children inevitably spill liquids such as milk, juice, paint, glue, syrup, and water. These events are heavily loaded with social knowledge. Parents often admonish that spilling is undesirable because it spoils things or makes the place dirty and because it involves the waste of things that cost money. The term *spilling* is also used to refer to objects that behave like liquids to some extent, such as flour and crumbs.

Young children often spill things simply because they cannot anticipate the reactions of objects. When they spill a cupful of milk, for example, it may not occur to them quickly to right the cup in order to stop the source of the flow. When they finally get a sponge to wipe the table, it does not occur to them to look at the floor to see if it might need wiping. Cleaning up a spill can thus be a physical-knowledge activity in itself. When children have spilled something, the best thing to do is to say, "What do you need to do?" or "Can you get the mop/sponge?"[6]

---

[6]The reader may wish to read Piaget (1932, Chapter 3) on expiatory sanctions and sanctions by reciprocity to find out why this is the best thing to say. A brief discussion of sanctions can also be found in Kamii and DeVries (1977).

The way young children use a mop or sponge reflects the limitation of their physical knowledge and intent to clean up. Preschoolers usually dip the sponge in a pail of water and carry it to the spill without squeezing the water out of it. The result is a trial of water and an additional mess. Even when the teacher cautions them to squeeze the sponge, they often do so while it is still in the water! One way to call attention to this problem is for the teacher to ask an experienced child to show the others the most effective way to squeeze the sponge. However, even when this technique has been mastered, they often end up "wiping" by moving the sponge back and forth on the table just because this action is in itself fun!

Young children are often not even aware that they are spilling something. We have observed this during water play—the big flood under the water table often goes completely unnoticed. Dripping paint all the way from the paint jar to the paper is another form of spilling of which the child may be unaware. In this situation, the teacher does well to ask tactfully, "Would you like me to show you how you can paint without dripping like this?"

One experienced teacher told us that she never succeeded in teaching children to brush crumbs off the table into their hands. This difficulty may be explained in terms of children's frame of reference and their desire not to hold in their hand things that are "dirty." For them, if the desired effect is to clean up the table, all they have to do is brush the crumbs off! The floor only vaguely exists in their frame of reference at this moment,[7] and, besides, they don't notice dirt on the floor or even the stickiness resulting from spilled juice! The best technique for handling this problem may, therefore, be to get a big wastepaper basket out and aim the crumbs into it.

A particularly difficult object for children to use in water play is the watering pot with a long spout (mentioned in Chapter 11) that a teacher bought to use with the Water Wheels. For example, when Diane, a four-year-old, poured with the wide opening instead of the spout (see Photograph 12.8), water coming out of the spout sprinkled David, who ran to tell the teacher. The teacher had not had the advantage of seeing what happened and responded by asking, "Did you ask Diane to be careful?" David shook his head. The teacher suggested, "Well, maybe we'd better go tell her." She took David by the hand and said to Diane, "Diane, David has something to say to you." He blurted out angrily, "You splashed me! You weren't careful!" Diane looked dazed. (In fact, she was completely unaware that she had splashed David.) Seeing that Diane was playing with the watering pot, and knowing the tendency for problems with this object, the teacher guessed that the problem had something to do with this. She said to David, "Let's

---

[7]This statement is based on observations such as the following: When a child climbed on a chair to reach something in the classroom, one of us asked him, "What are you standing on?" The child answered, "On a chair." To the next question, which was "What is the chair on?" he replied, "Nothing."

Photo 12-8.

watch Diane pour and see if we can figure out how to help her be careful. Are you making the water wheel turn with the water, Diane?" Diane proceeded to demonstrate by pouring with the water pot, and water spurted out of the top as well as the spout. The teacher laughed and said, "Look what's happening," pointing to the spout. "See, the water comes out the spout, too. Watch out so this water doesn't splash anybody."

The younger child carrying a puzzle under his arm, totally oblivious of the trail of falling pieces, can likewise be said to be "spilling" the pieces. In such a situation, the teacher can help children become conscious of the result of their action by asking, "What's happening to your puzzle?"

Dirty objects

When we say "dirty objects," we are referring, for example, to pots and pans that have been used for cooking, clothes that got dirty with paint, paint brushes that dried up because they were not promptly washed, tables that need to have old glue and crayon marks removed, and a floor into which playdough has been trampled. "Dirty" is a term loaded with social knowledge which young children cannot learn directly from objects. However, these kinds of dirt often provide the opportunity for physical-knowledge activities, or, more specifically, a chance to observe and compare the changes in objects. Soap cleans pots and pans, but will not get crayon marks off a table.

In washing pots and pans, children often see no reason to rinse them or to soap the outside of a bowl. The teacher will, of course, try calling these necessities to children's attention. If they still do not see the need, he or she may wisely decide not to nag them and instead rewash the dishes later. By insisting that children accomplish a task "correctly," adults can prevent them from developing initiative and autonomy. In dishwashing, too, children have to go through one way after another of doing things in their own way—the way that makes sense to them at each level of development.

Despite all precautions, children's clothing attracts paint, glue, batter, and grease; viewed positively, the problem of washing clothes may present an opportunity for learning. One teacher recounts how a child attempted to get paint off her dress by rubbing gobs of wet toilet tissue on the spot. Bits of paper stuck, and the mess then seemed incurable to the crying child. The teacher suggested that the child change clothes while she put the dress in the washing machine to see if the paint and paper would wash out. (Washing it by hand with the child would have been much better from the standpoint of building physical knowledge, but the teacher obviously did not have time for such a time-consuming project.)[8]

The cleaning of stiffened paint brushes is another project that can be turned into a physical-knowledge activity. Needless to say, a good time to make a "big deal" of the unusable brushes is group time. After an expression of regret, the teacher may suggest soaking the brushes in a bucket for a long time before washing out the paint. Children often go spontaneously to the bucket from time to time to test whether the brushes are soft enough to be washed.

When the teacher encourages children to try to figure out for themselves how to clean the tables, chairs, and floor, they begin to compare what is easy and what is hard to remove, and what technique works in one instance but not another. Dried paint, clay, and playdough can be washed or scraped. Glue on the table must be scraped with a knife. One teacher recounts that she had asked Ann, who had written on the table with a crayon,

---

[8]This is an example of a child's action which did not result in the desired effect. While the effect produced by the washing machine seems magical to a child, the little girl in this case still had an opportunity to compare what she did with what the machine produced.

to clean it off during cleanup time. (She knew that Ann had watched the removal of crayon marks before.) Later, when she noticed the crayon marks still on the table, she reminded Ann that she had asked her to clean it up. Ann, who had gotten a sponge and scrubbed the table with soap, screamed, "I *did* (try to) clean it up, you dummy!" The teacher then asked her if she could remember better ways to clean the table, and others who had gathered around said, "You can scrape it off or put nail polish remover on it." This scene later made a rich topic for discussion at group time. One of the older children demonstrated the two techniques, and everyone became impressed with how hard it was to get the marks off—and with the importance of not writing on the table with crayons.

Spilled flour reveals children's belief that sponges are for cleaning up everything! When they spill flour, four-year-olds immediately proceed to cake the counter, floor, and sponge with the sticky paste. The teacher can save this caked sponge and show it to the children whenever she has to explain why the small vacuum cleaner is the thing to use when flour is spilled.

Broken Objects

When objects are broken, the teacher can try to use this occasion in an educational way. For example, when Jess was upset because he found his wood "sculpture" broken, the teacher asked at group time if anyone knew how it got broken. Needless to say, she assured the group that there would be no punishment if anyone claimed responsibility. Ron timidly raised his hand, saying that he had done it but that it was an accident. The teacher congratulated Ron on his honesty and advised the entire group that, in a situation of this sort, it is best to tell the teacher or the owner immediately so that the group can think of a way to repair the object. Ron helped Jess glue the broken pieces back together, and both felt much better afterwards.

Some broken objects can unfortunately not be repaired, and this is part of the physical reality of this world. When Jess accidentally stepped on Ron's little car and demolished it, for example, Ron was inconsolable. At group time, the teacher and children talked about how sad Ron felt and what could be done to help him feel better. Among the suggestions children came up with was "Don't bring toys from home if they can break."

In Conclusion

We conclude Part III, "How to Go beyond This Book," with the mundane examples just given to emphasize once again the difference between "science education" and the child's construction of physical knowledge. Recall the example we presented in Chapter 1 of the "science-education" approach, in which the teacher attempted to teach by social transmission the knowledge about crystals accumulated by scientists over many centuries. This approach is based on the premise that since scientists have organized knowledge in a certain way, educators must teach it according to the same organizational principles. The category "crystals" makes sense to scientists, who can see certain commonalities among sand, sugar, and salt. However, even most adults have trouble explaining the similarity among sand, sugar, and salt. This ignorance reflects the blind acceptance of "scientific" terminology learned in the same way as arbitrary social knowledge.

Instruction, or the transmission of the cumulative knowledge from the past, has a legitimate place in the education of an individual. We are not saying that all individuals must reinvent the wheel, the steam engine, the airplane, and the atomic reactor. But there must be an indirect way to instruct that meshes with, and buttresses, the natural construction of knowledge that started in infancy. The ideas presented in this book are only the beginning of an attempt to develop such a way of teaching at the preschool level. Soon, we hope, more educators will delve into Piaget's recent research on causality (Piaget and Garcia, 1971; Piaget, 1972a, 1972b, 1973a, 1973b. 1974a, 1974b), which has remained largely unnoticed by them. We also hope that many more curriculum developers will experiment within a long-range constructivist framework to find better ways of teaching all other subjects at each grade level. One cannot expect an individual's autonomy to develop fully if a constructivist education is limited to the preschool years. The individual's intellectual autonomy can likewise not develop fully in science if the rest of his education is of a conformist nature.

The use of Piaget's theory beyond the preschool level implies drastic changes in the teacher's conception of the educative process. When the focus of teaching shifts from what the teacher does to *how the child constructs his own knowledge*, the center of the classroom will no longer be the subject matter or the method of teaching, and the teacher's thinking will undergo a revolution similar to the Copernican revolution.

The educational implications of Piaget's theory are not just a different way of reaching the same goal as traditional education. In order to foster autonomy schools will have to give up trying to fit the individual into a mold. The ideas presented in this book often face opposition in elementary schools, but we firmly believe, as stated in the discussion of objectives in Chapter 3, that those schools which take autonomy seriously will produce more adults with inquisitive, critical, and inventive minds. We also believe that the graduates of such schools are more likely to go on learning and developing the rest of their lives. These statements are only hypotheses at the present time, but hypotheses well worth testing in a longitudinal study.

Final Remarks

We would like to reemphasize that the accounts of activities presented in Chapters 4–10 are *not* models for teachers to follow. They are only ways in which certain teachers at specific points in their own development attempted to use Piaget's theory with particular groups of children. Teachers must, therefore, go beyond this book by constructing for themselves their own ways of applying the broad principles outlined in Chapter 3.

It may be helpful to mention that as we have observed teachers begin to use Piaget's theory, we have sometimes noticed two initial phases of change. The first is one in which they feel paralyzed in the classroom. We have often heard remarks such as, "I used to be able to teach without thinking about *why* I was doing what I did. Now I stop to think and find that I don't know what to do." A second, later reaction is to try too hard with too many interventions. The reader may have recognized in Chapters 4–10 questions that were gratuitous or intrusive. These seem to stem from the teachers' new consciousness of rationale combined with the old habit of teaching by talking.

With experience, it usually becomes possible for the teacher to decenter and think more in terms of what the children are thinking, and this decentering results in more appropriate intervention. When the teacher thus grows out of the initial phases of reconstructing his/her way of thinking about teaching, he or she finds a new excitement and a new confidence that comes from having the theoretical tools necessary to analyze his/her practice.

Bibliography

Books, Journals, and Films

CANEY, STEVEN. *Steven Caney's Toy Book*. New York: Workman Publishing, 1972.

CANEY, STEVEN. *Steven Caney's Playbook*. New York: Workman Publishing, 1975.

CAPT, CLAIRE-LISE, LILIANE GLAYRE, and ARIANE HEGYI. *Des Activités de Connaissance Physique à l'Ecole Enfantine*. Unpublished mémoire de licence, University of Geneva, 1976.

DEVRIES, RHETA, and LAWRENCE KOHLBERG. *Constructivist Early Education: Overview and Comparison with Other Programs*. Washington, DC: National Association for the Education of Young Children, 1990 (first published in 1987).

DUCKWORTH, ELEANOR. "The Having of Wonderful Ideas," *Harvard Educational Review*, 1972, *42*, 217–231.

ENGELMANN, SIEGFRIED, E. "Does the Piagetian Approach Imply Instruction?" in *Measurement and Piaget*, ed. Donald Ross Green, Marguerite P. Ford, and George B. Flamer. New York: McGraw-Hill, 1971.

FLETCHER, HELEN JILL. *The Big Book of Things to Do and Make*. New York: Random House, 1961.

FURTH, HANS G. *Piaget and Knowledge*. Englewood Cliffs, NJ: Prentice-Hall, 1969.

GINSBURG, HERBERT, and SYLVIA OPPER. *Piaget's Theory of Intellectual Development*. Englewood Cliffs, NJ: Prentice-Hall, 1969.

HILDEBRAND, VERNA. *Introduction to Early Childhood Education*. New York: Macmillan, 1971.

HILDEBRAND, VERNA. *Guiding Young Children*. New York: Macmillan, 1975.

INHELDER, BÄRBEL, and JEAN PIAGET. *The Growth of Logic from Childhood to Adolescence*. New York: Basic Books, 1958 (first published in French in 1955).

INHELDER, BÄRBEL, and JEAN PIAGET. *The Early Growth of Logic in the Child*. London: Routledge and Kegan Paul, 1964 (first published in French in 1959).

INHELDER, BÄRBEL, HERMINE SINCLAIR, and MAGALI BOVET. *Learning and the Development of Cognition*. Cambridge, MA: Harvard University Press, 1974.

KAMII, CONSTANCE. "Evaluation of Learning in Preschool Education: Socio-Emotional, Perceptual-Motor, Cognitive Development," in *Handbook on Formative and Summative Evaluation of Student Learning*, ed. Benjamin S. Bloom, J. Thomas Hastings, and George F. Madaus. New York: McGraw-Hill, 1971.

KAMII, CONSTANCE. "An Application of Piaget's Theory to the Conceptualization of a Preschool Curriculum," in *The Preschool in Action* (1st ed.), ed. Ronald K. Parker. Boston: Allyn and Bacon, 1972a.

KAMII, CONSTANCE. "A Sketch of the Piaget-Derived Preschool Curriculum Developed by the Ypsilanti Early Education Program," in *History and Theory of Early Childhood Education*, ed. Samuel J. Braun and Esther P. Edwards. Worthington, OH: Jones, 1972b.

KAMII, CONSTANCE. "A Sketch of the Piaget-Derived Preschool Curriculum Developed by the Ypsilanti Early Education Program," in *Revisiting Early Childhood Education*, ed. Joe L. Frost. New York: Holt, Rinehart and Winston, 1973a.

KAMII, CONSTANCE. "A Sketch of the Piaget-Derived Preschool Curriculum Developed by the Ypsilanti Early Education Program," in *Early Childhood Education*, ed. Bernard Spodek. Englewood Cliffs, NJ: Prentice-Hall, 1973b.

KAMII, CONSTANCE. *Number in Preschool and Kindergarten*. Washington, DC: National Association for the Education of Young Children, 1982.

KAMII, CONSTANCE. "Autonomy: The Aim of Education Envisioned by Piaget," *Phi Delta Kappan*, 1984, 65, 410–415.

KAMII, CONSTANCE. *Young Children Reinvent Arithmetic*. New York: Teachers College Press, 1985.

KAMII, CONSTANCE. *Young Children Continue to Reinvent Arithmetic—2nd Grade*. New York: Teachers College Press, 1989.

KAMII, CONSTANCE, and LOUISE DERMAN. "The Engelmann Approach to Teaching Logical Thinking: Findings from the Administration of Some Piagetian Tasks," in *Measurement and Piaget*, ed. Donald Ross Green, Marguerite P. Ford, and George B. Flamer. New York: McGraw-Hill, 1971.

KAMII, CONSTANCE, and RHETA DEVRIES. "Piaget for Early Education," in *The Preschool in Action* (2nd ed.), ed. Mary Carol Day and Ronald K. Parker. Boston: Allyn and Bacon, 1977.

KAMII, CONSTANCE, and RHETA DEVRIES. *Group Games in Early Education*. Washington, DC: National Association for the Education of Young Children, 1980.

KAMII, CONSTANCE, RHETA DEVRIES, MAUREEN ELLIS, and RAUL ZARITSKY. "Playing with Rollers: A Pre-School Teacher Uses Piaget's Theory," a film produced under the auspices of the Office of Instructional Resources Development, University of Illinois at Chicago Circle, 1975.

KAMII, CONSTANCE, and NORMA RADIN. "A Framework for a Preschool Curriculum Based on Some Piagetian Concepts," *Journal of Creative Behavior*, 1967, *1*, 314-324.

KAMII, CONSTANCE, and NORMA RADIN. "A Framework for a Preschool Curriculum Based on Some Piagetian Concepts," in *Educational Implications of Piaget's Theory*, ed. Irene J. Athey and Duane O. Rubadeau. Waltham, MA: Xerox College Publishers, 1970.

KARMILOFF-SMITH, ANNETTE, and BÄRBEL INHELDER. "If You Want to Get Ahead, Get a Theory," *Cognition*, 1975, 3, 195–212.

KOHLBERG, LAWRENCE, and ROCHELLE MAYER. "Development As the Aim of Education," *Harvard Educational Review*, 1972, 42, 440–498.

LEEPER, SARAH HAMMOND, RUTH J. DALES, DORA SIKES SKIPPER, and RALPH WITHERSPOON. *Good Schools for Young Children*. New York: Macmillan, 1974.

LICKONA, THOMAS. in *ERIC/ECE NEWSLETTER*, 7, No. 3 (January 1974), 4.

LOCKE, JOHN. *Essay Concerning Human Understanding.* Oxford, England: Oxford University Press, 1947 (first published in 1690).

MCKINNON, J. W., and J. W. RENNER. "Are Colleges Concerned with Intellectual Development?" *American Journal of Physics*, 1971, 39, 1047–1052.

PIAGET, JEAN. *Language and Thought in the Child*. London: Kegan Paul, 1926 (first published in French in 1923).

PIAGET, JEAN. *The Child's Conception of the World*. New York: Harcourt and Brace, 1929 (first published in French in 1926).

PIAGET, JEAN. *The Moral Judgment of the Child*. New York: Harcourt, 1932.

PIAGET, JEAN. *The Child's Conception of Movement and Speed*. London: Routledge and Kegan Paul, 1970 (first published in 1946a).

PIAGET, JEAN. *The Child's Conception of Time*. London: Routledge and Kegan Paul, 1969 (first published in French in 1946b).

PIAGET, JEAN. *The Psychology of Intelligence*. London: Routledge and Kegan Paul, 1950 (first published in French in 1947).

PIAGET, JEAN. *To Understand Is to Invent*. New York: Grossman, 1973 (first published in 1948).

PIAGET, JEAN. *La Transmission des Mouvements*. Paris: Presses Universitaires de France, 1972a.

PIAGET, JEAN. *La Direction des Mobiles Lors de Chocs et de Poussées*. Paris: Presses Universitaires de France, 1972b.

PIAGET, JEAN. *La Formation de la Notion de Force*. Paris: Presses Universitaires de France, 1973a.

PIAGET, JEAN. *La Composition des Forces et le Problème des Vecteurs*. Paris: Presses Universitaires de France, 1973b.

PIAGET, JEAN. *The Grasp of Consciousness*. Cambridge, MA: Harvard University Press, 1976 (first published in French in 1974a).

PIAGET, JEAN. *Réussir et Comprendre*. Paris: Presses Universitaires de France, 1974b.

PIAGET, JEAN, and ROLANDO GARCIA. *Understanding Causality*. New York: Norton, 1974 (first published in French in 1971).

PIAGET, JEAN, JEAN-BLAISE GRIZE, ALINA SZEMINSKA, and VINH BANG. *Epistémologie et Psychologie de la Fonction*. Paris: Presses Universitaires de France, 1968.

PIAGET, JEAN, and BÄRBEL INHELDER. *The Child's Construction of Quantities*. London: Routledge and Kegan Paul, 1974 (first published in French in 1941).

PIAGET, JEAN, and BÄRBEL INHELDER. *The Child's Construction of Space*. New York: Norton, 1948 (first published in French in 1946).

PIAGET, JEAN, and BÄRBEL INHELDER. *Mental Imagery in the Child*. New York: Basic Books, 1971 (first published in French in 1966a).

PIAGET, JEAN, and BÄRBEL INHELDER. *The Psychology of the Child*. New York: Basic Books, 1969 (first published in French in 1966b).

PIAGET, JEAN, BÄRBEL INHELDER, and ALINA SZEMINSKA. *The Child's Conception of Geometry.* London: Routledge and Kegan Paul, 1960 (first published in French in 1948).

PIAGET, JEAN, and ALINA SZEMINSKA. *The Child's Conception of Number.* London: Routledge and Kegan Paul, 1952 (first published in French in 1941).

PITCHER, EVELYN G., MIRIAM G. LASHER, SYLVIA G. FEINBURG, and LINDA A. BRAUN. *Helping Young Children Learn.* Columbus, OH: Charles E. Merrill, 1974.

READ, KATHERINE H. *Nursery School* (6th ed.). Philadelphia: Saunders, 1976.

SCHWEBEL, MILTON. "Formal Operations in First-Year College Students," *The Journal of Psychology,* 1975, 91, 133–141.

SINCLAIR, HERMINE. "Piaget's Theory of Development: The Main Stages," in *Piagetian Cognitive-Development Research and Mathematical Education,* ed. Myron F. Rosskopf, Leslie P. Steffe, and Stanley Taback. Reston, VA: National Council of Teachers of Mathematics, 1971.

SONQUIST, HANNE, and CONSTANCE KAMII. "Applying Some Piagetian Concepts in the Classroom for the Disadvantaged," *Young Children,* 1967, 22, 231-246.

SONQUIST, HANNE, CONSTANCE KAMII, and LOUISE DERMAN. "A Piaget-Derived Preschool Curriculum," in *Educational Implications of Piaget's Theory,* ed. Irene J. Athey and Duane O. Rubadeau. Waltham, MA: Xerox College Publishers, 1970.

STANT, MARGARET A. *The Young Child.* Englewood Cliffs, NJ: Prentice-Hall, 1972.

TAYLOR, BARBARA J. *A Child Goes Forth.* Provo, UT: Brigham Young University Press, 1964.

TODD, VIVIAN EDMISTON, and HELEN HEFFERNAN. *The Years Before School.* New York: Macmillan, 1970.

ZAFFO, GEORGE. *The Big Book of Real Boats and Ships.* New York: Grosset and Dunlap, 1951.

Programs and Materials for Science Education

African Primary Science Program. Newton, MA: Education Development Center, 1973. (*Wheels* is one of the booklets of this program.)

Elementary Science Study. Distributed by the Webster Division, McGraw-Hill Book Co., St. Louis. The following are parts of this program cited in this book.

> *Lights and Shadows,* 1963
>
> *Mobiles,* 1966
>
> *Musical Instruments Recipe Book,* 1971

Science—A Process Approach. Distributed by Ginn and Company, Xerox Distribution Center, Carlstadt, NJ, 1967.

Science Curriculum Improvement Study. Distributed by Rand McNally Co., Chicago, 1966.

Science 5/13. New York: Macdonald Education, 1972.

Catalogs Cited

Childcraft Education Corp., Edison, NJ, 1976.

Community Playthings, Rifton, NY, 1976.

Creative Playthings, Princeton, NJ, 1976.
Ideal Toy Corp., New York, 1975.
Mead School Products, Atlanta, 1973/74.

Toys Cited

"Don't Break the Ice," Schaper Manufacturing Co., 1969.
"Don't Spill the Beans," Schaper Manufacturing Co., 1967.
"Jumbo Tiddledy Winks," Milton Bradley, 1963.

Index

About the Authors

Constance Kamii is Professor in the School of Education at the University of Alabama at Birmingham. She previously held a joint appointment in the College of Education, University of Illinois at Chicago and in the Faculty of Psychology and Sciences of Education, University of Geneva, Switzerland. Following receipt of her Ph.D. from the University of Michigan in 1965, she was a research fellow under Jean Piaget at the International Center of Genetic Epistemology and the University of Geneva.

Rheta DeVries is a former public school teacher who is now Professor of Human Development and Family Studies at the University of Houston, where she is also Director of the Human Development Laboratory School. She previously taught at the University of Illinois at Chicago and at the Merrill-Palmer Institute. She received her Ph.D. from the University of Chicago and did postdoctoral work at the University of Geneva, Switzerland.